THE POLITICAL THEORY OF CHRISTINE DE PIZAN

Women and Gender in the Early Modern World

Series Editors: Allyson Poska and Abby Zanger

In the past decade, the study of women and gender has offered some of the most vital and innovative challenges to scholarship on the early modern period. Ashgate's new series of interdisciplinary and comparative studies, 'Women and Gender in the Early Modern World', takes up this challenge, reaching beyond geographical limitations to explore the experiences of early modern women and the nature of gender in Europe, the Americas, Asia and Africa. Submissions of single-author studies and edited collections will be considered.

Titles in the series include:

Publishing Women's Life Stories in France, 1647–1720
From voice to print
Elizabeth C. Goldsmith

Maternal Measures
Figuring caregiving in the early modern period
Edited by Naomi J. Miller and Naomi Yavneh

Marie Madeleine Jodin 1741–1790
Actress, philosophe *and feminist*
Felicia Gordon and P.N. Furbank

The Political Theory of Christine de Pizan
Kate Langdon Forhan

The Political Theory of Christine de Pizan

Kate Langdon Forhan

Routledge
Taylor & Francis Group
LONDON AND NEW YORK

First published 2002 by Ashgate Publishing

Reissued 2018 by Routledge
2 Park Square, Milton Park, Abingdon, Oxon OX14 4RN
711 Third Avenue, New York, NY 10017, USA

Routledge is an imprint of the Taylor & Francis Group, an informa business

A Library of Congress record exists under LC control number: 2001095424

ISBN 13: 978-1-138-73007-6 (hbk)
ISBN 13: 978-1-138-72998-8 (pbk)
ISBN 13: 978-1-315-18953-6 (ebk)

Contents

Preface

Christine de Pizan presents an intriguing paradox to historians of political ideas. She held no political office and her work was not influential on any political theorist living today. Her world – with its passion, grandeur, misery and hardship – has long since passed away, and many would add a cheerful farewell to the Dark Ages. Some might argue that she is of interest merely as an anomaly – the only significant female writer on politics before the early modern era. By contrast, in the disciplines of women's studies and French literature, she has inspired tremendous intellectual debate, to the extent that Margarete Zimmermann has referred it as a battle between the Christinophiles and the Christinoclasts.

The purpose of this book is to present the political paradoxes of Christine de Pizan, one of the most prolific political writers of the Middle Ages. She was a woman in a man's world, an Italian at a French court, the daughter of a civil servant in a world structured by social class. The quintessential outsider, she wrote a dozen political treatises that dared to instruct the ruling classes on how to govern themselves and their kingdoms. Her corpus of political works includes five works designed to educate the male ruling class, commonly known as mirrors for princes, two works expressly for princesses and a treatise on warfare. To these must be added other works that defy the categories of literary genres by incorporating political ideas into imaginative poetry, allegory and prose, including a nationalistic panegyric on Joan of Arc. Despite this amazing productivity as an overtly political writer, Christine is virtually unknown outside the fields of French literature and women's studies, in which, until recently, her political works have inspired relatively little interest. It is to address this lacuna in the history of political philosophy that this work is directed. My goal is to outline in a systematic and comprehensive way the political theory of Christine de Pizan, in part to address the puzzle of her thought, to be sure, but also to situate her ideas within the history of political ideas in general.

To do so, I discuss the traditional concerns of political theorists, such as justice, law and social class, in thematic fashion, rather than examining each of her political works separately. I chose this format, despite its inherent difficulties, because I would like to propose a view of Christine de Pizan as offering a sustained and internally consistent political theory, showing both the development and the continuities in her ideas. Thus, Chapter One is devoted to the historical context in which Christine lived and wrote. While some might argue that such extensive treatment is unnecessary, I believe that Christine de Pizan's work was always deeply integrated into the circumstances of events around her. Indeed, as I hope will become clear in these pages, some of the apparent paradoxes in her thought stem from her desire to address contemporaneous political problems. In Chapter Two, I contextualize her views by discussing related concepts in the works of her predecessors. In particular, I have highlighted the two most visible writers in the mirror for princes tradition in which she wrote, John of Salisbury and Giles of Rome. Familiarity with these two influential minds will allow us more clearly to see Christine de Pizan's use of that tradition to promulgate her own views. In Chapter Three, I discuss the dominant understandings of the nature of political community and compare them with Christine's ideas. Chapter Four situates Christine's concept of kingship within medieval currents. Chapter Five takes up the critical question of law and its relationship to the abiding problem of justice. Chapter Six introduces Christine's most startling contribution to political thought, found in her views on war. Finally, in the Conclusion, I readdress the paradox of Christine's position in the history of political ideas.

Situating Christine's intellectual contribution to the history of political theory in this fashion will, I hope, be useful to scholars of literature or women's studies who are not familiar with the history of political thought. My primary audience, however, is political scientists and political theorists, especially those concerned with contemporary political issues who are unfamiliar with French political history and medieval political thought. In doing so, my aspiration is to demonstrate that Christine's ideas, and indeed medieval political thought in general, do have significance for the modern era. We tend to see only the disjuncture between her world and our own. After all, ours is a determinedly secular society, hers a religious one; ours is doggedly democratic, hers aristocratic. But her thought has genuine relevance for us, on several counts: first, hers was a society in transition. New class structures, new occupations and new aspirations were appearing behind the crumbling structures of the late medieval world. Although couched in the language of the *auctores*, the authorities of the classical world, her solutions to the problems of her society are decidedly her own. Many contemporary observers have noted that many modern societies are in crisis, too – in danger, as one author put it, of 'imploding'. Perhaps Christine de Pizan has something to teach us about politics in an unstable world, where institutions appear to have lost their effectiveness and leaders have apparently surrendered to the most venal and corrupt practices.

Secondly, Christine de Pizan was an outsider: a woman in a world dominated by men, an Italian at a French court, a member of a professional class in a world that was rigidly hierarchical. Her 'difference' may give her the perspective to observe her society more objectively. Her personal vulnerability allows her to see politics more clearly, as those who are most vulnerable might see our own. Thirdly, she was a shrewd observer of royal government in a country that was emerging as a nation-state, where new concepts and practices in law, justice, administration and politics in general were in the process of development. She writes on the threshold of a new era, called by us 'early modern' or 'Renaissance'. Her works are of considerable interest to the historian because of her lively and insightful descriptions of life around her, but the astute reader can discern valuable observations that reveal her prescience of things to come.

In conclusion, it must be noted that Christine de Pizan is really not that obscure. Her prestige in her own lifetime was high, and she could count among her friends many notable writers and thinkers. Her literary legacy is considerable, in part because of her amazing productivity, but also because of the influence of her patrons. The majority of her works in prose were commissioned by members of the nobility, especially the royal family, and account books demonstrate that she was paid liberally for them. Her reputation continued well into the modern period; in fact the first recognition of her political works dates to the nineteenth century, in Raymond Thomassy's important *Essai sur les écrits politiques de Christine de Pisan* (1838).

While Christine de Pizan was not a political theorist of the rank of Plato or Hobbes, she had a considerable gift of synthesis, that is, of adapting the great political ideas of her favourite authors to the needs of the society around her. Like Machiavelli after her, she refreshed ancient and conventional political concepts and genres of political writing that had been elaborated by her predecessors, modifying them to conform to the conditions of her own world, often subverting the conventional wisdom in the process. Her success varied. As political conditions worsened in the early fifteenth century, her pleas for responsible government became more pessimistic and more personal, until her retreat, after the siege of Paris, into the comparative peace of a convent at Poissy.

The 'rediscovery' of Christine de Pizan by scholars of French and women's studies has only begun to bear fruit for political scientists and intellectual historians in the form of new editions and translations of her work into modern French and English. As of this writing, only three of her multiple mirrors for princes are available in English, and several of her works are not available in modern critical editions. Her *Livre de prod'homie de l'homme/Livre de prudence* has not even been transcribed from the manuscript, although scholars can hope that Eric Hicks's critical edition will be available soon. Students can take inspiration from the fact that there is much work to be done on the political thought of Christine de Pizan. My own desire is that this book will awaken sufficient interest in Christine's political ideas that its conclusions will soon be superseded by new work in the field.

Acknowledgements

Despite an interest in mirrors for princes of the European Middle Ages dating back to my dissertation on the *Policraticus*, my first encounter with Christine de Pizan came about through a chance telephone call when a colleague at another university asked my help in tracing the exact source in the *Policraticus* for one of Christine's citations. I became fascinated by this remarkable political thinker who was so little known outside the field of French literature and women's studies. To academics in those disciplines, her prodigious output of didactic, ethical and political works was of relatively little interest compared with other genres in which her achievement was also enormous, creative and significant, and thus where significant work was awaiting scholars. By contrast, I wished to examine Christine de Pizan's political theory because it was relatively unknown yet clearly tied to major traditions of political writing and because it was widely respected among her contemporaries. An eminent political theorist of the period confessed to me that he had never heard of Christine de Pizan, despite having written a masterwork evaluating the period in which she lived. In short, Christine de Pizan represents a missing link, a lost chapter in the history of political thought, that I attempt to explore in this book.

Over the last ten years I have worked on Christine's political thought, presenting conference papers and articles, and benefiting greatly both from the International Christine Society, whose very first meeting I attended, and from the insights of many Christine scholars, including Professors Ros Brown-Grant, Eric Hicks, Angus Kennedy, Christine Reno, Jeff Richards, and the doyenne of 'Christiniana', Charity Cannon Willard, among many others.

My thanks to the National Endowment for the Humanities and Siena College for the fellowship that allowed me a year-long sabbatical to work on this project. I am especially grateful to the Nederman–Dox Scholar-in-Residence Program in Tucson, Arizona, where scintillating dinner conversations provided a foil for the quiet of my quarters in the Whetmore Wing, furnishing a superb environment in which to write. Also important was my time as a visiting scholar at the Department of Political Science at the University of Arizona, and I thank both the chair, Professor William Mishler, and members of the department, especially Cary J. Nederman, for their hospitality. Gary Thompson and the faculty of the Siena College library have moved mountains of books for me, and the Companions and Members of Convivium, Siena's Center for Medieval and Early Modern Studies, have been consistently helpful and supportive.

Like all scholars, my debt to the generosity of others is enormous: Two anonymous readers provided valuable insights and assistance on both style and substance. Professor Eric Hicks has very generously shared not only his transcription of *Prod'homie*, but also his breadth of knowledge and his sense of humour. My translations from *Prod'homie* come from his text. Professor Pam Clements read an early draft of my work and has been very generous with comments and information. To Cary J. Nederman I owe a great debt. Without his encouragement, enthusiasm and provocation, this work never would have been written. He is a splendidly generous scholar. Erika Gaffney of Ashgate Press has not only been a pleasure to work with but has become a friend. My far greatest debt is to a Renaissance man, Joseph Paul Cousins, PhD, MD – scientist, political activist, father, dancer, chef, healer and husband extraordinaire – to whom this book is dedicated.

Note on the Texts

For the convenience of a non-specialist audience, every effort has been made to take quotations from previously published translations into English of Christine's works, even if these have only been published as excerpts. Where there is no English translation of a work by Christine or indeed another medieval writer, I have used French or Latin critical editions or modern French translations, again in the interests of accessibility for the general reader. Translations of these materials are my own.

A canny businesswoman, Christine was well aware that the marketability of her work was increased by lavish production that would befit additions to a bibliophile's treasures. She is one of the few late medieval authors who has left us some account of her choice of artists, and of her respect for them. Christine's perfectionistic attention to this aspect of her work resulted in sumptuous manuscripts illustrated by carefully executed illuminations, many of which have been studied by art historians who have been particularly intrigued by Christine's use of illustrations to underline the force of her arguments. Sandra Hindman's magisterial study of *Othéa*, for example, demonstrates the importance of paying close attention to the illuminations as they emphasize, and even reveal, Christine's message. Thus, the importance of the relationship between text and image in Christine's work should be emphasized particularly for historians and theorists, whose examination of primary sources rarely takes them beyond a critical edition to the actual physical manuscript. Christine de Pizan is one political thinker for whom examination of the manuscripts themselves is extremely helpful and revealing. Finally, not all of Christine's manuscripts were prepared with illuminations. *Corps de policie* and *Prod'homie/Prudence*, for example, do not have any, nor is it apparent why they do not.

Chronological List of Works and Short Titles[1]

1399–1402
Numerous poetic works, including *Cent Ballades, Virelays, Rondeaux*, etc.
L'Epistre au dieu d'amours (verse)
Le Debat de deux amants (verse)
Le Livre des trois jugements (verse)
Le Livre du dit de Poissy (verse)
L'Epistre d'Othéa [*Othéa*] (verse)
Enseignements a son filz (verse)
Proverbes moraux (verse)

1401–1402
Le Livre des epistres sur le Roman de la Rose (prose)
Le Dit de la rose (verse)

1402–1403
Le Livre du chemin de longue estude [*Chemin*] (verse)
Dit de la pastoure (verse)
Une Oroison Nostre Dame (verse)
Les Quinze Joyes de Nostre Dame (verse)
Une Oroison de la vie et passion Notre Seigneur (verse)

1403
Le Livre de la mutacion de fortune [*Mutacion*] (verse)

1 The most extensive bibliographic study of Christine's works is by Angus Kennedy, *Christine de Pizan: A Bibliographic Guide* (London: Grant & Cutler, 1984), which was updated by Kennedy as *Christine de Pizan: A Bibliographic Guide, Supplement I*, in 1994. See also Edith Yenal, *Christine de Pizan: A Bibliography* (Metuchen: Scarecrow Press, 1989).

1404
Une Epistre a Eustache Morel (prose)
Le Livre des fais et bonnes meurs du sage roy Charles V [*Charles V*] (prose)

1404–1405
Le Livre du duc des vrais amants (prose and verse)
Le Livre de la cité des dames [*Cité des dames*] (prose)
Le Livre des trois vertus or *Le Trésor de la cité des dames* [*Trésor*] (prose)

1405
L'Avision Christine [*Avision*] (prose)
Le Livre de la prod'homie de l'homme or *Le Livre de prudence* [*Prod'homie/Prudence*] (prose)
Le Livre du corps de policie [*Corps de policie*] (prose)
Epistre a Isabeau de Baviere, reine de France (prose)

1402–1407
Autres ballades (verse)

1407–1410
Une Complainte amoureuse (verse)
Sept psaumes allegorisés (prose)
Cent ballades d'amant et de dame (verse)

1412–13
Le Livre de la paix (prose)
L'Avision du coq (lost)

1414–1418
L'Epistre de la prison de vie humaine (prose)

1420
Les Heures de la contemplation (prose)

1429
La Ditié Jehanne d'Arc (verse)

Descendants of Jean II, King of France

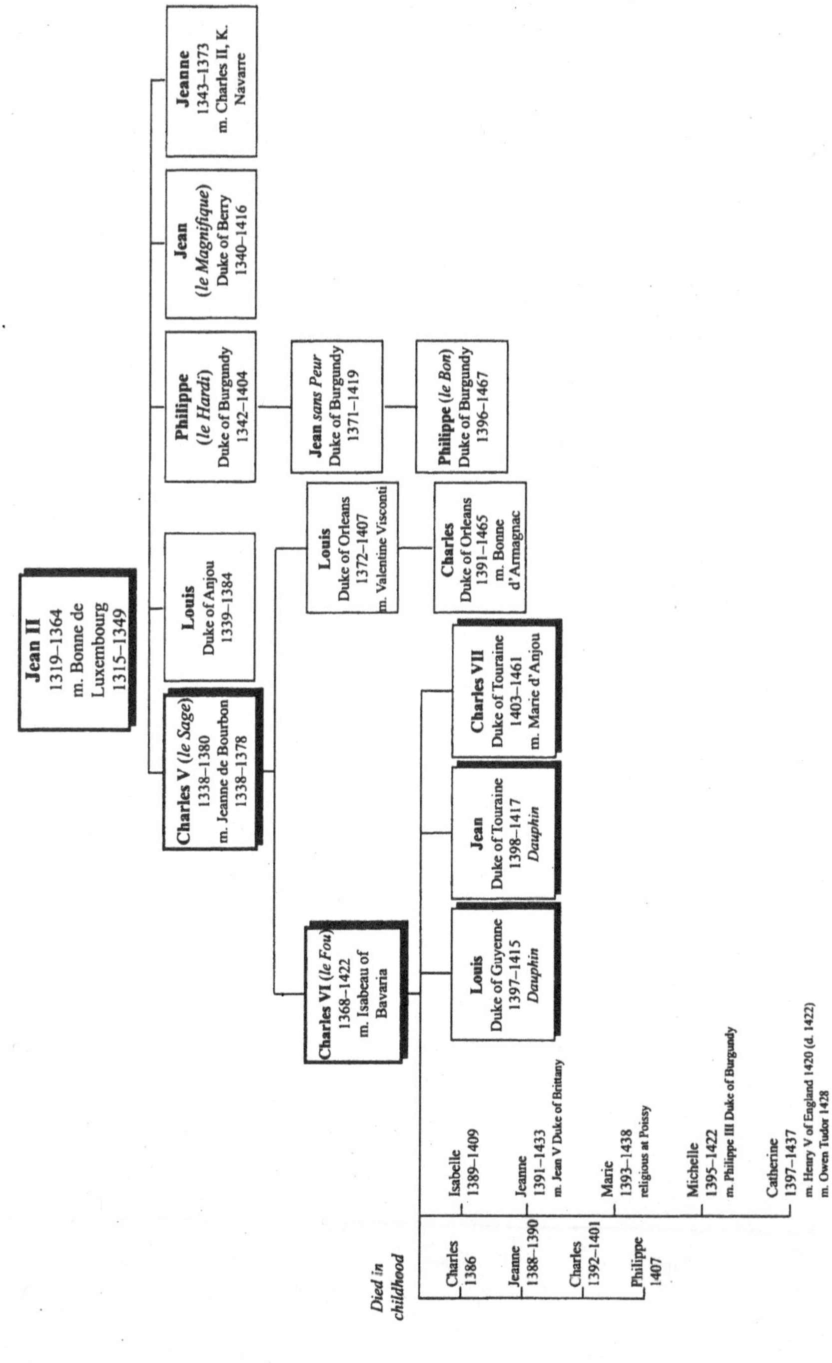

For Joseph

. . . a sweet thing is marriage . . .

CHAPTER ONE

Alone am I

. . . I have no great treasure to make you rich, but a measure of good advice . . .

Perhaps it was amidst the swirling leaves of autumn 1418 that Christine de Pizan said farewell to the world.[1] The convent gate at Poissy closed behind her, and she moved within to begin another life – not of deprivation, but certainly of silence and order.

Thus ended the public career of one of the most remarkable, yet paradoxical, women of the fifteenth century. Called variously 'France's first professional writer', included among 'first feminists', considered by some 'a prude', a 'bluestocking', a 'conservative',[2] Christine de Pizan was born in 1364 in Venice, but from the age of four she spent her entire life in France, primarily in Paris. An extraordinary witness and commentator on French political and social life, through her insights she provides us with a window on the world of the late fourteenth and early fifteenth centuries in France. This troubled, chaotic, yet evocative era has also been characterized variously by some of the most widely read twentieth-century historians. Christopher Allmand describes the 'breakdown of the historic feudal order'. Barbara Tuchman refers to the 'calamitous' fourteenth century. P. S. Lewis alludes to 'crisis' and J. Russell Major depicts the 'failure' of political institutions. Michel Mollat, writing of

1 Christine entered Poissy sometime after late January 1418. She dated her letter to the queen, *L'Epistre de la prison de vie humaine*, 'escript a Paris', 20 January 1418. The Burgundian army entered Paris on 28 May 1419. In the *Ditié de Jeanne d'Arc*, written 31 July 1429, she refers to having lived at Poissy for eleven years.

2 The literature on Christine de Pizan is enormous. Among works in English, the best place to begin is probably Charity Cannon Willard's magisterial and influential *Christine de Pizan: Her Life and Works* (New York: Persea Books, 1984), both for its biographical detail and its superlative contextualization of Christine's work. It includes a discussion of Christine's reputation in its last chapter, especially pp. 222–3. The best-known negative view of Christine can be found in Sheila Delany's article, 'Mothers to Think Back Through: The Ambiguous Example of Christine de Pizan', in Laurie A. Finke and Martin B. Schichtman (eds), *Medieval Texts and Contemporary Readers* (Ithaca, NY: Cornell University Press, 1987), 177–97.

the lives of the poor during this period, says, 'Confusion reigned everywhere'. William Chester Jordan, describing the great famine of the early fourteenth century, writes that the 'fear and ravages of famine weakened civility and decency, affection and trust . . . and encouraged . . . transformations of community life'.[3] Johan Huizinga, in his germinal work on the later Middle Ages, characterizes the period as autumnal, as though its light were dying out as it faded into oblivion. In the new translation of his masterwork, Huizinga remarks that 'a general look at the French-Burgundian world of the fifteenth century gives the primary impression of a fundamentally somber mood, a barbarian splendor, bizarre and overloaded forms, an imagination that had become threadbare . . .'.[4] Nor is this dark vision of late medieval France limited to some modern scholars; Christine de Pizan's contemporaries, such as Eustache Deschamps, draw our attention to the stresses of the period, with its eschatological expectations:

> Time of mourning and of temptation,
> Age of tears, of envy and of torment,
> Time of languour and of damnation,
> Age that brings us to the end . . .
> Time without honour and without true judgement.[5]

While this may in part be literary affectation, it also expressed some deeply felt melancholy, or poets like Deschamps would not have found so much favour. On the other hand, perhaps Huizinga's *fin de siècle* gloom overstates the case.[6] From our perspective it is possible to see the positive side as well; indeed, one could well ask if Christine was a witness to the waning of the Middle Ages or

3 Christopher Allmand, *The Hundred Years War* (Cambridge: Cambridge University Press, 1988), 7; Barbara Tuchman, *A Distant Mirror: The Calamitous Fourteenth Century* (New York: Knopf, 1978); P. S. Lewis, *Later Medieval France: The Polity* (London: Macmillan, 1968), 376; J. Russell Major, *Representative Institutions in Renaissance France* (Madison: University of Wisconsin Press, 1960), 10; Michel Mollat, *The Poor in the Middle Ages* (New Haven: Yale University Press, 1986), 198; William Chester Jordan, *The Great Famine: Northern Europe in the Early Fourteenth Century* (Princeton: Princeton University Press, 1998) [5].

4 Johan Huizinga, *The Autumn of the Middle Ages* (Chicago: University of Chicago Press, 1996), 383.

5 Eustache Deschamps, *Œuvres complètes* (Paris: Societé des anciens textes français, 1878–1903), i, 113. For this and other examples, see Huizinga, *Autumn of the Middle Ages*, 32–5.

6 For a recent review and analysis of Huizinga's scholarly influence see Edward Peters and Walter P. Simons, 'The New Huizinga and the Old Middle Ages', *Speculum*, **74** (1999), 587–620. For an important overview of contemporary medieval studies, see Paul Freedman and Gabrielle Peters, 'Medievalisms Old and New', *American Historical Review*, **103** (1998), 677–704.

the beginning of the Renaissance, a revitalization of culture and art that freed European culture from dark superstition. Was the crisis the decline of feudalism or the growth of centralized bureaucratic power? Was the age experiencing the death of an international culture or the birth of the nation-state? All of these questions have been argued by many scholars from many disciplines, often fighting their own battles of historical periodicity. Whatever the interpretation or search for the ultimate meaning of this epoch, to any observer, events of the fourteenth and early fifteenth centuries in France reflected significant changes in almost every aspect of life.

Perhaps the most fundamental challenge faced at the outset of this period was the havoc caused by population loss, agricultural disasters, plague and their collateral effects. In 1328 the population of France was estimated at some 2,500,000 'hearths', about fifteen million people. Between 1348 and 1450 it fell by an astonishing 50 to 70 per cent, so that by 1450, when the population began to increase again, there were fewer than ten million people.[7] Population losses of this magnitude cannot be explained by a single factor, and indeed multiple causes are most probable, forging an interlocking chain of malnourishment, infertility, delayed marriage and unusually high death rates due to disease. The earliest contributor, before 1348, was a series of major agricultural catastrophes resulting in poor harvests. Over-abundant rainfall in 1315 and 1317 caused meagre harvests, diseases in animals, and a shortage of sun-dried salt essential to food preservation, which led to famine, especially in 1321 and 1322.[8] Henri Pirenne gives the example of Ypres: between May and October of 1316 this town of 20,000 people buried 2,800 – 14 per cent of its population – in six months.[9] Hunger drove people off the land, crime and vagabondage increased and with them came widespread despair.[10]

This recurring pattern of flood and famine became the norm, which in part explains the exceptional vulnerability of children and peasants to the first great wave of plague, which arrived in Marseilles in mid-March of 1348. Despite rudimentary quarantine via abandonment, exclusion and ostracism in some villages and towns, the plague had worked its way north to Paris by that same summer, where its devastation lasted until the end of autumn 1349. The mortality

7 Elisabeth Carpentier and J.-P. Arrignan, *La France et les Français, XIVe et XVe siècles* (Paris: Orphys, 1993), 35.

8 For details and further discussion of the demographic implications of the cycles of agriculture catastrophe and disease, see Jordan, *Great Famine*; see also Allmand, *Hundred Years War*, 10; Mollat, *Poor in the Middle Ages*, 192–250; Georges Duby, *Histoire de la France urbaine* (Paris: Seuil, 1980), v, esp. 514–43.

9 Henri Pirenne, *Economic and Social History of Medieval Europe* (New York: Harcourt Brace, 1937), 192. See also Jordan, *Great Famine*, 146.

10 Jordan, *Great Famine*, 112–13; Allmand, *Hundred Years War*, 120.

rate for those infected was very high, as much as 60 to 80 per cent. Between 1347 and 1350, a third of the population of Europe died.[11] Destruction of this magnitude caused great social distress and dislocation, with its own consequent effects on both birth rates and infant mortality. It also increased economic pressures. All across Europe, the loss of able-bodied farm labourers and artisans meant that milk was not churned, cheeses not turned, bread ovens grew cold and grain was not harvested. Taxes and tithes were not paid, prices for food skyrocketed and the cost of labour soared. Contemporary observers commented on the demanding and presumptuous attitudes of the surviving labourers and their seemingly outrageous demands. Mollat writes of a fourteenth-century witness who remarked, 'The little people, men and women, owing to the excessive abundance of things, were no longer willing to work in their usual occupations. They demanded the most expensive and delicate food . . . Most things cost twice as much as before the plague, if not more.'[12] Peasants ran away, attracted to the cities. One historian has found that between 1330 and 1360, 74 per cent of the labourers streaming into the city from the countryside were unskilled.[13] Legal disputes increased over property ownership and inheritances. Apprentices lost masters; masters lost apprentices. A contemporaneous observer, Gilles li Muisis, wrote that 'the widespread mortality of 1349 killed so many farmers and vintners, so many workers of every trade . . . that there was a great lack. All the workers and their families demanded exorbitant wages.'[14] These pay increases were occurring across Europe. Before the Black Death, an English ploughman might earn 10 shillings a year; a century later, he could make 4 pounds. Wages in Florence increased by 100 per cent; an English day labourer's pay increased by 135 per cent. The wages paid to labourers working on the Hôpital Saint-Jacques increased by 100 per cent between 1348 and 1353. While Michel Mollat estimates that wage increases for the poor ranged from 100 per cent in rural areas to 150 per cent in cities and towns, these higher wages benefited those in cities the most, especially weavers, who, given their association with both shipping and flea-bearing animals, were particularly hard hit by plague.[15] Even the mendicant poor – those who could not work, and thus were dependent on charity – benefited from gratitude and perhaps fear of hell among the plague survivors. Bequests and alms increased, at least during the early part of the period. But even in

[11] Pirenne, *Economic and Social History*, 193. For general information on the impact of the plague, see Philip Ziegler, *The Black Death* (New York: Harper & Row, 1971).

[12] Mollat, *Poor in the Middle Ages*, 198.

[13] Quoted ibid., 244.

[14] Ibid., 198.

[15] Ibid., 199.

charity, improvements were not lasting; changing attitudes towards poverty and the poor are reflected in a shift away from the distribution of alms to individuals and towards bequests benefiting institutions.[16]

A number of historians point out that this increase in wages may only have been temporary since the cost of living increased as well, due in part to a shortage of money in addition to the paucity of food. Social dislocation and unrest were perhaps an inevitable consequence. Governments throughout Europe tried to regulate prices and wages. In France, in particular, ordinances attempted to control economic and social upheaval. While wages were set a third higher than in the pre-plague period, laws also forbade piecework, required the unemployed to work, and refused services to vagabonds, who as an itinerant element of society were looked upon with suspicion.[17] Yet even with wage and price controls, through the later fourteenth century it became increasingly difficult for skilled workers to earn enough to support a family. Public order was jeopardized by these stresses; the heightened economic and social insecurity caused by inflation, currency devaluation and wage restrictions, compounded by the effects of war, led to increases in crime and to civil disturbances that were often crushed with brutality, such as the uprising by the Jacquerie in 1358.[18]

The trauma of plague also increased the desire for a scapegoat on whom this calamity could be blamed. Sometimes the poor themselves were held responsible. On 17 April 1348 the provost of Narbonne noted that 'paupers and mendicants' accused by mobs of poisoning wells and food supplies had confessed to obtaining poisonous potions from unknown persons who had paid them to do so. Mob anger led to drawing and quartering for such offences, as well as anger directed at usurers and the wealthy. Jews were also blamed. A contemporaneous commentator, Jean de Venette, a Carmelite in Paris, recounts with disapprobation the widespread burning of Jews as punishment for the plague. In April of 1348 forty Jews were burned at Toulon; in Strasbourg, 900 were killed on 14 February 1349. Consequently, on 6 July 1351 a papal bull in protection of the Jews was promulgated in a response to this massacre of innocents. But even after this initial horrifying experience, the plague did not disappear but returned sporadically with varying degrees of virulence: in 1361, when the wealthy were more likely to be infected, and again in 1369, 1374, 1382, 1390 and 1400. Other infectious diseases took their toll on a population already vulnerable, especially between 1410 and 1425.[19]

16 Miri Rubin, *Charity and Community in Medieval Cambridge* (Cambridge: Cambridge University Press, 1987).

17 Mollat, *Poor in the Middle Ages*, 203; Pirenne, *Economic and Social History*, 193.

18 Carpentier and Arrignan, *La France et les Français*, 51–2.

19 Ibid., 35–6.

Civil disorder, alluded to above, was another significant social disruption. The *menu peuple* were outraged and fearful from the aggravated assault of devaluations, rising prices and increasing taxes to pay for the war. Allemand calculates that 'the subsidy demanded in Normandy in the winter of 1347–1348 cost the agricultural worker, living on his smallholding in the countryside, the equivalent of about thirty days paid work'.[20] These ordinary farmers were also subjected to 'taxes' extracted by warring bands of soldiers and unemployed mercenaries and their leaders, a consequence of the general lack of law and order under a series of weak kings. Such predators turned parts of France into wasteland, so that in whole regions 'there was no longer to be heard a cock-crowing or a hen clucking' because anything edible had been stripped from the peasants.[21]

The incompetence of King Jean II (1350–64) and the breathtaking ransom of 3,000,000 livres demanded of the people of France to buy their king's freedom from his English captors increased the financial strain. Later, the all-too-brief respite of the reign of Charles V from 1364 until 1380 was followed by a compounding of misfortunes under Charles VI (1380–1422), whose poor mad mind made him incapable of controlling the jealous machinations of the rival coteries that surrounded him and devastated his country during the forty-two years of his reign. All three reigns witnessed increased civil disorder and discontent. The revolt led by Etienne Marcel (1358) involved both the poor and artisans, primarily in Paris, although Marcel hoped for support from the justly dissatisfied in other cities experiencing unrest, including Toulon, Montbrison, Rouen, Troyes, Amiens and Arras. The uprising of the Jacquerie included peasants and artisans, but also merchants and miscreant soldiers as well. Mollat attributes these rebellions to abuses of power. Lewis sees them as a consequence of the failed attempt to re-establish the control of the Estates over a system that was clearly corrupt. Rebellions reflected 'a clear hostility to the court and a passion for reform of the administration'.[22]

These events and other civil unrest added to the general sense of insecurity and fear that governed society; nor were those fears unfounded, since popular revolts recurred periodically throughout the era – 1375, 1378, 1382, 1383, 1393, 1413, 1418 – all saw riots, rebellions and violence in the streets. At times, these uprisings seem to have been explosions directed at the general lawlessness of society as a whole; for others, historians point to more specific

20 Allmand, *Hundred Years War*, 126. On political unrest generally in this period see E. Charpentier and M. Le Mené, *La France du XIe au XVe siècle: population, société, économie* (Paris: Presses universitaires de France, 1996).

21 Pirenne, *Economic and Social History*, 194.

22 Mollat, *Poor in the Middle Ages*, 203–205; Lewis, *Later Medieval France*, 335.

grievances, such as the gap between rural and urban economies, heavy taxes, especially the tax to pay King Jean's ransom or Charles V's hearth tax, or specific changes in working conditions or hours. Nor were these limited to France, but in fact reflect a pattern across Europe. In any case, tensions were exacerbated between rich and poor, or rather between those who were fed and those who went hungry. Now in a generally apocalyptic mood, the 'angry poor', as Mollat calls them, were further frightened by prophecies of trouble to come.

The third factor was the Great Schism in the papacy, from 1378 until 1417, which fed eschatological fears. In a society that was both hierarchical and conventionally pious, the papal bull *Unam sanctam* promulgated by Boniface VIII in 1302, which stressed the spiritual primacy of the pope, was terrifying – for anyone who feared to have chosen the wrong pope. '[I]t is altogether necessary to salvation for every human creature to be subject to the Roman Pontiff'.[23]

Charles V played a pivotal role in this conflict, as we shall see, but the lesson of the Schism was that the Church was itself increasingly and visibly a tool of warring factions, instead of playing a role as mediator between them. The general lack of credibility, the legacy of corruption and the rise of lay piety all reflected and reinforced the inability of religion or religious institutions to deal adequately with the stresses on society, and in fact compounded them, providing an additional challenge to stability, thus augmenting rather than alleviating the anguish of this period.

These interrelated events had profound effects on political, social and economic life in ways that would radically alter late medieval France in almost every fashion imaginable. The trauma of these experiences must have been devastating to individual persons subjected to them. To us, they signal changes that from our perspective seem improvements – after all they are harbingers of the 'early modern'.[24] But the profound pessimism, the discouragement and despair of contemporaneous observers of these events serves as a reminder to us that French writers had reason to look with nostalgia to a more prosperous past.

By far the greatest factor was the senseless conflict referred to by historians as the Hundred Years War (1337–1453). It caused enormous loss of life, both directly, as at Agincourt, and indirectly through disruption of the economy, destruction of agricultural rhythms, despoliation and seizure of crops and

23 R. N. Swanson, *Religion and Devotion in Europe, c.1215–c.1515* (Cambridge: Cambridge University Press, 1995), 3.

24 However, it must be remembered that the decline of the standard of living and in social and political protections for women, children and working-class people was to continue, and reached its nadir between 1700 and 1750, the so-called Enlightenment. Thus, the view that the breakdown of the old order was progress can only be a retrospective and long-term one. To contemporary observers the increase in general misery was inescapable.

livestock, and diversion of resources. A true war of attrition,[25] the Hundred Years War was a complex struggle with origins dating to the twelfth century. The term itself comes from the late nineteenth century and categorizes together – not without reason – a series of wars that lasted well beyond a century. Beginning in 1066 with the Norman Conquest, France and England had been closely linked for generations in law and institutions, shared a language and religion, and had cultural ties that had allowed a truly international culture to develop that peaked in the late twelfth or early thirteenth century, with constant traffic between monasteries, schools and universities and the great houses of both lands, linking the ruling families of France and England through a web of marriage and feudal relations. In the following centuries, these two cultures began to diverge, evolving in different directions. Parallel to the increasing divergence in their languages, so too other institutions were evolving in separate directions. Changing views of inheritance, property, sovereignty and the feudal relationship, and family rivalries not far removed from the tradition of blood-feud added to burgeoning economic competition and complicated the relations of two emergent nation-states. In the first stage of this competition, culminating in the Treaty of Paris in 1259, France had been the victor, whereby England had renounced its claims to Normandy, Maine, Poitou, Anjou and Touraine but had retained its possession of Aquitaine (Guyenne), held as a fief of the French crown. Yet France's growing economic strength threatened English interests in Flanders, controlled by the dukes of Burgundy, and in Aquitaine, which was nominally under the English king as Duke of Aquitaine. In 1337 Edward III of England (1327–77) laid claim to the throne of France by right of inheritance through his mother, Isabelle of France, a daughter of Philippe IV. As a direct descendant, Edward argued, his claim was better than that of the ambitious and tough Philippe VI (1328–50), who although only the nephew of the king, had been personally named his heir on the late king's deathbed. A common explanation for the development in the quarrel is that France was following the Salic law of exclusively male succession in this, whereas England had a different legal tradition. Sarah Hanley has argued in a fascinating article that the articulation of Salic law used to justify the exclusion of women as heirs to the throne dates only from the early fifteenth century, originating from the hand of the same Jean de Montreuil whose misogyny was to be criticized by Christine de Pizan.[26]

As punishment for his disloyalty, Philippe VI 'confiscated' Guyenne from Edward. This event set off a second cycle in the war that did not end with the

25 Janet Coleman, *Medieval Readers and Writers, 1350–1400* (New York: Columbia University Press, 1981).

26 Sarah Hanley, 'Identity Politics and Rulership in France', in M. Wolfe (ed.), *Changing Identities in Early Modern France* (Durham, NC: Duke University Press, 1997), 78–94.

antagonists' deaths but continued into the next generation. This stage of the conflict France lost, with the defeat at Crécy and capture of Jean II of France in 1346. Held for ransom by his English captors at enormous cost to the French population, the apparently charming but inept king never reigned again. The disastrous events of his reign appeared ready to end with the treaty of Brétigny in 1360, but the treaty was never fully implemented, and respite from this second active phase of the Hundred Years War began only with Jean's death in 1364 and the accession to the throne of his son.[27]

Charles V is one of those extraordinary figures who seems to appear in spite of all the circumstances that shape an individual. Not his father's son in either intelligence or judgement, he came to the throne apparently determined to provide the kingdom with good rule. His intentions were undoubtedly complex. The safety of his own throne and the integrity of his dynasty were linked to an emerging national consciousness that had a rich symbolic content of which he seems to have been well aware. Since much of our knowledge about his character, aspirations and goals comes from sources within his own court, and especially from Christine de Pizan's laudatory biography completed in 1404, it is difficult to determine how much was conscious myth-making on his part and that of his biographers, and how much of his reputation reflects the golden glow of hindsight. In any case, he seems to have grasped both the symbolic and real problems of rule early and dealt with them effectively. As a consequence, the sources tell us, he began to assemble the elements that he believed were most important, especially wise advisers from both the present and the past. To this end, he had his staff search for young talent from the universities of Europe and he also began to build a library that would contain the known wisdom of the world, not just for his personal use, but for others as well. While Charles V came from a family of noted bibliophiles, more than just a desire for luxury goods and status symbols seems to have been involved in his desire for new translations into French of classic works on government and other sciences deemed important to rule, such as astrology and cartography. This seems to have been a conscious effort, as Nicole Oresme, both an adviser and one of Charles's most prestigious authors, attests: 'The king desired, for the common good, to have [these works] translated into French so that he and his advisers could better understand them, especially the *Ethics* and the *Politics*.'[28]

27 For the reign of Charles V generally, see Françoise Autrand, *Charles V: le Sage* (Paris: Fayard, 1994).

28 '[L]e Roy a voulu, pour le bien commun, faire les translater en françois afin que il et ses conseilliers et autres les puissent mieulx entendre, mesmement Ethiques et Politiques'; Nicole Oresme, *Le Livre de politiques d'Aristote* (Philadelphia: American Philosophical Society, 1970), 99.

As a consequence, Charles V commissioned both new copies and translations of all the great works believed worthy and significant for consultation. These included vernacular translations of Aristotle's *Ethics*, *Politics*, *Economics*[29] and *On the Heavens*; Vegetius' *Treatise on the Military Arts*; numerous works by other classical Roman authors, including Valerius Maximus, pseudo-Seneca and Livy; translations of Christian political thought, including Augustine's *City of God*, John of Salisbury's *Policraticus* and Giles of Rome's *On the Government of Princes*, as well as copies of more recent vernacular political works including the influential *Songe du vergier*, *Li Livres dou tresor* by Brunetto Latini and a translation of Petrarch's *Remedies of Both Kinds of Fortune*. Nor were all of these volumes political or philosophical. The Bible itself was translated by Raoul de Presles in about 1375.[30] A thirteenth-century scientific encyclopedia by Bartholomaeus Anglicus was translated as *Le Livre des propriétés des choses* by Jean Corbechon; the *Catalan Atlas*, several astronomical books and the revived *Grand Chroniques de France* were only a few of the works commenced, purchased or otherwise collected by Charles V. The first inventory of the library by its 'guardian', Gilles Malet, described 910 items on the three floors of the north-west tower of the Louvre, called the Falconry. The most valuable luxury editions were held amidst the precious objects from the royal collections in the stronghold of Vincennes.[31]

The library project spurred a real interest, as well as competition, among other members of the royal family, most especially the king's brothers. The dukes of Burgundy, Anjou and of course Jean, Duke of Berry, were notable collectors, and a passion for books was shared by their heirs. The fashionable quest for books as luxury goods was augmented by the increase in the numbers of literate lay persons from the developing professional class of lawyers and government officials.[32] This increased demand expanded the visibility and

29 Until the sixteenth century, this authentic fourth-century classical work on the household was believed to be by Aristotle himself.

30 Late medieval vernacular translations of the Bible were numerous, including Jerome's Latin Vulgate itself. On the eve of the Reformation, some 250 vernacular-language translations of the Bible existed.

31 Leopold Delisle, *Recherches sur la librairie de Charles V* (Paris, 1907; repr. Amsterdam: G. Th. van Heusden, 1967). Discussions of the library project can be found in Willard's *Life*, especially 28–9, but also in Claire Richter Sherman, *Imaging Aristotle: Verbal and Visual Representation in Fourteenth-Century France* (Berkeley: University of California Press, 1995), 6–12. The Bibliothèque Nationale de France has an exhibit on the era of Charles V illustrated with manuscript illuminations selected from his collection. As of this writing, it can be found at www.bnf.fr.

32 Coleman argues that literacy extended well into the middle classes and indeed could be considered a characteristically defining element of that class. Cf. *Medieval Readers and Writers 1350–1400*, 63 ff.

productivity of the Parisian book market, especially highlighting the work of illuminators, well beyond the confines of Paris. Certainly manuscripts produced in Paris during this period had worldwide audiences.

The companion project of Charles V was the recruitment of the best minds that could be persuaded to enter his service either formally or informally. Notable thinkers cultivated by Charles included Jean Buridan, Raoul le Presles, Jean Foulechat and Jean Froissart, whose chronicles remain a major primary source for medieval scholars. Foremost among these must be Nicole Oresme, a Norman by birth, dean of Notre Dame, both translator and commentator on Aristotle's political and scientific works, and one of the most important – and understudied – political theorists of the late Middle Ages. His commentary on the *Politics* is referred to by James Blythe as 'exceptionally original' and Blythe points out that Oresme's suggestions were actually implemented by Charles V, something few political theorists can claim.[33] Oresme's discourse *De moneta* is the earliest discussion in Europe of monetary policy, and is especially strong on dealing with inflation. Oresme's work in mathematics and astronomy inclined him to a heliocentric view of the solar system and his attitude towards astrology was cautionary, despite dealing with a king who subscribed wholeheartedly to astrology as an asset for rulers.[34]

Part of this new government initiative included what we would consider administrative recruitment. In 1364, the year of Christine de Pizan's birth in Venice, the two major centres of intellectual talent were the University of Paris and the University of Bologna. Bologna's reputation was enhanced by its status as the premier school of medicine and of civil law and by the fact that many of its faculty and students were lay persons and thus free of the constraints imposed by the Church or by religious orders, which allowed them to take positions elsewhere. Tommaso da Pizzano was a graduate of the University of Bologna, which, according to Charity Cannon Willard, he left in 1357 to take a position in Venice, where he married Christine's mother, daughter of Tommaso Mondino da Forlì. In 1365 he decided to accept a position at the court of Charles V as physician, or as Christine herself describes it, as 'philosopher, savant, and counselor'.[35] It seems that his primary attraction for Charles was his training

33 James Blythe, *Ideal Government and the Mixed Constitution in the Middle Ages* (Princeton: Princeton University Press, 1992), 203–204.

34 On Oresme, see Susan M. Babbitt, *Oresme's Livre de politiques and the France of Charles V* (Transactions of the American Philosophical Society, 75, pt. 1; Philadelphia: American Philosophical Society, 1985), as well as the introduction to Menut's critical edition of Oresme's *Le livre de politiques*; and Blythe, *Ideal Government*, 203–42.

35 Christine de Pizan, *Christine's Vision*, trans. Glenda McLeod (New York: Garland Publishing, 1993), 153.

in astrology as part of natural science. Tommaso da Pizzano was thus a member of that new and rising class of literate lay officials at court, whose living depended primarily on the largesse of the king. While scholars of Christine de Pizan have always assumed that her origins were thus 'middle class', or simply accepted at face value her own claim to nobility, recent studies of the Pizzano family by Nikolai Wandruszka indicate that Christine's claim to be 'born of noble parents' was not idle boasting; in fact her family can be traced to 1249 and were probably of the lower nobility, later absorbed into the rising urban upper classes in the fourteenth century.[36]

In any case, Tommaso decided to bring his young family with him to Paris, and in December 1368 Christine de Pizan and her family were presented to the king at the Louvre. Christine adopted France with a passionate intensity. Despite her later financial difficulties, she was to live in France for the rest of her life.

As Christine's story opens in 1364, France was about to enter into a momentary state of comparative political calm. Charles V's successful campaigns to restore the geographical integrity of his kingdom, as well as the discernible wisdom of his political and military appointments, resulted in relative political and economic stability compared with the reigns both immediately before and after his own. These years were not without economic pressures and social instability – some of which were the direct consequence of Charles's policy choices. For example, although during the imprisonment of Jean II Dauphin Charles had been advised by Nicole Oresme to make greater use of the Estates General, they met only during these early years and the lack of their approval for the heavy tax burden was a major contributing factor to the popular uprising led by Etienne Marcel. Charles V also had a significant impact on the papal schism. Even the accounts of his admirer, Christine de Pizan, reflect an uneasiness with the consequences of his role in this divisive and dangerous conflict, which was not reconciled until 1417. As she notes in the biography:

> We know that King Charles V, as we saw above, never resolved delicate problems without taking counsel of wise clerks and other discreet men of integrity. He observed this just rule in the affairs of the Church, because the schism was . . . a great weight on him. This was, indeed, a serious and dangerous business that demanded a great deal of circumspection.[37]

But relative improvement is better than none at all, and in retrospect, the reign of Charles V must have seemed an island of civility, peace and prosperity

36 Nikolai Wandruszka, 'Christine's Family Origins', in Eric Hicks, *Au champ des escritures* (Paris: Champion, 2000), 111–33.

37 Christine de Pizan, *Le Livre des faits et bonnes moeurs du roi Charles V le Sage*, ed. Eric Hicks and Thérèse Moreau (Paris: Stock, 1997), 285.

when compared with the events that followed. It was during this period that Christine came to France. To some degree, all of Christine de Pizan's works are autobiographical, and her own account of her upbringing and education during this period is a fascinating one. We are left with a picture of an intelligent and observant young woman, 'indulged and pampered as a child',[38] particularly attached to and admiring of her father, receiving a fairly conventional upbringing for her age, her class and her sex. Having been given the opportunity to study, she later regretted not having taken better advantage of it. 'I was too young and foolish to drink my fill . . . Alas when I had those learned masters beside me, I did not give much thought to study!'[39]

In later life, reflecting further on the delights as well as the importance of education for both men and women, she remarked with typical humour: 'One day, a man criticized my desire for knowledge, saying that it was inappropriate for a woman to be learned, as it was so rare, to which I replied that it was even less fitting for a man to be ignorant, as it was so common.'[40]

Assiduously wooed by a number of suitors, Christine's marriage at fifteen to a young Picard nobleman, Etienne du Castel, who served the king as a secretary and notary, was a singularly happy one. Tenderly, she confides that

> A sweet thing is marriage,
> I can well prove it by my own experience.[41]

These happy, busy years saw the births of three children. Marie, the eldest, would one day become a nun at the Royal Convent at Poissy. Jean du Castel, Christine's son, would follow his father's footsteps in the royal service. Evidently the third child, also a boy, died sometime after 1390 but before 1399.[42] But the death of Charles V in 1380, and the consequent gradual decline of her father and his fortunes no doubt diminished her happiness. The new king, Charles VI,[43] was only eleven at his father's death. Highly vulnerable in the quarrelsome court, he was caught in the unpleasant conflict and competition between his ambitious uncles, Louis of Anjou, Philippe of Burgundy, Louis of Bourbon and Jean of Berry. Louis of Anjou had been named regent, and two of

---

38 Christine de Pizan, 'L'Avision Christine', in *The Writings of Christine de Pizan*, ed. Charity Cannon Willard (New York: Persea Books, 1994), 16.

39 Ibid.

40 Ibid.

41 'Ballade XXVI', in *Writings*, ed. Willard, 51.

42 In *L'Avision Christine* she refers to being left a widow with three small children. Later in the same work she refers to her joy at being reunited with Jean after three years, 'whom Death had left her only son'. 'L'Avision Christine', *Writings*, ed. Willard, 19.

43 For the reign generally, see Françoise Autrand, *Charles VI: la folie du roi* (Paris: Fayard, 1986).

his brothers, the dukes of Burgundy and Bourbon, were the prince's guardians. All four promptly acted with their usual disdain for the *bien commun*, Louis by seizing the treasury and some eighty of the manuscripts from his dead brother's collection in the royal library. His brothers, not to be outdone, demanded the immediate coronation of the young Charles, whereupon the new king's uncles divided France among themselves. The Duke of Burgundy controlled not only his duchy but Flanders, and thus the English cloth trade. The Duke of Berry set himself up in luxurious style, controlling a third of France and inaugurating a building programme that increased taxes throughout his territories. Louis of Anjou controlled much of the south, where he too managed to alienate the populace by adding to already burdensome taxes. As regent, he had reinstated the taxes that Charles V had abolished, thus his reputation was low everywhere. Louis's empire-building ambitions were nothing new. He had always desired Italy, which aspiration may have played a role in the fateful decision by Charles V not to recognize the newly elected Italian pope in 1378, an act that contributed to the Great Schism. Anjou's son would later be crowned king of Naples, although he never reigned.

By 1388 the young king had had enough of these machinations and he threw off his uncles' controls, reinstating some very able former ministers who had been out of favour after the death of Charles V. Hopes rebounded that the newly emancipated king would govern well. The 'marmousets', as these advisers were nicknamed by their enemies,[44] pressed for peace, and finding the young Richard II of England similarly inclined, French and English envoys signed a truce on 18 July 1389. Both sides were optimistic and enthusiastic; Charles VI naively hoped to turn his energies to a Crusade, while his English counterpart seems to have been a francophile and wary of war's enormous economic and social costs as well.

But Christine's personal hopes were shattered with the deaths in quick succession of her father some time in 1387 and her young husband in 1390. The disintegration of her family's fortunes is well known, told both by Christine herself in her accounts in both *L'Avision Christine* and in *Mutacion de fortune*, and by her biographers, and need not be retold here. But the first attack of madness[45] in Charles VI in 1392 added enormously to the dysfunction of the kingdom, and many of Christine's personal troubles could be attributed in part

44 The group was known disparagingly as the 'marmousets' from their lined, elderly and perhaps disapproving faces. Their unattractive nickname, with its weasel-like connotations, has caused them to receive less than their due as advisers. Their ideas for institutional and political reform went unheard.

45 The king's health is discussed in Autrand, *Charles VI* and in R. C. Famiglietti, 'The French Monarchy in Crisis 1392–1415' (Ph.D. diss., City University of New York, 1982).

to the political and institutional weaknesses that were further revealed by the king's incapacity. Pleas for justice for widows and the powerless are a prominent theme in her political works, resonating with personal experience as she tried to recover her husband's unpaid salary, the sums of money owed to him, and the principal of funds invested with an unscrupulous merchant for her children's futures:

> Troubles surged upon me from all sides, and as is the common lot of widows, I became entangled in legal disputes of every sort. . . . How vividly I remember many a chilly winter morning spent in that palace, shivering from the cold while waiting for those representing me so I could remind them of my case or urge them to action, only to hear at the end of the session decisions that made me burst with outrage, or else puzzled me; but what hurt even more was the expense I could ill afford.[46]

She tried to keep up appearances. 'Under my fur-lined cloak and fine surcoat that was carefully mended but seldom replaced, I was often shivering.'[47] Bitter and difficult years passed, fourteen in all, but her rediscovery of the joys of reading the philosophers led her to experiment with her own writing, primarily at first as a mechanism for dealing with her grief and loss:

> Since I lost my love, by foul Death betrayed,
> Grief has struck me, which has to perdition led,
> All my good days, and so my joy has fled.[48]

Working out her personal grief, as well as the fears and insecurities of a woman struggling with the responsibilities of a family alone, was a lengthy process. Her poems reveal an honest immediacy, and a touch of anger. Her most famous poem reflects this struggle:

> Alone am I and alone would I be
> Alone by my lover left suddenly
> Alone am I, no friend or master with me,
> Alone am I, both sad and angrily,
> Alone am I, in languor wretchedly,
> Alone am I, completely lost doubtlessly
> Alone am I, friendless and so lonely.[49]

Within France, the presence of a weak king exposed opportunities for graft, corruption and general opportunism throughout the government. During the 1390s Philippe 'the Bold', Duke of Burgundy, ruled with a firm hand as regent during the king's episodic madness, but the king's younger brother, the talented

---

46 'L'Avision Christine', in *Writings*, ed. Willard, 11–12.

47 Ibid., 12.

48 'Rondeau III', in *Writings*, ed. Willard, 53.

49 'Ballade XI', ibid., 41.

Louis of Orleans (1371–1407), was in control when the king was sane. The jealousies, ambition and cupidity of the king's uncles were augmented in the younger generation – particularly in the king's much abler brother, Louis, and in his cousin, the prospective Duke of Burgundy, Jean sans Peur (John the Fearless) – which generated rivalries that would soon tear the country apart.

Court life continued with a febrile intensity that seems remarkably undiscerning of the widespread problems in the kingdom, and oblivious to the turmoil in England. Richard II preferred peace to war with France, which blackened his reputation in the eyes of those whom knighthood and nascent nationalism inclined to battle. Popular uprisings and the terror of those who saw Richard's overtures to the rival pope as hell-bent ultimately made him so unpopular that Henry Bolingbroke was able to seize the throne in 1399. Christine's son Jean was caught in this conflict by virtue of having been taken to England by the Earl of Salisbury as a companion to his twelve-year-old son. In Christine's view, '[m]isfortune . . . brought calamity down upon the said King Richard of England, as is well known. The good count [Salisbury] remained loyal to his rightful lord and as a result was beheaded, which was an act of grave injustice'.[50] Young Jean du Castel was taken into the household of Henry V and treated generously, but Christine was uneasy under the circumstances and managed to bring the boy safely home, although it cost her some of her works, an event that will be discussed at more length in a later chapter.[51] While the French exclaimed in horror at the regicide, the overthrow of Richard II does not seem to have aroused in them any desire to unite and settle their own differences.

In fact, the opposite was the case. Caught up in the pursuit of pleasure, the French court was increasingly insensible to the unrest and dissatisfaction in France. Charles VI had developed a taste for luxury, 'encouraged in his taste for pleasure by his beautiful, sluttish wife'.[52] Paris had the desperate gaiety of other *fin-de-siècle* periods. In this milieu, competitions were staged between court poets, who lauded the romanticism of a chivalric ideal that was very far from the lived reality. Poetry was as much a part of court life and the expectations of courtiers as were the other virtues of chivalry, a form of entertainment that originated much earlier both in France and in England.

Willard believes that Christine de Pizan began to write in verse somewhere around 1394, perhaps following the instructions for writing verse in Eustache Deschamps's then recent treatise on poetry. Christine herself dates the beginning of her career from 1399, which saw her poetry becoming known at the French

50 'L'Avision Christine', ibid., 19.

51 Ibid.

52 Desmond Seward, *The Hundred Years War* (New York: Athenaeum, 1978), 138.

court, and even beyond, in England and even in Milan, through the wife of Louis of Orleans, Valentine Visconti. 'Thus the first Duke of Milan in Lombardy heard of me, perhaps in a way more flattering then I deserve, and offered me a generous lifetime income if I would come live in his land.'[53] In these circles, particularly the ducal court of Louis of Orleans, to whom some of her early works were dedicated, Christine was able to associate with a number of influential and respected members of the intelligentsia, including Gilles Malet, the former royal librarian, who was now responsible for the duchess's household; wise old Bureau de La Rivière, who had been an experienced and authoritative adviser to the late king; Guillaume de Tignonville, whose *Ditz des philosophes*, a translated compendium, was an important source of classical quotations; and the revered poet himself, Eustache Deschamps, also called Eustache Morel.

Many of Christine's early poems were frothy nothings to celebrate the new year or St Valentine's Day or May Day.

> Now has come the joyous month of May,
> So gay, with such sweet delights,
> As these orchards, hedges and these woods,
> All decked with leaves and blossoms,
> And all things rejoice
> Among the fields all flowered and green,
> Nothing is troubled or grieving,
> In the sweet month of May.[54]

Such light occasional poetry would please her patrons, and perhaps provide a quick supplement to her income as well. At this early stage of her career, between 1399 and 1402, Christine's works were primarily in verse, on ostensibly light and courtly themes, but with serious undertones. For example, Ballade XXXIV, quoted above, ends on a darker note:

> For him, whom I mourn I weep often,
> For him, from whom I have no help;
> The painful grief of love I now more strongly
> Feel . . . .

This period was very fruitful, consisting almost entirely of poetry on courtly themes with a few exceptions: her moral proverbs, an advice book written for her son Jean, and the fascinating *Epistre d'Othéa*, where her transition from court poet to public intellectual and political pundit can be observed. Then, in 1399, she criticized the *Roman de la Rose* for its negative view of women. Christine's *Epistre au dieu d'amours*, composed in 1399, mocks the amorous

53 'L'Avision Christine', in *Writings*, ed. Willard, 20.

54 'Ballade XXXIV', ibid., 44.

boasting of vain courtiers, who belittle women and dispute their virtue. Cupid argues that these views were the consequence of shallow and vulgar sentiments by poets like Jean de Meun. It is unlikely that Christine anticipated the reaction to her criticism of the misogynistic *Roman de la Rose*, which ignited the 'Quarrel of the Rose' and thrust Christine into the centre of court life, inaugurating her later carefully constructed career as a professional writer. The resultant debate became public and involved several of the major intellectual figures of the day, including Jean Gerson, Chancellor of the University of Paris and a significant philosopher, theologian and moralist; Pierre d'Ailly, also a significant theorist; Jean de Montreuil; and Guillaume de Tignonville, and the association may even have reached Geoffrey Chaucer in England before his death. Christine's poem was very successful; it circulated widely and was translated into English by Thomas Hoccleve, the first of several of her works to be translated.

The position that Christine articulated in the Quarrel was one that she sustained throughout her career. Despite the use of allegory and the general erudition of misogynistic poetry, she argued that its real impact was to corrupt and degrade the reader by desensitizing him or her to a debased view of human beings. The titillation and glorification of behaviour that was crude, abusive, irresponsible and uncontrolled seemed to Christine not only wrong but dangerous to society. As Helen Solterer observes, by emphasizing the transition from verbal violence to real violence, readers can more clearly see the potentially harmful consequences of abusive language and their own complicity in them.[55] Given the state of the court of Louis of Orleans, and indeed of France in general, this was not a particularly prudish view, although it might appear so when reading the correspondence in the abstract.[56] Like all of Christine's views, however, the quarrel must be seen in context. The growing gap between the chivalric myth and the increasingly brutal reality of noble conduct was having an impact more generally on literary forms in both England and in France. Some writers, like Philippe de Mézières, exaggerated an already saccharine myth. Others, like Chaucer, treated the codified values of chivalry with humour. Christine, by contrast, confronted the problem of brutal behaviour head on, in this case by challenging a supposedly romantic view of women that actually vilified them. In her later didactic works, she would continue this process of emphasizing the impact of artistic creations on the mores of public life and

55 Helen Solterer, *The Master and Minerva* (Berkeley: University of California Press, 1995), 151 ff.

56 For a fuller discussion of the Quarrel see Eric Hicks, *Le Débat sur le Roman de la Rose* (Paris: Champion, 1977), Kevin Brownlee, *Rethinking the Romance of the Rose* (Philadelphia: University of Pennsylvania Press, 1992); Joseph Baird, *The Quarrel of the Rose: Letters and Documents* (Chapel Hill: University of North Carolina Press, 1978).

attempt to guide them in more appropriate directions. In her biography of Charles V, for example, she deliberately reframed the concept of chivalry to emphasize values that she believed it lacked.

Her position vindicated – in some eyes at least – after 1402, she began to treat other more serious subjects, still in verse. Her first mirror for princes dates from this period – the evocative *Epistre d'Othéa*, which was presented to Louis of Orleans. Resembling the much later emblem books of the sixteenth century, it is composed of one hundred *textes* explicated by an accompanying *glose* and *allégorie*. In some redactions, although not the earliest, each chapter is illustrated by a sumptuous illumination. As will be discussed in a later chapter, this complex work functions as a mirror for princes, with the goddess Othéa tutoring the recalcitrant Hector of Troy.

In 1404 Christine composed her first lengthy prose work, *Le Livre des faits et bonnes moeurs du roi Charles V le sage*, followed in short order by *Le Livre de la cité des dames*, *Le Livre des trois vertus*, also called *Le Tresor du cité des dames*, *Le Livre de prod'homie/prudence* and *Le Livre du corps de policie*. This was an extraordinarily productive period in her life. Given the labour-intensive and time-consuming nature of book production in the fifteenth century, as well as the lengthy process of actually committing ideas to words, it is amazing that she produced so many works in less than a decade. It is also significant that she began to turn from poetry to prose. Christine herself says that she began 'to forge pretty things' in 1399, and as her skill improved, turned to 'more noble' subject matter,[57] perhaps because of her heightened sense of urgency, faced with the deteriorating political situation. While her prose works include much more borrowing both from each other and from established authorities, such as Valerius Maximus, and reflect at times the haste in which they were written, they indicate a concern for more serious subjects and a darker mood.[58] As a simple observation, this is valuable enough, but it does not answer why she would become more preoccupied by ethical and political matters. In an entirely different context, W. H. Auden once remarked that the movement of a writer from prose to verse indicated, he thought, an increase in the serenity of the author.[59] Perhaps, in this case the opposite is true: Christine's preoccupation with the dreadful political situation was taking its toll. To paraphrase Auden, both the time and the energy to count syllables were missing. In both France and England, poets and other intellectuals were attempting to

---

[57] *Christine's Vision*, trans. McLeod, 119.

[58] Rosalind Brown-Grant, *Christine de Pizan and the Moral Defence of Women* (Cambridge: Cambridge University Press, 1999), 5.

[59] Dag Hammarsjkold, *Markings*, with introduction by W. H. Auden (New York: Knopf, 1968), xx.

bring some sanity to the political situation. Philippe de Mézières had written to the young Richard II urging him to pursue peace, and his *Songe du vieil pèlerin* was an allegorical dream vision on France. Geoffrey Chaucer's works were very much addressed to the political environment, and 'The Tale of Melibee' – also in prose – can be read as an anti-war statement.[60] By 1405 the conflict between the Duke of Burgundy, Jean sans Peur, and his increasingly bitter antagonist, Louis of Orleans, and his ally Isabeau of Bavaria, was reaching a crisis point. Jean Gerson and other distinguished intellectuals attempted to intervene in the conflict; thus Christine was certainly not alone in her pleas for good government and her fears about the deteriorating political situation.

Several other factors undoubtedly contributed to Christine's exceptional productivity during this time. Her financial situation had stabilized and her children were provided for adequately. Her growing reputation as a court poet was significant. Her beautifully produced works were also held in high esteem among the royal bibliophiles. Certainly, as she acknowledges herself, some of her success was due to the novelty of her position as a woman poet in a world dominated by men artistically as well as politically. 'I had by this time achieved some fame, since many of my works had been given as gifts – not by myself but by others – to princes in foreign lands, and these were regarded as new works written from a woman's perspective. As the proverb says, novelty pleases . . .'.[61]

However, the transition from court poet to political adviser, no matter how circumspect or beautifully embellished her voice, is more difficult to explain. There is no question that this period was one in which the desire for pleasure at court burned with a feverish energy while the political situation was rapidly unravelling. Was it her own sense of concern that turned her to didactic writing? Did she have some sense that there was interest in a call to reform the political situation? Had she begun to command high enough prices or favours for her works that she could afford to expand her repertoire? Was it her very real love and pride in France? While such speculation is fascinating, the only documentation scholars have is to be found in Christine's own voice as revealed in her prologues and in the extant account books. Whatever combination of reasons, whether a sense of urgency or nationalism, economic exigencies, or increased confidence in her right to speak seriously, in any case, *Le Livre du*

60 See K. L. Forhan, 'Poets and Politics: Just War in Geoffrey Chaucer and Christine de Pizan', presented at the annual meeting of the American Political Science Association, 2000; forthcoming.

61 'L'Avision Christine', in *Writings*, ed. Willard, 19–20. This passage, like so many in Christine's work, deserves serious consideration, since it challenges many of the stereotypes about the period.

corps de policie, the last of her political works from this period, was finished before November 1407, and was dedicated to the young dauphin, Louis of Guyenne, who was then living under the influence of the Duke of Burgundy. The *Livre du corps de policie* can be so precisely dated because it refers to Louis of Orleans as still living.

On 23 November 1407 Louis of Orleans was attacked by a group of armed ruffians, including Raoul d'Anquentonville, who was later charged with his murder. Information spread very quickly that Jean sans Peur was behind the attack, and indeed he blurted out a confession two days later. In his defence of the assassins, Jean Petit argued that the murder was justified on the basis of tyrannicide, and it is certainly clear that Louis of Orleans, despite his considerable talent, had been as neglectful of his responsibilities as Christine's mythical Hector, and had paid the same price. The Duke of Burgundy was banished from court for a while but was back within the year. The elimination of his rival did not, of course, resolve the conflict since that was caused as much by the king's incapacity as by the jealous ambitions of the antagonists. France was divided into two factions: the Burgundians and now the Armagnacs, so called because Louis of Orleans's son, eleven-year-old Charles, had married Bonne, the daughter of Bernard, Count of Armagnac, who now acted as protector and advocate for his young son-in-law. Jean of Burgundy's talents as a ruler and his promises of financial reform brought him the support of the Parisian bourgeoisie and academics, while the Armagnacs were supported by the 'establishment': royal officials, the nobility – at least those outside of Burgundy – and the rest of the royal family.

Christine's *Livre des faits d'armes et de chevalrie* dates from this later period. This is an innovative political work, most remarkable for Christine's articulation of the standards of just war. It was commissioned by the Duke of Burgundy, who had the young dauphin, Louis of Guyenne, under his control. The dauphin was an heir worthy of his troubled family. Apparently lazy and spoiled, he had little taste or talent for military leadership, unlike his cousin, Jean sans Peur. It is possible that this work on military life may have influenced him, since he played a positive role in the negotiation of the treaty of Auxerre in 1412.

Christine, optimistic that the moral and political authority of the late king's brothers could bring about a cessation of hostilities, wrote a formal letter, *La Lamentation sur les maux de France,* to the Duke of Berry, who had as yet sufficient neutrality between the factions that he might have been able to intercede had he chosen to extricate himself from his treasures. He failed to take action, however, and the propaganda war between the two parties intensified.

By 1411 Jean of Burgundy had taken control of Paris; the Armagnacs then assembled an army, and with the Duke of Berry, last survivor of the wise king's brothers, besieged the city. At the same time, Jean was negotiating commercial treaties with the English king, Henry IV, as well as offering his daughter in marriage to the king's heir. Four Flemish cities changed hands; and some 800 English troops and 2,000 archers came to France under the English Earl of Arundel. Charity Cannon Willard believes that the Armagnac claim that there was a treaty between the English and Burgundy to exchange troops for commercial interests was Armagnac propaganda, since there is no documentary evidence to substantiate that assertion. Other historians assume that a pact was made, operating under the theory that the simplest explanation suffices even without explicit documentation. In either case, combined with Jean's 3,000 men, they were able to avoid the Count's troops and thus break the Armagnac blockade of Paris, entering the city together. Jean had the king outlaw the dukes of Orleans and Bourbon, but pressures for peace brought negotiations. The dauphin, Louis of Guyenne, the Duke of Anjou and the Count of Savoy were able to negotiate among the parties, resulting in the treaty of Auxerre, 22 August 1412. Christine dedicated her *Livre de la paix* to the then seventeen-year-old dauphin with clear but cautious optimism for his future and that of France.[62]

The peace party, headed by the dauphin, was in the ascendant, when with a turn of Fortune's wheel, Jean sans Peur was brought down by a popular uprising. The Cabochian revolt began with a list of grievances presented by Simon Caboche, head of the butcher's guild, but over the weeks that followed mob violence intensified, including the invasion of the dauphin's chambers, the seizure of several persons who were close to the ruling family, and threats to the dauphin himself. Financial and administrative reforms were enacted in the Cabochian ordinance of 26–27 May 1413, but the threat to the dauphin's safety caused him to appeal to the Armagnacs for aid, and both Cabochians and Burgundians left the city. *Le Livre de la paix* refers to many of these events, since it was written in two parts, with the Cabochian uprising occurring after Part One was completed but before Part Two. It was presented to the Duke of Berry for New Year's Day in 1414 and praises the prince for his role as peacemaker. Mob violence was now seen by Christine as an extremely dangerous aspect of political life, which represents a tempering of the view presented in *Corps de policie*, written only five years earlier, where she recommends that the common people's complaints be presented to the king via intermediaries from the merchant class. By contrast, *Le Livre de la paix* presents much sterner warnings about the advisability of controlling the common people, as we shall see in a later chapter.

62 The dauphin was born on 20 January 1395.

On 3 October 1413 the Cabochian reforms were abolished, the Duke of Burgundy was banished, and the Armagnacs were optimistically preparing for his military defeat in spring of 1414. But the young, ambitious and relentless Henry V of England invaded France, and the ensuing Battle of Agincourt, 25 October 1415, deprived the French of much of its leadership through death or imprisonment. Among the French victims were the Duke of Bourbon, the Duke of Burgundy's two brothers, most of the Armagnac leadership, and significantly, Charles d'Albret, Constable of France and commander-in-chief. The young Charles of Orleans would remain a hostage for twenty-five years. Both the Duke of Burgundy and Louis of Guyenne survived, but only by the expedient of having been elsewhere at the time.[63]

Sadly, Louis of Guyenne's potential as future king went unrealized. In December of the same year he died, and in early 1416 the Duke of Berry died as well. The political instability and anxiety these deaths caused in the aftermath of Agincourt cannot be underestimated. For example, the Bourgeois de Paris, whose style is laconic and understated, remarks that the prices of food had doubled, that the Armagnacs were 'without pity', and alludes to rumours that the king's son had been poisoned.[64] As a consequence of the death and destruction, the Count of Armagnac, a singularly brutal man but one of the few surviving leaders with military experience, had been named Constable of France. His repressive leadership was sufficient spur to cause the Duke of Burgundy to begin negotiating an alliance with Henry V in late 1416. The new dauphin, Louis's younger brother, Jean of Touraine, died in April 1417, leaving yet another young and inexperienced brother, Charles, as the royal hope, while the English invaded that same summer. The Armagnacs were effectively penned into Paris by Burgundian forces, when, under the protection of the Armagnacs, the future Charles VII was named dauphin. France had to deal with yet another great schism: on the one hand, a rival government centred around the queen and the Duke of Burgundy, on the other the competing regime of the new dauphin in Armagnac-controlled Paris. At the beginning of the new year, on 20 January1418, Christine dedicated her *Epistre de la prison de vie humaine* to Marie de Berry, duchess of Bourbon, who had lost husband, son, son-in-law, cousins and friends to death or imprisonment at Agincourt. That was a

63 In this Louis may have been following Christine's instructions. She argues the importance of having a professional and experienced war leader in battle rather than an inexperienced young prince at the head of an army. John the Fearless may simply have been too clever a tactician to be present. Willard comments that few 'princes had a tactical sense as good as his, and he may have foreseen the disaster' (Willard, *Life*, 192).

64 *Journal d'un bourgeois de Paris* (Paris: Librairie Générale Française, 1990), 90–91, 132.

very difficult year in Paris: food supplies were low, the English capture of Normandy and the terrible siege at Rouen made frightening the prospect of the English advance. On 28 May 1419 Burgundian troops entered the city by stealth, murdering suspected Armagnac sympathizers as they slept. The dauphin and his staff, including the young Jean du Castel, son of Christine de Pizan, and many other Parisians, fled.

Attempts at a peace were made, with meetings between the Burgundians and Armagnacs that summer, but the Armagnacs were planning their revenge for the bloodshed in Paris. On 10 September 1419, as he presented himself to the dauphin, Jean sans Peur, Duke of Burgundy, was hacked to death as he knelt in homage. Disgust at this butchery alienated many from the dauphin, especially Jean's son, the new Duke of Burgundy, Philippe the Good, who hated the Armagnacs even more than he loathed the English, with whom he formally aligned himself in December 1419. He and the English began negotiations with the queen at the rival court in Champagne, where the oblivious Charles VI was titular monarch. In an extraordinary act of personal and maternal treachery, Queen Isabeau disowned her son, the dauphin Charles, declaring him illegitimate, and the English Henry V was named the king's heir and regent of France. To further strengthen his claim on the French throne, Henry was to marry Charles VI's daughter. One popular historian has called this treaty France's 'greatest humiliation', comparable to the defeat at the hand of the Nazis in 1940.[65] Poor old Charles VI, despised and neglected by his family, entered his capital in September 1420, with his sole surviving son disinherited and in flight. The optimistic Parisians greeted their king and Henry V with joyful celebrations, but a hard winter followed and suffering was intense. The English were to occupy the city for the next fifteen years.

Of Christine herself we know little during these years. Safely in the convent at Poissy with both her daughter and Princess Marie de France, she was not cut off from the news; her son Jean du Castel was a secretary to the exiled dauphin and was named by him to a post as ambassador to Spain, but, sadly for Christine, Jean died about 1425, like his father a young man, only forty-two years old. His widow and their three children were not able to return to Paris until 1431. During this arduous time only one work by Christine is known, a religious meditation in the *vita Christi* tradition called *Les Heures de contemplation sur la passion de Notre Seigneur*. The sadness and difficulty of this period was surprisingly alleviated by the sudden appearance of a new young, passionate and charismatic military commander of the French, known in English as Joan of Arc. Christine's last work was *Le Ditié de Jeanne d'Arc*, dated 31 July

[65] Seward, *Hundred Years War*, 182.

1429. It is nationalistic in tone, celebrating the woman who had been able to overcome the English (when no man had been so able) and to lead the then thirty-year-old dauphin to coronation as Charles VII.

It was long believed that Christine may have died before the denouement of this story, Joan's capture by the English in May 1430 and her trial and execution in May 1431. The defeated and discredited Charles VII would not return to Paris until 1437. We do not know the exact date of Christine's death since the records at Poissy were destroyed when the convent passed into government hands at the Revolution.[66] The last public record comes from the memoirs of Guillebert de Mets, who in 1434 referred to her in the past tense. If she died around 1430, it was in her mid-sixties and at the end of a long and fruitful career. Her descendants continued in the royal service, and even in the twentieth century they still could be found in Paris. The nightmarish companion of Christine's life, the Hundred Years War, was as yet unresolved, however. Charles VII was recognized as king by Philippe of Burgundy at the treaty of Arras on 20 September 1435, and the French went on the offensive in 1442, attacking Aquitaine itself, which had been an English stronghold since the twelfth century. In 1445 Henry VI married Charles's niece, Margaret of Anjou, and the truce with the English was extended while Charles rebuilt his army. In 1449 Charles attacked Normandy, and then continued to drive the English north, until the battle of Formigny on 15 April 1450, which was the first decisive English defeat since 1314. This turned the tide definitively for the French. The final surrender of the city of Bordeaux, the heart of Aquitaine, to the French forces on 19 October 1453 ended the Hundred Years War and English control of the rich province. In the words of one historian, the war 'bankrupted the English government and fatally discredited the Lancastrian dynasty',[67] and much the same could be said for the credibility of government in France. But in addition, the French people suffered terribly, since the battles were fought on French soil. The churches and chateaux that were looted and burned, the fields that went unsown, the hamlets abandoned in a depopulated countryside were in France, not England. Culturally, two nations that had been linked by traditions, religion, language and education now fomented a jingoistic hatred and contempt for each other that would itself sow further seeds for later conflicts. After the defeat at Agincourt, there was a distinct change in the kind of language used by both French and English to speak of each other; contempt and arrogance were intensified, translated into chauvinistic abuse. The wasted resources and political and economic dysfunction had tremendous consequences for the

66 Today, the still partially standing convent buildings house the French national Musée des Jouets in what is now a Paris suburb.

67 Seward, *Hundred Years War*, 263.

history of France. The ducal power of Burgundy was destroyed and the commercial centres of Flanders came under influences hostile to France. Representative government languished and fiscal reform was centralized and bureaucratized. French political theorists, distraught by the weakness of rule, saw the powerful monarchy they hoped for become a reality in the absolutism of 'l'État c'est moi'. Medieval France had disappeared.

CHAPTER TWO

An Introduction to the Mirror for Princes

No one can look into this mirror . . . without achieving clear self-knowledge.

Christine de Pizan's influence and competence as a political writer derive in part from her deep familiarity with the mirror for princes genre of didactic literature. Her political mirrors include *L'Epistre d'Othéa*, *Le Livre des fais et bonnes meurs du roy Charles V le sage*, *Le Livre de prudence* and/or *Le Livre de la prud'homie de l'homme*, *Le Livre du corps de policie*, *Le Livre de fais d'armes et de chevalrie* and *Le Livre de la paix*. Not limited to works for men in her concern for education, she wrote a mirror for princesses, *Le Trésor de la cité des dames*, also called *Le Livre des trois vertus*. *Le Livre de la cité des dames,* perhaps her best-known work, can be read as providing models of political, moral and spiritual leadership. To these works could be added two other books of instruction, *Enseignements de Christine à son filz* and her *Proverbes moraux*. All of them were advice books for rulers, or at least ruling classes.[1] Nor did this exhaust Christine's interest in politics. At least two of her formal letters, *Epistre a Isabeau de Baviere* and *La Lamentation sur les maux de France*, plus the *Ditié de Jehanne d'Arc*, are obviously political in scope and content, although they belong to other genres. In order better to understand the intellectual context in which Christine is situated, a brief discussion of the development of the mirror for princes and Christian political thought is important.

---

1 Some might prefer to place her book on chivalry and her moral proverbs into the genre of courtesy books, that is, mirrors written for courtiers. In the taxonomy of mirror literature, I consider those directed to members of the ruling classes as part of the mirror for princes genre. While I would include *Cité des dames* as a mirror, some scholars disagree. See the discussion of the mirror genre in this chapter as well as Brown-Grant, *Christine de Pizan and the Moral Defence of Women*, 130–31, and Glenda K. McLeod, *Virtue and Venom* (Ann Arbor: University of Michigan Press, 1991).

In His image

Early Christianity in the post-Pauline era was not immediately concerned with political questions. The imminence of the 'end times' and the influence of Manicheism and other renunciatory movements made concern about the political world tangential to the real concern of a growing religious movement that saw itself as separate from the world. The adoption of Christianity by Emperor Constantine as the official religion[2] of the Empire threw Christian theologians into deep questioning about the nature of the true believer's relation to the world and to political power. These questions were addressed by the remarkable figure of St Augustine of Hippo, whose attempts to wrestle with the relationship between the Christian and the world gave birth to *De civitate dei*, in which he drew a picture of Christians in the world but not enslaved by it or its values, and the Christian ruler as responsible for a higher order of things. As Christian belief spread into northern and western Europe, particularly France and England, the warrior codes of blood feud and bride-capture intermingled with ancient survivals of Roman civilization and ideals to become the amalgam that we call medieval society. A rich and creative stew, medieval Christian culture was remarkably adaptable to the innovations of social and political organization that were developing, yet Christian political thinkers were seemingly not aware of – or refused to acknowledge – their own innovations. All of their creations would be cloaked in the grave words and deeds of the much admired ancestors of the classical world whose direct heirs they saw themselves to be. While most kinds of writing during the patristic and early medieval period, whether sermons, rules for monastic communities, hagiographies and the like, had political consequences and implications, political writing, as distinct from these genres, began in its earliest form as instructions for political leaders on how to govern, most especially, how to combine Christian morality, Roman political ideas and pagan political structures into effective rule. Thus was born the mirror for princes.[3]

---

2 While Constantine (*c.*280–337) adopted Christianity as the religion of the state, he did not himself become a Christian until his baptism on his deathbed. The Edict of Milan dates from 313.

3 For an introduction to the mirror for princes genre, especially in France and England, see Leslie K. Born, 'The Perfect Prince', *Speculum*, **3** (1928), 470–504; Dora M. Bell, *L'Idéal éthique de la royauté en France au Moyen Age* (Geneva: E. Droz, 1962), Jacques Krynen, *Idéal du prince et pouvoir royal en France à la fin du Moyen Age, 1380–1440* (Paris: Editions A. et J. Picard, 1981); Cary J. Nederman, 'The Mirror Crack'd: The Speculum Principum as Political and Social Criticism in the Late Middle Ages', *The European Legacy*, 3/3 (1998), 18–38; Wilhelm Berges, *Die Fürstenspiegel des hohen und späten Mittelalters* (Stuttgart: Hiersemann, 1952).

As a genre of political writing, there are three major stages in the development of the mirror for princes. The earliest Christian mirrors[4] in the European West can be found in the attempt to select ideas from patristic sources, most notably Book V, chapter 24 of Augustine's *De civitate dei*, and to collect them together as a single work or handbook, which often included classical authorities like the fragment of Cicero's *De res publica* commonly referred to as *Somnium Scipionis* as well. To these collections were added various scriptural injunctions and excerpts from commentaries like that of Macrobius, the whole bound together and circulated as advice books on rule. An alternative format to these earliest mirrors was the letter of instruction, such as Claudian put into the form of an epistle from Emperor Theodosius to his son Honorius, written in 398,[5] or the well-known manual written in 841 by Lady Dhuoda for her son William. The letter form, combined with citations from various authorities, shaped the distinctive character of all later mirrors: the combination of a unique personal and personalized engagement with the individual being addressed, coupled with quotations from well-known authors, even if those quotations are out of context, poorly understood, or simply fabricated.

The second stage of mirror writing was inaugurated by John of Salisbury in his monumental and influential *Policraticus* (1159), dedicated to then royal chancellor, Thomas Becket. These later works, written in the twelfth and thirteenth centuries, were highly original adaptations of classical ideas to medieval contexts. The twelfth-century renaissance, of which John of Salisbury was both an exemplar and a catalyst, ushered in a whole new phase of mirror writing. In part this had to do with the institutionalization of rule from a kind of family enterprise to something very like a kingdom, if not yet a state. Indeed, the itinerant kings of the early twelfth century, with their personalized justice and the extraction of what looks more like gifts or extortion than taxes, dramatically changed by the end of the century, so that there were real permanent institutions staffed by paid 'bureaucrats' receiving and accounting for the wealth of the kingdom in a much more centralized and institutionalized way. Despite the anachronistic nature of these terms, they help us to appreciate the enormous distance that separates the kingdom of Henry I (d. 1135) from that of his grandson, Henry II (d. 1189) and his heirs. Not only were methods of public administration being developed both in England and on the Continent, they

4 There is a parallel tradition of Byzantine mirrors with different conventions and a far different history. It may have influenced the development of Muslim and Persian mirrors, a subject that is virtually unexplored.

5 For a discussion of Claudian's letter, see P. D. King, 'The Barbarian Kingdoms', in *The Cambridge History of Medieval Political Thought*, ed. J. H. Burns (Cambridge: Cambridge University Press, 1988), 123–53.

were codified and regularized, in works such as clerk Richard Fitznigel's instruction manual for the Exchequer, *Dialogus de scaccario*, written about 1177. As David Luscombe remarks:

> The authors of the *Leges Henrici primi* and the *Constitutio domus regis*, like their successors who prepared the *Dialogus de scaccario* and the common law treatise known as Glanvill, provided manuals for professional lawyers and bureaucrats; they go beyond the task not only of edification but also of reliance on custom, practice and memory.[6]

Between France and England we can also see many elements of a shared common culture and language, at least in elite circles. Similarities were far greater than we often imagine. Anglo-Norman courtiers understood their French counterparts. Clerics were part of a universal European intelligentsia that had studied at the same universities and shared – at least in theory – both values and language. Poets and scholars moved effortlessly between French and English courts. About 1160 Marie de France performed at the court of Henry II of England, just as many years later Christine de Pizan would be invited to the court of Henry IV, perhaps to replace the recently deceased court poet and civil servant, Geoffrey Chaucer.

This common culture and shared political concerns inspired a torrent of political writing aimed at 'princes' – a singularly elastic term – of every variety. Indeed, mirror literature expanded over the next two centuries to include mirrors for other social classes and positions, including courtiers, princesses and even housewives.

The idea of the mirror

The mirror is a magical invention and its reflective ability has given it great power as a metaphor in Western thought, and it evoked a complex series of images for the medieval reader.[7] It implied the use of the mirror as a part of the

6 D. E. Luscombe, 'Introduction: The Formation of Political Thought in the West', in *Cambridge History of Medieval Political Thought*, ed. Burns, 157–73. For the bureaucratization of medieval administration during this period see Joseph Strayer, *Medieval Statecraft and the Perspectives of History* (Princeton: Princeton University Press, 1971); C. Warren Hollister and John W. Baldwin, 'The Rise of Administrative Kingship', *American Historical Review*, **83** (1978), 867–905; also Kate Langdon Forhan, 'The Twelfth-Century "Bureaucrat" and the Life of the Mind: John of Salisbury's Policraticus' (PhD diss., Johns Hopkins University, 1987). R. L. Benson and Giles Constable (eds), *Renaissance and Renewal in the Twelfth Century* (Cambridge, Mass.: Harvard University Press, 1982) includes several chapters relating to this theme.

7 For a discussion of the mirror image, see Ritamary Bradley, 'Backgrounds of the Title *Speculum* in Medieval Literature', *Speculum*, **29** (1954), 100–15; Benjamin Goldberg, *The Mirror and Man* (Charlottesville: University of Virgina Press, 1985).

process of self-examination. Just as we look in the mirror to inspect ourselves, so too a mirror allowed the reader an opportunity for self-reflection. Furthermore, the idea of the mirror also refers to a spiritual dimension. The Christian's responsibility in the world was to 'mirror' Christ and at one's highest development to be a reflection of God even in the most pedestrian of daily activities. A mirror also provides a model for comparison with examples of virtuous behaviour. The saints and martyrs presented such exemplars of behaviour and belief.

Developed for an elite audience, the mirror for princes drew on the richness of this mirror imagery, drawing both on Christian and classical sources for their *exempla* but also for the very virtues they valued. Elaborate schemes of virtues were developed, but the best known were the four cardinal virtues: justice, fortitude, temperance and prudence, which had been identified by many classical authorities, especially Cicero and pseudo-Seneca's *Formula for an Honest Life*,[8] and by some very early Christian ones, such as Augustine and Macrobius. Aristotle's discussion in the *Ethics* and *Politics* was unavailable until the thirteenth century and thus had little direct influence during this formative period, but a tradition of 'underground Aristotelianism'[9] certainly prepared the way for the integration of the ethical ideas of Aristotle into the mirror tradition. These virtues of 'practical wisdom' had been identified as the 'political' virtues as early as Peter the Chanter in the late twelfth century and their application to rulers was an important source in this rich and cumulative body of literature, which by the fourteenth century had become so conventionalized that it could be conveyed by images alone.[10]

The third stage of development, beginning with the fourteenth century and extending well into the sixteenth, includes works like Machiavelli's *Il principe* (1513) and Erasmus' *Institutio principis christiani* (1516). In the later stages of development in particular, variations from the standard themes and usages are doubly expressive of their author's views, since they stand out quite distinctly from the mirror's rich if conventional backdrop. These include, first, the author's

8 Long thought to have been a work of Seneca, *Formula vitae honestae* was written by Martin of Braga (d. 580).

9 For a discussion of the infiltration of Aristotelian political ideas into the West before the rediscovery of these texts, see Cary J. Nederman, *Medieval Aristotelianism and its Limits: Classical Traditions in Moral and Political Philosophy, 12th–15th Centuries* (Variorum; Aldershot: Ashgate, 1997). See also Kate Langdon Forhan, 'Reading Backward: Aristotelianism in the Political Thought of Christine de Pizan', in Hicks (ed.), *Au champ des escriptures*, 359–82.

10 As discussed in Kate Langdon Forhan, 'The Ciceronian Prince: Text and Image in the Mirror of Princes', presented at the annual meeting of the American Political Science Association, Washington, DC, 1991.

claim to be unfit by his or her qualifications or background, but resolute in writing nonetheless, either at the request of the prince or for his good.

For example, from 1159, we have:

> I, a plebian man, am only capable of honouring you by making a shrill sound upon rustic pipes with the uncultured language of this book, like a pebble tossed on to your piles of honours; while [this book] has none of the elements known to please, yet it cannot displease because it is written out of devotion.[11]

From 1513:

> . . . and although I deem this work unworthy of Your Highness's acceptance, yet my confidence in your humanity assures me that you will receive it with favour, knowing that it is not within my power to offer a greater gift than that of enabling you to understand in a very short time all those things which I have learned . . .[12]

Christine too followed this tradition, as can be seen, for example, in *Corps de policie*, where she writes 'I humbly supplicate [you] not to take wrongly nor disdain such a small intelligence as mine, that such a humble creature dares to speak about the way of life for higher ranks . . .'.[13]

The humility topos results in reliance on ancient authorities for advice rather than daring to speak one's own unworthy thoughts and reveals the second important convention: the writer is 'merely' passing along the wisdom of others, in the form of stories of the ancients, from Livy, Valerius Maximus, Plutarch or other classical sources, interspersed with political concepts from Aristotle, Cicero or Seneca on justice, good rule, tyranny or law.

The problem of authority in medieval literature is well known. The general distaste or disapprobation of originality or creativity was an important part of philosophers who believed themselves, as the *Metalogicon* states, to be 'dwarfs standing on the shoulders of giants' as the direct heirs of a classical world they saw as the foundation of their own. This is an important point in understanding not only medieval political thought but its psychology as well. Unlike our vision of a linear and ever upward progress, medieval persons often saw the world in a downward spiral, where things had been good in the past, but had been declining ever since in values, culture and morality as the world grew closer to senescence. The medieval reader had respect and nostalgia for this long-lost world and so in a sense, all medieval thought was 'conservative' because it

11 John of Salisbury, *Policraticus: Of the Frivolities of Courtiers and the Footprints of Philosophers*, trans. Cary J. Nederman (Cambridge: Cambridge University Press, 1990), 5.

12 Machiavelli, *The Prince*, trans. Quentin Skinner (Cambridge: Cambridge University Press, 1988), 3.

13 Christine de Pizan, *The Book of the Body Politic*, trans. Kate Langdon Forhan (Cambridge and New York: Cambridge University Press, 1994), 3–4.

looked back with regret and longing to the past. This slightly melancholy temperament (which in extreme form was called *accidia*) was in part itself a literary affectation, but it was also a felt even when unarticulated world-view. This is not to argue that all thought had this melancholy wistfulness, in fact vigorous and energetic minds like those of John of Salisbury or Giles of Rome were grappling with complex issues and their ideas were decidedly creative and fresh. But they were couched in the language and authority of the past.

A third convention concerns the key figures to whom much authority was given in the mirror for princes, a list that includes Aristotle, Seneca, Plutarch, Cicero and Boethius. Yet while Aristotle appears to be obvious, his political works were unavailable well into the thirteenth century. Plutarch's influence seems disproportionate given his extant corpus of works, and although Seneca's works were plentiful, his era seems so different from anything medieval that it is difficult to understand how captivating his readers found him. But prayers were addressed to God on behalf of these three pagans, and works by many now anonymous medieval authors were ascribed to them, attesting to their prestige. They were regarded not only with respect but affection, as can be seen from Dante's picture of their afterlife and Pope Gregory's famous plea for the soul of Trajan. While all three classical philosophers left important literary legacies and their ideas had impact on the formation of medieval culture, they were held in particular esteem by writers in the mirror tradition because they were all thought to have been teachers or advisers to rulers so monumentally important that they were emblematic of aspects of kingship: Aristotle was tutor to Alexander the Great, model of the warrior king. Plutarch advised Trajan, the archetype of the virtuous king, and Seneca was tutor to Nero, who, once the restraining hand of his teacher was removed through forced suicide, became the exemplar of the tyrant or evil king. An ambitious royal adviser was well served by invoking the authority of these *auctores*.

Cicero[14] and Boethius carried a different kind of weight. In the medieval view, both were philosopher-statesmen who counselled unjust kings and then paid for their integrity with their lives. In Cicero's case, the story was well known: his reputation as a honorable political leader, his exile, and ultimately his death for his opposition to Mark Antony after the assassination of Caesar, gave weight to his reputation for virtue and thus as an princely adviser. *De officiis* and *Somnium Scipionis* were much read and admired. *Scipio's Dream* in particular was extremely influential. Preserved thanks to Macrobius' powerful commentary when most of the rest of the text of Cicero's *Republic* was lost, it

14 Cicero was usually called Tully in the Middle Ages. There is some evidence that Christine de Pizan was not aware that Tully was the same person as Cicero. The mythic status was conferred on Cicero.

describes a heaven peopled with honourable political leaders, who merited their reward because they had chosen the highest way of life on earth – public service. This gave weight to a view that the ideal statesman epitomized the princely virtues of fame, honour and glory, but also that his heavenly reward would be for his achievements on earth. Thus, he is to despise 'the talk of the rabble' and to keep his eye on the prize of renown.

The moral of the story of Boethius was equally pointed. A statesman in the employ of Emperor Theodoric, he was falsely accused of conspiring against the emperor and ultimately was executed by being bludgeoned to death. The *Consolation of Philosophy*, written in his prison cell, is ironic but advisable reading for anyone in political life. Its most famous motif is that of the wheel of Fortune that changes one's life from pinnacle to depths in a moment. The wheel was a powerful symbol of the impermanence of life and permeated medieval culture as a consequence.

While some scholars may believe it historically inaccurate and overly sentimental, nevertheless this association between adviser and royal patron played an important role in the development of the kind of secular sainthood that these mythologized advisers enjoyed. The image of the ideal statesman martyred for his integrity took on spiritual resonances, illustrated by the death and canonization of Thomas Becket (d. 1170). The religious qualities of rule, as we shall see in the chapter on kingship, spilled over to rulers, and so we see the canonization of kings known more for their craft than their piety, like Charlemagne, canonized in 1165.[15] In 1400, this conventional relationship between tutor and royal pupil would be used by Christine de Pizan in her *Epistre d'Othéa*, where Prince Hector of Troy, believed to be the founder of the French monarchy, is tutored in statecraft and the political virtues by Othéa, goddess of wisdom and prudence. Christine also 'canonized' a secular political leader as an ideal king in her biography of Charles V.

The purpose of all mirrors for princes, however, is the transformation of the immature or irresponsible prince into the model king. The author might stress a physical transformation, therefore have the mirror address questions about the prince's upbringing; his diet, leisure, education and daily schedule. The most famous mirror of this type is Giles of Rome's *De regimine principum*. Other mirrors emphasize the moral and political transformation of the prince, like John of Salisbury's *Policraticus*, or even Machiavelli's *Il principe*. Christine's *Corps de policie*, which very closely observes the traditional mirror forms, follows both models, relying specifically on Giles of Rome and John of Salisbury.

The conventions also included an ideology of rule, which typically embraced a few key ideas: the king ruled for the good of his people, administered justice

15 Charlemagne was canonized by Pascal III to please his patron, Frederick Barbarossa.

by 'treating equals equally', was generous to friends, firm but just to enemies, and was a courageous and personal leader in battle. The models chosen for the ideal prince included both classical and Christian exemplars: Alexander the Great as the warrior king and Emperor Trajan of Rome as the just and merciful king from the classical tradition, and David and Solomon in parallel roles from the biblical tradition. The individual authors of mirrors often attributed their points to the *auctores* directly, or glossed the ancient texts, and then illuminated their chosen ideas by *exempla* that concentrated the reader's attention on particular features or attributes of rulers or court life from the classical period. At times they invented their sources; Seneca, Aristotle, Plutarch and others had works attributed them.

Over the centuries, the development of the mirror was a cumulative process. While many of the *exempla* and stories in mirrors by Walter Map, Vincent of Beauvais and John of Salisbury come from either *florilegia* or direct acquaintance with favourite sources like Livy's *Ab urbe condita and Vegetius' Epitoma rei militaris*, later mirrors combed earlier ones, or, as access to classical texts improved, newer sources like Aristotle's *Politics* and the ubiquitous Valerius Maximus. Certain stock characters and illustrations appear: Caesar as a shrewd military strategist, courtiers likened to bees, the dream of Nebuchadnezzar, the wonderful story of the revolt of the body's members against the stomach, Nero as miserly as well as unjust are only a few examples.

As could be expected given this customary and conventional use of authority, the specific political content of some mirrors is similar and even derivative. But the vast majority of works are a fascinating window into a distant but intriguing world. They represent an attempt to reach out from the specialized world of law, university or curia to an essentially lay but powerful audience. The uniformity of the genre's conventions allows the individuality of perspective to show up more clearly against this conventional backdrop. Certain mirrors stand out in the tradition because they mark a new understanding of classical authors or concepts, or a new adaptation of the tradition to particular historical exigencies, or, of perhaps even greater interest, because they actually invent the authorities or texts used to convey the author's own political ideas. In some cases, the authorities and the conventions of the genre are turned upside down. This 'subversion' of the genre can be found in a number of mirrors, including those of both Machiavelli and Christine de Pizan.[16]

---

16 See Nederman, 'The Mirror Crack'd', and Kate Langdon Forhan, 'Christine de Pizan and the Mirror Tradition', in Zimmerman and De Rentiis (eds), *The City of Scholars*, 189–96; also Forhan, 'Subversion of the Princely Ideal: Prudence, Pragmatism and the Political Works of Christine de Pizan' prepared for Royaume de Femynie: Femmes et Pouvoirs en France à la Renaissance in Blois, France, 13–15 October 1995.

While the list of extant mirrors for princes is long, several of them were inordinately influential either because of the significance of the author or authorities or because they provided uniquely useful information to be appropriated. The two most influential, either directly or indirectly, for Christine de Pizan are John of Salisbury's *Policraticus*, and Giles of Rome's *De regimine principum*. A few words about each will be very helpful in understanding a tradition to which she contributed so extensively.

John of Salisbury and the *Policraticus*

John of Salisbury's *Policraticus* was the first medieval and Christianized attempt to reconcile the demands of practical politics with an equally exigent moral philosophy, on the model of the great *Republic*s of Cicero and Plato. The towering reputation of the *Policraticus* itself stems in part from its originality in several areas. An extensive education in the classics had left John deeply impressed by the political ideals of Greek and Roman authors, especially Cicero. The articulate, well-educated and virtuous Ciceronian statesman was to be the model for the twelfth-century public man, but a transformed and Christian one. Secondly, another classical theme, the idea of virtue as moderation rather than asceticism, is invigorated and Christianized by John, who desired to see the virtues practised in a revalidated public life. Third, despite being written by a cleric, the work is intended for a non-monastic audience. The *Policraticus* is about human nature and purpose, and the highest good that can be achieved, a good that must be possible to achieve in the world of politics. The *Policraticus* was intended for those who, like Thomas Becket, to whom the work is dedicated, and John himself, lived in the centre of the turmoil, excitement, power and temptation of a medieval court.

The most influential contribution of the *Policraticus* was in its development of the corporate metaphor. In contrast to the vague allusions in the work of Peter Damian or Bernard of Clairvaux, the *Policraticus* elaborates a full-scale metaphor that not only influenced the development of later political theory, as in Hobbes's famous frontispiece in *Leviathan*, but also permeates our language in metaphorical expressions such as 'head of state'. The metaphor reflects the reorientation of political life. In the twelfth century, the dominant images used to describe the polity emphasized hierarchy and subordination to authority. By changing the metaphor used to describe politics, John showed that its true nature is 'polycratic', and he emphasized the interdependence of political actors, whether groups or individual persons. His metaphor of the body politic, a far more elaborate version of the metaphor than had ever appeared before, validates political life. In John's work, the head, that is, the prince, and the soul, which represents the clergy, are shown to be indispensable to the well-being of the body, as are the feet, or peasantry. John's use of the metaphor grounds the relationship between church and state, of ruler and ruled within the context of this larger metaphor, stressing neither duality nor subordination, but interdependence. This striking new use of a powerful political metaphor then enables John to address problems of political violence, the nature of justice and the concept of liberty within a larger context of the whole society and its relationship to the philosophic good.

The influence of the *Policraticus* was comprehensive and profound. Even as late as the fifteenth and sixteenth centuries, legal scholars in Italy and France continued to refer the book.[17] As a leading model for the mirror of princes, the *Policraticus* was copied by others and important to the development of the idea of courtliness. In the twelfth century alone, the *Tractatus contra curiales et officiales clericos* of Nigel Wireker (*c.*1190) explicitly acknowledges the work of his predecessor. Lotario Segni, the future Innocent III, incorporated passages into his *De miseria humanae conditionis*, which also appeared about 1190. Gerald of Wales wrote a work entitled *De principis instructionis* (*c.*1220), in which he quotes from Book IV. There is also the use of the *Policraticus* as a sourcebook of quotations from classical culture, specifically about political ideas. For example, Linder states that of the three known versions of the legend of Trajan and the widow, John's was the most widely disseminated, and it is found in the very influential works of Dante.[18] Of great importance is the dissemination, in John's amended form, of classical concepts of justice, law and virtue, and particularly of the ancient ideal of political life as important both for the individual and the community. Gaines Post claimed that John anticipated the discovery of Aristotle's *Politics* by over a hundred years, particularly by suggesting that human nature is essentially political.[19] While there are limits to John's Aristotelianism, his fundamental recognition of a positive role for political life is a classical ideal not found in other early Christian theorists. Furthermore, John's classical scholarship, and his knowledge and love of the works of pagan philosophers, are apparent throughout the *Policraticus* and account for his work's great influence, especially in the Italian Renaissance.

Secondly, John's attribution of the metaphor to a fictional letter from Plutarch to Trajan gave that invented text, the *Institutio Trajani*, an independent life as

---

17 For the later influence of this work on political ideas, see the introduction to Webb's critical edition, John of Salisbury, *Policraticus*, ed. C. C. I. Webb (Oxford: Oxford University Press, 1909); Amnon Linder, 'The Knowledge of John of Salisbury in the Late Middle Ages', *Studi medievali*, ser. 3, **18** (1977), 319–22.

18 Linder, ibid., 325.

19 John's close acquaintance with Cicero's works would lead him to this 'Aristotelian' conclusion. This is clearly an example of 'underground Aristotelianism'. See Nederman, *Medieval Aristotelianism and its Limits*.

a piece of classical wisdom. The *Institutio Trajani* appears as a separate work beginning in the fourteenth century and was the only Plutarch (pseudo or otherwise) known and taught well into the fifteenth century.

Thirdly, original political concepts developed in the *Policraticus* were also widely disseminated. The doctrine of tyrannicide was often quoted, although at times knowledge of its author was lost. As we have seen, Jean Petit's defence of the assassination of Louis, Duke of Orleans, makes use of John of Salisbury's arguments on tyrannicide and stimulated voluminous discussion on the problem of political assassination.[20]

Giles of Rome and *De regimine principum*

Like John of Salisbury, Giles of Rome is an exemplar of his age and was a catalyst for both innovation and the transformation of the political ideas of his era.[21] Born about 1243 (and perhaps as late as 1247), he is also known in the literature by two other forms of his name, Aegidius Romanus and Egidio Colonna.[22] A prolific scholar and writer, his works covered a wide range of subjects, and his teaching, according to James Blythe, became the educational standard for the Augustinians. Amidst all this prodigious activity, following the famous philosopher-teachers of the mirror for princes tradition, Giles was believed to have served as tutor[23] to the sons of Philippe III of France and wrote his own mirror between 1277 and 1279 for one of those sons, who became Philippe IV in 1285. We have the author's own statement on the motivation and purpose of his book *De regimine principum*: 'Your grace has requested me to compose a book on the education of princes or the government of kings.'[24]

20 See especially the discussion in Linder, 'Knowledge of John of Salisbury', 349–53.

21 On *De regimine* in particular, see Charles F. Briggs, *Giles of Rome's De regimine principum: Reading and Writing Politics at Court and University, c. 1275–c.1525* (Cambridge and New York: Cambridge University Press, 1999). For Giles's political ideas, see Blythe, *Ideal Government*.

22 Or even Columna. This adds to the general confusion when dealing with library catalogues. The Library of Congress still uses the Latin form, but the much simpler Giles of Rome, which stems from the French documents of the period, has come into general use.

23 Briggs believes that the evidence that Giles was the princes' tutor 'can be neither proven nor disproven' and briefly discusses some of the evidence (*Giles of Rome*, 9), The *Cambridge History of Medieval Political Thought* biography of Giles states that this is 'unlikely', but without attribution or documentation (p. 669). The confusion about whether Giles was actually tutor to Philip's sons or to the heir in particular may come in part from the mirror tradition of philosopher tutors. It would certainly increase the credibility of Giles's own mirror if later he was believed to have been tutor to a prince.

24 As quoted in *Li Livres du gouvernement des rois: A XIIIth Century French Version of Egidio Colonna's Treatise De regimine principum, now first published from the Kerr MS*, ed. Samuel Paul Molenaer (New York: AMS Press, 1966), xviii.

De regimine was the first complete mirror written under the influence of the triad of Aristotelian texts that dealt with the 'practical wisdom' of the Philosopher; the *Ethics*, the *Economics*,[25] and the *Politics*. The mirror reflects this influence even in its organization. The first book, like the *Ethics*, establishes the ends of human society and the virtues that are appropriate within it. It deals therefore with the governance of the human soul, but in this case, with an emphasis on rulers. Secondly, Book Two deals with economics in the classical sense, that is, the appropriate governance of the household. Finally, like the *Politics*, Book Three deals with the governance of the kingdom.

It would, however, be an oversimplification to dismiss this work either as a paraphrase of Aristotle or as vulgarized Thomism. One of the longest mirrors in the tradition (and perhaps as a consequence, as yet untranslated into modern English),[26] it is an elaborate examination and blueprint for every aspect of royal life. It was meant to be a compendium or handbook of everything that a king needed to know in order to rule effectively, ranging from discussions of the diet, leisure, training and education of the young prince to the organization of his household and kingdom, to his relationship with his wife and his council, to practical advice on statecraft, including pragmatic advice on government in time of war, military recruitment, training, weaponry, fortifications and naval warfare. Comparable in subject matter in many ways to the previous generation's *Li Livres dou tresor* (*c.*1267) of Brunetto Latini, it is much more sophisticated in terms of its political theory.[27]

---

25 Until it was demonstrated by Lefèvre d'Etaples in 1506 that events in Book II postdated Aristotle's death in 322 BC, the entire *Economics* was believed to be authentic. According to its editor, Albert Menut, Book I may indeed date from antiquity and the entire work had to have been compiled in its present form no later than the twelfth century. The rosy glow of all things Aristotelian thus surrounded it no less than its authentic companion texts. See the introduction to Nicole Oresme, *Le livre de yconomique d'Aristote*, ed. and trans. Albert D. Menut (Philadelphia: American Philosophical Society, 1957).

26 There is a recent edition of the middle English translation: *The Governance of Kings and Princes: John Trevisa's Middle English Translation of the De regimine principum of Aegidius Romanus*, ed. David C. Fowler, Charles F. Briggs, and Paul G. Remley (New York: Garland Publishing, 1997). A short selection from Book 3 was translated in Cary J. Nederman and Kate Langdon Forhan (eds), *Medieval Political Theory: A Reader. The Quest for the Body Politic, 1100–1400* (London and New York: Routledge, 1993; repr. Indianapolis, Ind.: Hackett, 2000), 149–52.

27 Latini's work is also structured on Aristotle's practical wisdom, but from different sources. It predates the translation into Latin of the *Ethics* by William Moerbeke, and thus provided a handy compendium for those who did not know Greek. Its first book is on natural history; the second is a simplified paraphrase and synopsis of the *Ethics*, and the third, on rhetoric, comes largely from Cicero's *De inventione* and concludes with practical advice on governance in republican Italy. See Brunetto Latini, *Li Livres dou tresor*, ed.

In part, its practical advice contributed both to the success and the esteem in which the work was held, but *De regimine* also owes its influence to its ability to blend the medieval understanding of the importance of law and good government with Aristotelian ideas about the best regime. There are two aspects of Giles's political theory that should be emphasized, given Christine de Pizan's use of this monumental work as a source: first, his emphasis on the middle class and its role in providing political stability; secondly, his emphasis on strong monarchy, which has stimulated most of the controversy surrounding Giles's political thought.

The stability necessary to a kingdom is discussed in Book III of *De regimine*. As in Aristotle's *Politics*, this analysis occurs in the context of deliberation on the best regime within the ideal society. For Giles, one of the most important characteristics of the good community itself is the presence of a large middle class. A society in which there are extremes of wealth will foster undesirable behaviour: 'The very rich will not know how to conduct themselves towards the very poor and thus will injure them and do them harm for no reason. Those who are poor will not know how to behave towards the rich and will think unceasingly about how to rob them and to deprive the rich of their goods.'[28] Since, by definition, the middle class is the mean between two extremes, 'if the population is made up of many middle-class persons, they will achieve that rational mean, and can live together according to reason, as the fourth book of the *Politics* says'.[29]

But in addition to these theoretical preferences, for Giles there are more pragmatic reasons for encouraging the growth of a large middle class and discouraging great extremes of wealth through the regulation of inheritances and real property. Exploitation, on the one hand, and ignorance, on the other, lend themselves to political instability, or in Giles's words, the absence of 'equity and justice'. In language that Rousseau will echo five centuries later, the political atmosphere will be poisoned by the fact that 'the very poor will envy the rich, and the rich will have contempt for them. No society survives long where there is a lot of envy and contempt.'[30]

Giles's strong preference for monarchy is much more than a mere adaptation of Aristotle's best regime. Giles's distinction between political regimes is based

---

Francis J. Carmody (Berkeley: University of California Press, 1947) and *The Book of the Treasure*, trans. Paul Barrette and Spurgeon Baldwin (New York: Garland Publishing, 1993).

28 Nederman and Forhan, *Medieval Political Theory*, 150.

29 Ibid.

30 Ibid., 151. Cf. Jean-Jacques Rousseau, 'Discourse on Political Economy' and 'Discourse on the Origins of Inequality', in *The Basic Political Writings*, trans. Donald A. Cress (Indianapolis, Ind.: Hackett, 1987).

on the identity of the legislator rather than the structure of the system. When the king himself makes the law or rules by his own will for the good of the citizens, then it constitutes *regimen regale*. Alternatively, *regimen politicum* is a regime in which the king rules by laws that the citizens have made. While both political systems are legitimate forms of government, he argues that only *regimen regale* is ordained by God and is therefore the best for the common good. Using a complex Augustinian hierarchical analogy, Giles describes three levels of regal rule: God governs the universe on the cosmic level, and reason and the intellect govern the person on the individual level. Between them, as a kind of bridge between the heavenly and the earthly, the king rules over the people.[31] By analogy, it is preferable to be ruled by the king, that is, under *regimen regale*, rather than by the law of citizens, under *regimen politicum*, because it is the more rational system.

While Giles's distinction between the good king and the tyrant resonated with medieval readers, Giles also argues that faced with the evils of tyranny or lawlessness, rule by a bad king is preferable, because of the much greater evil that comes from disobedience to the prince: 'If it is considered how much good comes from kingship, not only when kings rule rightly, but even if in some ways they behave tyrannically, the people should endeavour to obey. Some tyranny on the part of the prince is more tolerable than the evils which arise from disobedience to the prince.'[32]

Giles's emphasis on the importance of monarchy, particularly his preference for regal monarchy, has been understood as an indication that he was an advocate of an unrestrained sovereignty. As Blythe points out:

> On almost every point on which Thomas Aquinas desired limitations of kingship – law, election, and 'tempering' among others – Giles comes down on the side of uncontrolled rule. He gives the impression of being a supporter of absolute monarchy, unwilling to allot any function or power to other segments of society. The Carlyles interpret Giles in this way, as a repudiator of the medieval tradition of limited kingship.[33]

---

31 See *De regimine principum* ii. 1. 14, and Blythe, *Ideal Government*, 68–76. On Augustinian hierarchical analogies between body and soul, see Kate Langdon Forhan, 'The Not-So-Divided Self: Reading Augustine in the Twelfth Century', *Augustiniana*, **42** (1992), 95–110.

32 'Si ergo consideretur quantum bonum advenit ex rege; non solum regibus recte regentibus, sed etiam dato quod in aliquo, tyrannizarent, studeret populus obedire illis. Nam magis est tolerabilis aliqualis tyrannides principantis, quam sit malum consurgit ex inobedientia principis.' *De regimine principum libri III* (Rome, 1556; repr. Frankfurt: Minerva, 1968), iii. 2. 34.

33 Blythe, *Ideal Government*, 61.

Yet Blythe correctly argues that this fails to take into account the context in which Giles was writing. While in part his preference may be in deference to a princely audience, that is not a sufficient reason for Giles's position. In a significant insight, Blythe points to the tension between Aristotelian and Augustinian views of the origins and purposes of political authority as an explanation. Fundamentally, Blythe argues, Giles wanted to resolve this dichotomy. After the thirteenth century, medieval political thought is often assumed to be an attempt to reconcile Christian theology with classical philosophy, a formulation that is often more polemical than useful. But the problem can be understood much more concretely as between Augustinian political ideas on the one hand and traditional medieval concepts articulated through Aristotelian political theory on the other:[34]

> Giles wanted to believe both that government resulted from sin and that it was a natural outgrowth of human nature. He wanted a regal king who ruled by his own rule, and yet he wanted law to prevail and the king to be bound by council. He wanted both a sovereign king and one basing his power on the consent of the people. He wanted to see the state as a natural outgrowth of the family, but he also wanted it to result from a social contract of its citizens.[35]

This is not merely a conflict between Augustinian and Aristotelian ideas in the abstract, but also accurately reflects the fundamental weakness of the French monarchy. The king was simultaneously challenged by decentralized authority and by powerful liegemen, including the French king's most important vassal, the King of England, who in fact controlled much of the territory of France. Giles's discussion of Aristotle's typology of regimes is especially interesting given the conceptual conflict between a desire for a strong centralized monarchy and the traditional means of limiting a tyrant's power. As would Christine de Pizan much later, Giles used the city-states of Italy as his example of rule by the many. In Blythe's words: 'Giles, alone of Aristotle and the Medieval Aristotelians, rejects any role for the multitude, either for expediency or for their wisdom, but he does substantially dilute the king's unlimited power by requiring him to take counsel with the wise few – who together can know more than the one.'[36] This is exactly the emphasis we shall see with Christine

34 Kempshall argues that this conflict also concerned competing notions of the common good. To accept the Augustinian notion, according to Kempshall, would be to give temporal authority over spiritual goods. To privilege Aristotle raised even more complex issues, placing 'the relationship between nature and grace, moral and theological virtue, at the centre of political controversy'. M. S. Kempshall, *The Common Good in Late Medieval Political Thought* (Oxford: Clarendon Press, 1999), 266.

35 Blythe, *Ideal Government*, 62.

36 Ibid., 70–71.

de Pizan. While monarchy is best, it is a mediated monarchy because the wise king listens to the experts, and acts accordingly.

Giles of Rome's monumental *De regimine principum* was the most influential mirror of princes after the thirteenth century. Early vernacular translations into French, English, Italian, Spanish, Catalan, Portuguese, Swedish, German and Hebrew, as well as the number of extant Latin manuscripts and early printed editions[37] testify to the esteem and popularity of the work. Krynen believes that its significance stems from its status as 'the first work in the genre to be free of a monastic and literary culture derived from scriptural and patristic sources. Augustine, Ambrose, Gregory, and even the Latin moralists that were made to agree with the inspired teachings of the Fathers and Saint Bernard are absent from this work.'[38]

While Krynen may overstate the innovativeness of the secular character of his work, Giles's *De regimine* has a much more pragmatic and utilitarian flavour than many earlier mirrors. The translation in 1296 by Henri de Gauchi of *De regimine* into a simplified vernacular version, meant to be read aloud,[39] shows the increasing authority of the Philosopher and the significance attributed to his political ideas. Like most medieval translations, *Li Livres du gouvernment des rois* modifies the original text, changing its organization or omitting an exact citation for the attribution 'le Philosophe dit', but the work was immensely useful in the development of a secular intelligentsia based on a science of government. This vernacular version is most likely the text with which Christine was familiar.

Giles's 'mock Aristotelianism', as George Sabine puts it, or what Walter Ullmann considers superficial support of an 'ascending'[40] theory of kingship, is not a precursor of seventeenth-century absolutism; rather it is an expression of one of the most fundamental characteristics of medieval political thought: its intense pragmatism and willingness to adapt the theory – whether Aristotelian philosophy, Roman law, or Augustinian theology – to the changing needs and situations of the contemporary context. It is a salutary reminder to any theorist, as well as historians of political thought; politics is the wisdom of philosophy put into practice, as Aristotle would have it. No medieval political theorist was wrote in a vacuum. What is remarkable is that this same tension between a

37 Eleven editions were printed between 1473 and 1617. The library of Charles V alone had ten copies in one form or another. See Jacques Krynen, *L'Empire du roi: idées et croyances politiques en France, XIIIe–XVe siècle* ([Paris]: Gallimard, 1993), 179, 187. See also *Li Livres du gouvernement des rois*, ed. Molenaer, p. ix.

38 Krynen, *L'empire*, 183.

39 Ibid., 180.

40 Blythe, *Ideal Government*, 62.

normative preference for what we might anachronistically call constitutionalism and the need for a workable political system is also found in Christine de Pizan's political works.

CHAPTER THREE

The Body Politic

... everyone should come together as one body of the same polity, to live justly and in peace.

Christine de Pizan's political thought paradoxically couples a progressive defence of women with what some have characterized as a regressive view of social class. In this chapter, her view of the political community as a whole will be explored. The examination of Christine's historical and intellectual context in the preceding chapters develops an appreciation of the experiences and ideas that shaped her political theory. While some political writers seem to write from a perspective that is insulated from the vicissitudes of fortune, Christine always wrote from a deeply rooted sense of her own vulnerability, and thus of the contingent nature of life. The crises, both personal and political, that she faced fostered the major themes of her work. Central to her concern was the nature of the political community itself. In order to understand Christine de Pizan's construct of the community, this chapter begins with a general exploration of two of the dominant metaphors used in the Middle Ages to describe the community: the city and the human body. Very much a visual thinker, Christine was profoundly imaginative – in the literal sense – and often used metaphors as the catalyst for her ideas about community.

Metaphors are often used to describe the polity and political life. Some are ancient, like the ship of state or the beehive. Today, metaphors in politics are often derived from sport, business or warfare, as in 'winning the media game', 'selling a president' or 'waging a war on drugs'. These metaphors shape political vision. Assumptions about human interactions, about societal values, needs and priorities, and about relationships between various groups within society are both revealed and created by the words used to describe them. Examples abound. Every ill person ought to worry when the local hospital administration refers to doctor/patient encounters as 'throughput'. Every professor ought to be concerned when a college president refers to faculty as 'constituents' or students as 'customers'. The use of these terms reveals the president's analogues in thinking about the college over which he or she presides. A business or political metaphor will mould campus discourse in ways of which the participants are often completely unaware. Not only is the observation and analysis of political metaphors extremely important in understanding political life, but changes in the understanding or use of images can express uncharted social or political change. A society in transition or in crisis may respond to those forces by creating new metaphors or revalidating older ones. Of course, this is all a part of symbolic use of language, ideas and images that is certainly part of the human psyche. It may be manipulated by political handlers, pundits or spin doctors, or deliberately created by political strategists. The 'New Frontier' and 'Thatcher Revolution' have a wealth of meaning far beyond their status as slogans, as we are well aware.

A general exploration of the idea of the community in the Middle Ages relies very heavily on examination of the dominant metaphors used to describe it. The images of the city and of the human body have been influential in part because they were linked to the foundations of Christian society, the city to the classical world and the body to the Christian Scriptures. This chapter begins with a brief introduction to the history of each of these metaphors and Christine de Pizan's use of them, followed by a discussion of nationalism.

The city

The early Christian idea of community was affected by the need to understand the role that the Christian church would play within society. Until Christianity became the official state religion, Christian discussions of the community were limited to the community of the church, and the primary metaphor used is the Pauline description of the church as members of the body of Christ. 'For as in one body we have many members, and all the members do not have the same function, so we though many, are one body in Christ, and individually members one of another.'[1]

The image of the church as 'members', that is, limbs and organs of the body of Christ, each with different gifts and perhaps of different value, is one of the oldest and most enduring images within Christianity and predates any Christian state. Even today it remains a powerful metaphor and has been enlisted by some to argue for a hierarchical ecclesiastical organization that excludes or includes members on the basis of their gifts. Its use was confined by Christian writers to the Church in the early part of the first millennium; it would not be applied to the political community as a whole until much later.

1 Rom. 12: 4–5. See also 1 Cor. 12. Paul himself had a classical education and thus may have been familiar with the metaphor from Cicero or Aristotle.

By contrast, it was with the advent of a Christianity increasingly closely tied to the state, following the Edict of Milan in 313, that political imagery used by Christian writers began to change, just as society itself was changing. The sense of a crumbling civilization and of a world grown old profoundly affected both Christian and non-Christian writers. Some Romans, facing the disintegration of the empire, blamed political and social upheaval on the wrath of gods offended by their abandonment in the name of the new state religion. In 420 Augustine refuted their arguments, drawing on a new analogy of Christian community as a kind of baptized eternal city, like Athens, or even Rome. His monumental work, *De civitate dei*, provided a very evocative image for a world that saw the city as both the pinnacle of civilization and as the source of identity. The Roman, especially Ciceronian, *civitas* was a powerful metaphor to have chosen, evoking images of both privilege and safety. The celestial city was infused with the Augustinian appreciation of the 'mixed' life – active in the world, but not of it.

This new image became important conceptually for describing the medieval political community.[2] The celestial city, complete with battlements and turrets, would remain an evocative image well into Christine's own era, further enriched by illuminated manuscripts and the traditions of medieval art. Indeed, the image of the 'shining city on a hill' persisted into early American political thought, as the celebrated sermon by Governor John Winthrop attests.[3]

Christine's use of this image of a celestial city is far more elaborate and multi-layered than that of Augustine, who used it only to contrast the twin realms of secular and spiritual life and behaviour and to evoke a sense of belonging. Christine allegorizes the image in *Le Livre de la cité des dames*, providing the city with a foundation of reason, walls of rectitude, and pinnacles of virtue, and peopling it with great women of the past and present.

After Augustine and the fall of Rome, Europeans were inventing and developing new political and social structures. Over the next few centuries, a multitude of terms to describe the political community also developed, many adapted from Latin, such as *universitas* and *communitas*. Frankish or Norman practical associations with Roman experience were limited to be sure, but the use of these terms by non-Romans layered medieval institutions with classical associations.

By the twelfth century, with the resurgence of the study of Roman law in particular, the influence of legal terminology on political ideas had revitalized political imagery as well, incorporating new meanings to older political terms.

---

2 It is worth noting that the metaphor is 'backwards', as it were; that is, the community is being compared to a political unit, the city, rather than the opposite.

3 John Winthrop, 'A modell of Christian charity', 1630. *Old South Leaflets*, ed. S. E. Morison, no. 207 (Boston: Old South Association, 1916).

In consequence, those new images and Roman terminology framed one of the most important discussions – and conflicts – of the medieval period. The proper relationship between *sacerdotium* and *regnum*, or church and state, as the conflict is articulated, was at its heart a conflict over political legitimacy, authority and obligation. This conflict and its collateral effects profoundly shaped the Western world.

Robert Pullen (fl. *c.*1120–1146), like Augustine, used the biblical imagery of the Psalms to present a view of the church as a city, but a spiritual city that must be defended from its enemies. The prelates of the church were to be its defenders, and their weapon was to be the sword of the spirit, which is the word of God. This new metaphor, the twin swords of spiritual power and temporal power, allowed for shared responsibility between political and ecclesiastical rulers over the whole community. The scriptural foundation for the image came from the Gospels themselves. Having previously been instructed by Jesus to buy swords for their defence, at his arrest in the garden of Gethsemane Peter was forbidden by Jesus to use his sword to harm his captors. As first Pope, Peter was believed to have been given authority over all Christians, and by extension his successors also had the 'power to bind and to loose' throughout Christendom. But, on this view, although the Pope as spiritual ruler had the right to the sword, he did not have the right to shed blood, because that had been explicitly forbidden to Peter by Jesus. The other sword of the Gospel account belonged to the temporal power, to *regnum* rather than *sacerdotium*. While the two swords govern different domains, the soul and the body, both are from God and are deputed to the appropriate authority. Both powers need each other, and together they can bring peace through the use of temporal and spiritual punishments. A king should therefore obey a priest in matters concerning God's commandments, but the prelate is subject to the king, Pullen stipulates, in matters concerning secular affairs: no one should resist royal tyranny by force.

The concept of the two swords also had its limitations. While it was very powerful (and much quoted)[4] to explain and shape the appropriate relationship between the two sources of medieval political authority, it does nothing to elucidate the bonds linking rulers and subjects; thus it cannot function as an image of the whole community.

While the metaphor of the two swords seems unduly to privilege religious authorities, in fact, it does the opposite. It must be remembered that most ancient civilizations, whether Chinese, Mayan, Egyptian or Roman, were essentially theocratic. Peoples were governed by god-kings, prophet-kings or priest-kings;

4 The metaphor was employed most famously, and perhaps most perniciously, by Bernard of Clairvaux, who used it to preach the second Crusade. See Nederman and Forhan, *Medieval Political Theory*, 21.

seldom was there any other acceptable arrangement. The 'two swords' metaphor allows the creation of a civilization where god/priest/prophet and king are separate entities. Each has separate powers and domains. Those subject to *regnum* or *sacerdotium* had different economic, social and personal obligations; and in principle at least, neither was to infringe on the other. Because of the doctrine of the two swords, the church was forbidden to shed the blood of those persons accused of crimes under its jurisdiction, which made punishments incurred under church control much more humane than those of the secular arm, a point that was not lost on observers and may have hastened the development of more humane treatment of criminals under civil law. Corporal punishment could only be inflicted by the state. Trial by one entity precluded trial by the other, whence the principle developed in Western law that one ought not to be tried for the same offence twice. Secondly, although each entity tried every conceivable method to control the other, the tension between them legitimized separate spheres of influence, which ultimately became separation of church and state, and allowed the creation of a conceptual space for the idea of civil disobedience, an important characteristic of freedom of conscience in the West.

In retrospect, by the time of Christine de Pizan this particular intellectual and political conflict had been resolved. It is clear to modern scholars that by the fourteenth century church and state were distinct and that ecclesiastical dominance over temporal authorities had declined, if indeed it had ever existed except in the minds of ecclesiastical authorities. A number of important writers, such as John Wyclif (1330–1384), had articulated positions that favoured the authority of secular rulers. But the Church still occupied a privileged position, which conferred high status on clerics, even if they were of low rank at birth.[5]

While Christine de Pizan never uses the image of the two swords herself, its influence on the idea that secular and religious entities are separate, distinct and with their own roles and privileges was a part of the background of her era, and helped to foster the development of her functional view of the church. Christine saw the different components of society as valuable in part because of their functions within society. The church, far from being privileged, had duties and responsibilities, and could be reprimanded if those obligations were neglected. As she writes in *Corps de policie*: 'So the good prince ought to take care of all these things, because despite the fact that correction of people in the Church is not his to undertake, nonetheless what prelate, priest, or cleric is so great that he will dare withstand or complain about the prince who reproves him for his manifest vice or sin?'[6] This is a significant step towards a more

5 This evolution is traced by Brian Tierney, James Blythe and Walter Ullman, among many others. For complete references, see the Bibliography.

6 *Book of the Body Politic*, trans. Forhan, 13–14.

secularized and laicized view of society, which might not have developed without the compartmentalized categories provided by the 'two swords' image.

The body

One of the most fascinating and useful political metaphors ever imagined is the metaphor of the body politic. So useful and pervasive is it that we scarcely recognize it as a metaphor, referring to a leader's 'right-hand man' or to a 'head' of state without a second thought. Although its origins are much older, the twelfth century contributed significant development to this influential image, which simultaneously addresses problems of authority, legitimacy and obligation, but does so vertically, as it were. Society was hierarchical without question, but the proper relationship between classes or ranks was a complex one. The metaphor of the body politic, which owes its most powerful development to John of Salisbury, as we have seen, was used by many medieval writers to elucidate class relations. At its inception in the twelfth century, the body was clearly seen as imagery, but as Anthony Black points out: 'By the thirteenth century *corpus* did not necessarily imply any deliberate comparison with the human body any more than "body" does in this context today. The organic analogy was, however, a favourite rhetorical, literary and philosophical device.'[7]

Building on Robert Pullen's foundation, John of Salisbury used both the 'two swords' metaphor and the body metaphor in his *Policraticus*, but he extended the use of the corporate metaphor to apply to society as a whole, rather than exclusively to the Christian community. Moreover, he developed to a much greater degree the discussion about the obligations of those involved in an active life in the world as members of that body. While both Pullen and Augustine implied that a 'mixed' life of a cleric – both active and contemplative in one role – had as much or even more intrinsic value than the contemplative life, John of Salisbury extended the argument to validate the lives not only of those who were administrators or 'bureaucrats' in secular government, but also by implication the lives of all the laity.[8] In the hands of John of Salisbury, the metaphor of the body really became a metaphor of the body *politic* rather than ecclesiastic.

Part of the richness and utility of the metaphor came from a combination of factors. First, it had associations linking it to the Pauline metaphor of the early church. Secondly, its plasticity made it very evocative – in other words it could

7 Anthony Black, *Political Thought in Europe 1250–1450* (Cambridge: Cambridge University Press, 1992), 15.

8 This ideal of the mixed life in the *Policraticus* and its antecedents is discussed more completely in Forhan, 'The Twelfth Century "Bureaucrat"' and 'The Not-So-Divided Self'.

be very persuasive. Modern scholars have often assumed that this metaphor is an exclusively hierarchical one, perhaps because they have focused on its use in ecclesiastical writing. When applied to the state, the metaphor assumed importance historically and philosophically as validating an interdependence model of political organization. Thirdly, the alleged classical origins of the metaphor were extremely important to its legitimacy; in fact, John of Salisbury did not even allude to the Pauline texts as the authority for the metaphor. While we today attribute the origins of the metaphor to Cicero's *Republic* or to Aristotle's *Politics*, those works were unavailable in the twelfth century.[9] John attributed the metaphor to Plutarch, which allows the guidance offered the prince to be classical and civic, rather than scriptural and religious. He introduced the corporate metaphor in the midst of his argument that a prince's personal conduct is essentially political. John had his advice take the form of a letter for the instruction of the Emperor Trajan. 'A commonwealth, according to Plutarch, is a certain body which is endowed with life by the benefit of divine favor, which acts at the prompting of the highest equity, and is ruled by what may be called the moderating power of reason.'[10]

This citation furnished the foundation for an elaborate construction whereby John provided the reader with a description of the roles and responsibilities of each part of the body, along with counsels to the prince on the appropriate steps to keep the parts healthy, such as remuneration for soldiers and officials so that they would be less subject to the temptations of bribery and abuse of authority. Reflection on a tale that John used to illustrate the dangers of an unhealthy body may have inspired him to develop the metaphor so completely. This fable of the revolt of the members against the belly would later be used by Christine de Pizan in *Le Livre du corps de policie,* the appropriately named *Book of the Body Politic.*[11] For her, the moral of the story is clear: 'Likewise, when a prince requires more than a people can bear, then the people complain

9 While scholars differ on the most probable sources for the metaphor in the *Policraticus*, finding traces of it in Livy, Cicero and Aristotle, and Robert Pullen, many of these texts were unavailable to John; thus he is more likely to have been developing a complex allegorization of an interesting image than responding to the direct influence of a single classical author, and certainly not Plutarch.

10 *The Statesman's Book of John of Salisbury, being the Fourth, Fifth, and Sixth Books, and Selections from the Seventh and Eighth Books, of the Policraticus*, trans. John Dickenson (New York: Russell & Russell, 1963), 64.

11 John himself tells us that he first heard the story of the revolt of the members of the body from his friend and patron Pope Eugenius III, Nicholas Breakspear. This tale is found in the Roman translation of Aesop, in Livy's *Historia*, and – surprisingly perhaps – in the court poetry of Marie de France (*c.*1160). For this text, see 'Marie de France', in Nederman and Forhan, *Medieval Political Theory*, 24.

against their prince and rebel by disobedience. In such discord, they all perish together. And thus I conclude that agreement preserves the whole body politic.'[12]

Whatever its precise origins, use of the metaphor is appropriate, given three other important themes in John's work: first, the interdependence of all the members upon each other, even the least significant; secondly, the effect of the individual upon the community as a whole; and thirdly, the importance of the political life in general. The letter's ostensible Roman origins are essential to John because the letter bridges the chasm between classical and Christian views of politics. The metaphor is not restricted to the Church as in Paul, but is used to describe the entire political community, emphasizing John's desire to revalorize political life. But why then choose Plutarch as the author of his imaginary advice to princes? Because Plutarch was believed to be tutor to Trajan, the model prince of pagan antiquity, the prince so virtuous that Gregory the Great pleaded for his soul and Dante placed him in the paradise of the just.[13] As Beryl Smalley notes: 'Pseudo-Plutarch and Trajan made a bridge between profane and sacred teaching on statecraft, since Pope Gregory I had prayed for Trajan's release from hell on account of his justice and mercy to a poor widow.'[14]

John of Salisbury's fabrication of the letter allowed him to extend the metaphor (without reference to its Pauline analogue) from the church to the state. In his work, the head is the prince; the soul is the church; the heart is the senate; eyes, ears and tongue are the magistrates and governors; the hands are officials and soldiers; the sides are the prince's attendants; the stomach and intestines are the financial officers; and the feet are the farmers and artisans. While head and heart are still privileged, the metaphor is used by John to stress the interdependence of members of the political community. In fact his understanding of the good society really pervades the theoretical understandings of the Middle Ages; that is, the community works together with the king at the head, counsellors close at hand, and everyone else fulfilling their duties virtuously.

The organic analogy dominated as the preferred political image throughout the Middle Ages, appearing over and over in a variety of sources, sometimes completely conventionally, sometimes to argue for hierarchy, but always effectively. By the late Middle Ages, the metaphor was so deeply accepted that it was read into Aristotle's political works, especially following their translation

---

12 *Book of the Body Politic*, trans. Forhan, 91.

13 See *Paradiso* XX. 44–8 and *Purgatorio* X. 74 ff. Plutarch's status as Trajan's tutor may also be John's invention, since contemporary scholars find little connection between the two.

14 Beryl Smalley and P. R. L. Brown, *Trends in Medieval Political Thought* (Oxford: Blackwell, 1965), 92.

into Latin after 1280.[15] By the fourteenth century, Nicole Oresme had integrated the metaphor of the body politic into his glosses on Aristotle. This work, *Le Livre de politiques d'Aristote*, made for Charles V, is not really a translation in the modern sense. Heavily glossed, it is a vehicle for the discussion and interpretation of Aristotle's ideas, and the work made a significant contribution to the development of political thought in its own right, in part because of its incorporation into later works. In particular, Oresme plays with the body metaphor by merging it with Aristotle's idea of disproportionality in the state, finding in it a source of social and political transmutation or breakdown. The idea of proper proportion is critical to Aristotle's ethical theory, as is well known; courage, for example, is the 'virtuous' mid-point between rashness and cowardice. The virtuous mean – the proportionate centre between two extremes in the individual – also has its analogue in the state:

> Revolutions in the constitutions also take place on account of disproportionate growth; for just as the body is composed of parts, and needs to grow proportionately in order that its symmetry may remain, and if it does not it is spoiled . . . and sometimes it might even change into the shape of another animal . . . so also a state is composed of parts, one of which often grows without it being noticed as for example the number of the poor in democracies and constitutional states.[16]

As a translation, the Latin text – itself a thirteenth-century translation from the Greek by William Moerbeke – is rendered very literally by Oresme. However, in the very long commentary that follows the citation above, Oresme incorporated the whole of the body politic metaphor as found in the *Policraticus*, but citing Plutarch, rather than John of Salisbury. He then moves beyond the *Policraticus*, saying:

> Likewise, the polity is disordered and cannot endure long when if through taxes or bad agreements or laws that are badly made or badly enforced, one of the members of the body takes too much nourishment into itself, that is, wealth, which makes that member too large beyond just proportion. And such a polity is like a monster and a sick body.[17]

The idea of disproportion is understood by Oresme as being the consequence of a particular part of the body being overfed, while others are undernourished.

---

15 Forhan, 'Reading Backward'.

16 Aristotle, *The Politics*, trans. H. Rackham (London: W. Heinemann, 1932), 383 (1302^{b}33).

17 'Semblablement la policie est mal ordonee et ne peut durer longuement quant par exactions ou par malvés contracts ou par lays mal mises ou mal tenues un des membres attrait a soy trop de nourissement, ce est assavoir des richeces par quoy tel membre est fait trop gros oultre juste mesure. Et tele policie est aussi comme .i. monstre et comme un corps malade' (Oresme, *Politiques*, ed. Menut, 209).

Oresme's use of the corporate metaphor is atypical, but his understanding of the political body and its health profoundly influenced Christine de Pizan, as we shall see below. In general, as Black points out,

> the commonest use of the organic analogy was to draw attention to the different functions of different parts and then to insist that the king or ruler, as head, must be obeyed. But it could equally be used to point out the duties of rulers to other parts and the need for fraternal harmony. The message of the organic analogy was, none the less, most often conservative, whether against a tyrant or a rebellion.[18]

Yet as was noted previously, Cary Nederman has observed that despite their traditional and conventional stucture, in the later Middle Ages the number of 'subversive' mirrors increases, so that Machiavelli may be the apotheosis of a two-century trend rather than an exception to a traditional genre.[19] In sum, the organic metaphor was generally used to illustrate the typically medieval view of the good society and perhaps the best regime as well: the king as head over a well-formed body characterized by a distinct division of labour, with all parts contributing equally to the health of the whole.

Christine, the celestial city, and the body politic

Christine's preference for these two historically charged political metaphors is obvious, given the titles of two of her works, *Le Livre de la cité des dames* and *Le Livre du corps de policie*.[20] Evaluation of her use of them has inspired several heated exchanges. Sheila Delany claims that she manipulates them in order to reinforce conservative roles and values and concludes that Christine's views are decidedly regressive: 'As for my evaluation of Christine's social loyalties, this has been amply confirmed in . . . her *Livre des trois vertus* with its pragmatic counsel, its advertisements for herself (as author and governess), and its convenient revisionary theology . . .'.[21]

---

18 Black, *Political Thought*, 15

19 Nederman, 'The Mirror Crack'd'.

20 *Le Livre du corps de policie* is sometimes erroneously translated as *The Book of the Body of Policie*, based on the Middle English rendering. As for *Cité des dames*, in my own experience teaching it in translation to undergraduates in an introductory political theory course, students, particularly women, love it. Not recognizing the stories as retellings of myths or as 'fractured' history, they take the work at face value, amazed that women have played such an important role in historical progress. They are surprised to discover that a fourteenth-century woman was even literate. The naiveté of these readers is instructive to us, however, for it helps us to see how fresh the material is even today. To a medieval audience familiar with mythology, it must have been very effective.

21 Delany, 'History, Politics, and Christine Studies', in Brabant (ed.), *Politics, Gender, and Genre*, 193–206.

Conversely, others argue that Christine employs these images to present her own political theory. In her article 'The Subversive "Seulette"', Mary McKinley notes that 'Christine's departures from generic norms may be read as part of her rhetorical strategy, as moves calculated to strengthen her authority in a world where both authority and authorship were preempted by men'.[22] McKinley's position that Christine's manipulation of authoritative figures of speech and of genres is employed to reshape the dominant ideology tends to preponderate among Christine scholars. This manipulation is illustrated by *Le Livre de la cité des dames*, one of Christine's most familiar and best-loved works. As is well known, *Cité des dames* is a framed narrative in which Christine finds herself growing more and more depressed by some light reading that had been recommended to her. In an experience that many women have shared, she finds herself accountably discouraged without realizing that she is unconsciously picking up negative and hostile views of women and applying them to herself. She bursts out, wondering how it is that so many famous and authoritative authors view women so negatively: 'Just the sight of this book, even though it was of no authority, made me wonder how it happened that so many different men – and learned men among them – have been and are so inclined to express both in speaking and in their treatises and writings so many wicked insults about women and their behavior.'[23] Yet when she examines her own experience, she knows many women who are honourable, intelligent and virtuous. Then, in a moment of stunning psychological clarity on the part of the author, the character Christine decides that her empirical observation and experience must be false and the opinions of the authorities correct. How can women created in the image of God be so despicable?

> And I finally decided that God formed a vile creature when he made Woman, and I wondered how such a worthy artisan could have deigned to make such an abominable work, which, from what they say, is the vessel as well as the refuge and abode of every evil and vice. As I was thinking this, a great unhappiness and sadness welled up in my heart, for I detested myself and the entire feminine sex, as though we were monstrosities of nature.[24]

It is at this moment that the three ladies, the goddesses Reason, Rectitude and Justice, appear and instruct her to build a City of Ladies:

---

22 Mary McKinley, 'The Subversive "Seulette"', in Brabant (ed.), *Politics, Gender, and Genre*, 156. McKinley's view is echoed by other scholars in this same volume. See the articles by Christine Reno, Linda Leppig and Kate Langdon Forhan for examples.

23 Christine de Pizan, *The Book of the City of Ladies*, trans. Earl Jeffrey Richards (New York: Persea Books, 1982), 4–5.

24 Ibid., 5.

> So occupied with these painful thoughts, my head bowed in shame . . . I suddenly saw a ray of light fall on my lap, as though it were the sun . . . And as I lifted my head to see where this light was coming from, I saw three crowned ladies standing before me, and the splendor of their bright faces, shone on me.[25]

The ladies gently reprimand her for believing the contradictory words of the philosophers rather than her own experience: 'we have come to bring you out of the ignorance which so blinds your own intellect that you shun what you know for a certainty and believe what you do not know or see or recognize except by virtue of many strange opinions'.[26]

The work has been extensively studied, and rather than repeat or summarize the analyses of others, this examination will be limited to the relationship of the text to the traditions in which she writes – its 'metatheory', as it were. First, the very structure of the work, with its powerful opening images, implies an emphasis on experience and observation over the authoritative statements of the *auctores* of the past. Significantly, the reader is allowed to accept the validity of practical experience in questions of identity and consequently in the reading of politics and ethics. Secondly, the ironic aspect of Christine as author and Christine as character presents us with a charming, but subversive, paradox. This 'ignorant and irrational' woman of misogynist stereotype is so well-read that she can toy with the structures, allusions and ideas of the *auctores* on which she models her work, particularly the mighty St Augustine and the City of God, and the renowned and much beloved Boethius, whose Dame Philosophy is capped by not one but three consolers. Thirdly, to subvert a genre in this fashion points to considerable command and proficiency in the forms of discourse, coupled to the creative imagination that is one of Christine's most significant intellectual characteristics. In this particular case – one of her earliest pieces of didactic writing – Christine undermines the tradition of misogyny in literature by her clever manipulation of it. Her use of this adaptive methodology is consistent in most of her early political works. In a sense, it represents an extension of the humility topos. By speaking of herself as ignorant and foolish, she disarms her reader, paradoxically making her lessons more effective.

By contrast, Christine de Pizan makes no other real use of either the ideal or the reality of the city in her political writings. Her celestial and idealized city of ladies finds no counterpart in actual practice. The Italian city-states, the closest analogues to the cities of Augustine's world, do not appeal to her either as models of an ideal polity or as expressions of good government. No

---

25 Ibid., 6.

26 Ibid.

republican, Christine's ideal community is found in strong and authoritative monarchy. It is the image of the idealized celestial city of illuminated manuscripts that has captured her imagination, not a real political organization, such as Venice or Florence, as she notes in *Corps de policie*:

> There are cities and countries which are self governed and are ruled by princes which they choose among themselves. Often these make their choice more by will than by reason. And sometimes, having chosen them by caprice, they seem to depose them the same way. Such government is not beneficial where it is the custom, as in Italy in many places.[27]

Conversely, the corporate metaphor gets extensive use in Christine's works. Her use of the image to describe the political community appears not only in the aptly named *Livre du corps de policie*, but also is a referent in several other books, notably *Le Livre de la paix* and *Le Livre des bonnes meurs du roy Charles V le sage*. *Corps de policie*, a companion piece to *Trésor de la cité des dames*, was intended for the instruction of the 14-year-old dauphin, Louis of Guyenne. It incorporates the metaphor as a central organizing theme and refers to its supposed origins in Plutarch. But like the image of the city, the idea of the body politic is more a conception borrowed for its ability to evoke both a tradition and a visual image in this highly visual thinker, rather than a reinterpretation of the *Policraticus*. The admirable new critical edition of this work by Angus Kennedy draws attention to Christine's very medieval habit of stitching together phrases and *exempla* in *Corps de policie*, primarily, even overwhelmingly, borrowed from *Facta et dicta memorabilia* of Valerius Maximus. This was a popular work often mined by medieval writers for savoury quotes and stories, although it is definitely an acquired taste. The work was translated into French by Simon de Hesdin and Nicolas de Gonesse and presented to the Duke of Berry early in 1402. Heavily glossed by its translators, Simon de Hesdin and Nicolas de Gonesse turned a quite commonplace sourcebook of *exempla* into a political work in its own right, from which, in the words of Charity Cannon Willard: 'Christine quotes both the text and the commentary without always discriminating between them.'[28] Like Nicole Oresme's translations of Aristotle's *Politics*, *Ethics* and *Economics*, and Foulechat's translation of the *Policraticus*, Hesdin and Gonesse read into their source ideas and concepts not only foreign to their late Roman author, but traceable to medieval works of politics, in this case to Oresme's glosses on Aristotle.[29] A trademark of medieval writing, indeed of medieval intellectual

---

27 *Book of the Body Politic*, trans. Forhan, 92.

28 Willard, *Life*, 178.

29 This issue is elaborated in Forhan, 'Reading Backward'.

processes in general, was the gloss on the text, that is the expansion, interpretation and application of ideas from the great and famous authorities. This process required that the mere commentator keep in the background. A fourteenth- or fifteenth-century reader might easily mistake the gloss for the authoritaive text. Much would depend on the qualities of the actual manuscripts. For example, in the 'travelling' or personal editions of Nicole Oresme's translations of Aristotle's *Ethics* and *Politics* for Charles V, the glosses are virtually indistinguishable from Aristotle's text. A fourteenth- or twenty-first-century reader might easily mistake Oresme's original contribution for Aristotle's ideas. There is strong circumstantial evidence that Christine read Oresme's translation, but we may never know with certainty the intellectual and textual sources for her ideas about politics.

In any case, Christine made the metaphor of the body her own. In *Corps de policie* she follows her typical pattern of dividing the work in three, corresponding to the three estates she deems most important, the prince, the knights and nobles, and the common people:

> These three types of estate ought to be one polity like a living body according to the words of Plutarch who in a letter which he sent to the Emperor Trajan compared the polity to a body having life. There the prince and princes hold the place of the head in as much as they are or should be sovereign and from them ought to come particular institutions just as from the mind of a person springs forth the external deeds that the limbs achieve.[30]

This passage also provides an excellent example of how contemporary ideas about physiology have an impact on the political understanding engendered by the metaphor. In the twelfth-century usage, the prince was head, literally because he could see farther, given his higher placement in the body. Intelligence or reason was physically situated in the heart, where John of Salisbury placed the 'senate' or wise counsellors. For Christine, the king was head because he provided the mind that drove the physical force of the body. The king then held legislative power, setting the course for the entire nation, as in Giles of Rome's concept of *regimen regale*. This ideal role for the king recalls not only Christine's admiration for Charles V, 'the Wise', but also the traditional need in French political theory for a unifying head amidst discord:

> The knights and nobles take the place of the hands and arms. Just as a person's arms have to be strong in order to endure labor, so they have the burden of defending the law of the prince and the polity. They are also the hands because, just as the hands push aside harmful things, so they ought push all harmful and useless things aside.[31]

---

30 *Book of the Body Politic*, trans. Forhan, 4.

31 Ibid.

On this model, the knights – the *bellatores* of the 'three orders' – are a kind of executive power, defending the law and protecting the nation. The administration of justice is one of the most important elements in Christine's political theory, and in a kingdom where lawlessness and marauding bands of renegade soldiers are too often present, her emphasis on knights defending the law is critical:

> The other kinds of people are like the belly, the feet, and the legs. Just as the belly receives all that the head and the limbs prepare for it so, too, the activity of the prince and nobles ought to return to the public good, as will be better explained later. Just as the legs and feet sustain the human body so, too, the laborers sustain all the other estates.[32]

While, by medieval standards, Christine devoted a disproportionate amount of attention to the common people in both this book and its companion, *Trésor*, which some of her admirers see as protodemocratic,[33] in *Corps de policie* the emphasis is not really so much on the common people themselves as on the obligation that higher ranks have to them, and the inherent virtue and value of the poor. As she says in *Corps de policie*, there 'is no doubt that the estate of the poor which everyone despises has many good and worthy persons in purity of life'.[34] This reinforces not only the idea of interdependence within the body politic but also of the dignity of each member.

Social class

The connection between the organic metaphor and social class throughout the medieval period seems very obvious. The metaphor could be and was used not only to justify division of labour, but also the subordination of some groups within both the church and the state. The metaphor fails to reveal another important reality, however, and that is the permeability of social class. Although rigid distinctions were made, they were not caste-like distinctions. Rather, differences in rank, and thus in privileges and responsibilities, were justified to a certain degree by function. The three orders of medieval society – those who pray (*oratores*), those who fight (*bellatores*) and those who work (*laborares*) – because theoretically not based on any fixed attributes except for gender, did allow social mobility, especially for men, and movement into the ostensibly highest order, the clergy, was considered to be open to any legitimately born male of the requisite merits regardless of rank at birth. Women

32 Ibid.

33 For a view of *Trésor* as protodemocratic see Christine Reno, 'Christine de Pizan: At Best a Contradictory Figure?', in Brabant (ed.), *Politics, Gender, and Genre*, 171–92.

34 *Book of the Body Politic*, trans. Forhan, 109.

could also move into positions of authority that they were not born to by becoming members of religious orders. In the high Middle Ages, women could exercise influence through the prerogatives of various guilds, and even, as in the case of Christine de Pizan, independently of either religious orders or guild privileges.

For Christine de Pizan, as for her contemporaries, social class or rank was a reality that was rarely questioned. The issue was never whether or not social classes ought to exist but rather what the responsibilities, privileges and liberties were of each. Secondly, there was the political problem of enforcing those rights and obligations of rank. Traditionally, class distinctions were bolstered by tax policies and sumptuary laws that restricted access to certain goods, including particular kinds or styles of clothing, and luxury spices or wines. Sumptuary laws are often thought by moderns to be a way that medieval society enforced social norms of behaviour and status. While they certainly functioned to privilege elites, in the medieval view they were medically and socially prophylactic as well. As Johanna Moyer has pointed out, medieval medical ideas about balancing the humors meant that certain foods were considered risky in excess; thus restricting their consumption by particular classes was thought to increase social stability. For example, luxury foods like certain meats and wines overheated the body, causing surplus sanguinity, and thus could cause soldiers to be more warlike and inappropriately aggressive.[35]

During Christine's life the social body was completely disordered. Population losses, economic stress, public uprisings and the growing independence of the bourgeoisie precipitated much debate and many attempts to control change. The violent uprisings of the common people and the rapacious ways of itinerant soldiers could be understood as a consequence of disordered humours. Poorly digested foods corrupted the body both physically and morally, causing illnesses. Since luxury items were believed to increase the sanguine humour (blood) and predispose one to both illness and aggressive and violent behaviour, the cure for the individual was bloodletting, but for the body politic it was taxes. Retelling a story of one bourgeois woman's excesses, Christine comments that 'some remarked that Parisians have too much blood, the abundance of which sometimes brings on particular maladies (that is, great riches are capable of corrupting)'.[36]

---

35 Johanna B. Moyer, 'French Sumptuary Law and the Body in Medieval Thought, 1224–1571', paper presented at the fifth annual ACMRS conference, 18–20 February 1999, Tempe, Arizona.

36 Christine de Pizan, *A Medieval Woman's Mirror of Honor*, trans. Charity Cannon Willard (New York: Persea Books, 1989), 195.

Christine de Pizan approved of sumptuary laws and social norms of this kind not only because of the role they played in balancing the body politic, but also for purely practical reasons. Extravagance, social climbing, resentment and envy, and even the attention of tax assessors are the negative consequence of living ostentatiously. Thus, to wives of merchants she writes:

> Theirs is great folly to dress up in other people's costumes when all know who they really are, or to take on another's estate rather than being content with their own . . . But it is ridiculous to feel no shame in selling one's merchandise and carrying on business, and yet to feel shame at wearing the corresponding costume. It has its own luster for those who wear it appropriately; the merchant's place is good and honorable in France and every other country.[37]

This is not merely pusillanimity on Christine's part, but pragmatism. 'So no matter how great their wealth, it is better for them to wear suitable clothes – which can be handsome, rich and decorous – well adapted to their lives without any pretensions to being something other than what they are.'[38] Nor does she spare the nobility: 'Remember all this [extravagance in dress] comes from abundance of overweening pride, which reigns more today than ever before. Nobody accepts his true station in life but pretends to resemble a king . . . Such vanity of costume leads to other ridiculous behavior.'[39]

Christine's advice books directed at male audiences also advised moderation in food and drink, particularly for young princes, since it was believed that overly refined foods spoiled more quickly and provided inferior nourishment:

> And as for feeding them, some say that the child nourished on fine wines and foods will have better blood, and as a consequence will be stronger. That opinion is false, because dainty foods are earlier corrupted than others, according to Aristotle, nor do they strengthen a person's body as well as plain foods do. And we see this in our own experience, for the Bretons and the Normans are commonly fed plain food and they are not refined in their food and drink, but they are commonly stronger and tougher than other people.[40]

Social class is not only a diagnostic tool in ensuring the health of the body politic through mechanisms of social control, since each member of the body brings his or her own expertise and excellence to the whole society, but rank also signals a domain of knowledge. Thus, for example, both *Corps de policie* and *L'Epistre d'Othéa* advise the prince to listen to the counsels of soldiers when it comes to questions of warfare, and to 'the wise' or learned in areas of their expertise. Class distinctions are important to Christine because of her

37 Ibid., 196.

38 Ibid.

39 Ibid., 175–6.

40 *Book of the Body Politic*, trans. Forhan, 7.

functional view of society, but they do not constitute a belief that class or rank determines the value of the person. Charles V, the model king, for example, was praised for making political and administrative appointments on the basis of ability rather than rank. Criticized for his selection of 'un homme de rien' to a high administrative post, Charles is reported by Christine to have said, 'Know that the poor man, wise and trustworthy, merits more our esteem than the rich one who lives a foolish and shameful life.'[41] By this sharp rebuke, the model king, Charles the Wise, is revealed to be both pragmatic and virtuous in Christine's view. Just as the prince is wise to listen to counsellors of any rank, so too other social classes have an obligation to listen and to intercede.

Where Christine's advice is a striking departure from the conventional is in her view of the obligations of these other social classes and groups. For example, women have an active role to play in the pursuit of peace, beyond being the object of exchange in traditional marital alliances. In *Trésor*, princesses are given very clear instructions on the importance of their role as peacemakers in society: 'If any neighboring or foreign prince wars for any grievance against her lord, or if her lord wages war against another, the good lady will weigh the odds carefully.'[42] This is neither Pollyannaish optimism nor Jerrold's 'peace at any price', but pragmatic and experienced calculation of interests: 'She will balance the great infinite cruelties, losses, deaths, and destruction to property and people against the war's outcome, which is usually unpredictable. She will seriously consider whether she can preserve the honor of her lord and yet prevent the war.'[43]

In part, this role for high-born women is a natural consequence of Christine's gender theory of complementarity. Women are predisposed to be peacemakers because of their natural qualities of prudence and circumspection. This may confuse some American readers, used to associating feminism only with a 1970s liberal feminism that rejected essentialism, but is more consistent with European and social democratic views that indeed developed out of the corporate inheritance of Europe:

> The proper role of a good, wise queen or princess is to maintain peace and concord and to avoid wars and their resulting disasters. Women particularly should concern themselves with peace because men by nature are more foolhardy and headstrong, and their overwhelming desire to avenge themselves prevents them from foreseeing the resulting dangers and terrors of war. But woman by nature is more gentle and circumspect.[44]

---

41 *Le Livre des faits et bonnes moeurs du roi Charles V le sage*, ed. Eric Hicks and Thérèse Moreau (Paris: Stock, 1997), 229.

42 *Medieval Woman's Mirror of Honor*, trans. Willard, 86.

43 Ibid., 85.

44 Ibid., 86.

All women of whatever rank have an obligation to assist the unfortunate, an obligation with its origins in Christian piety. But a prudent woman of high social class also builds a network of allies among knights, prelates, lawyers, bailiffs and even merchants and artisans, so that if difficulties strike, her reputation as a woman of 'noble bearing and wisdom'[45] will maintain her credibility, and obtain their support. The pride of a princess might cause her to demur, believing it beneath her dignity to 'lavish attention on her lowliest subjects'. With gentle humour, Christine counsels that

> the more overtly considerate course is splendid not only for princes and princesses but for everyone . . . [D]espite the prince being the lord and master of his subjects, still the subjects create the lord, not vice versa. If people want to be troublesome, they will much more easily find someone else to take them on as subjects than a lord will find subjects to accept him as their ruler.[46]

Pragmatically, she argues that the difficulties of dealing with rebellion from within are far more costly to the prince than war, and that 'even if at any given moment he had the military power to destroy them, he would also destroy himself . . . "No one is lord in his country who is hated by his people"'.[47]

This web of mutual obligation, clearly spurred by self-interest, is also found in Christine's advice for men. The bourgeoisie is important to society, not only in providing wealth and commerce, but in interceding for the just demands of the commons. Thus in *Corps de policie* she advises that '[b]urghers and the wealthy must take care that the common people are not hurt, so that they have no reason to conspire against the prince or his council'.[48]

Christine's functional view of class and its interwoven tapestry of relationships and commitments gives a significant role to merchants and burghers in the economic and political systems of cities: 'These people ought to be concerned with the situation and needs of the cities of which they are a part. They are to ensure that everything concerning commerce and the situation of the population is well governed.'[49] The obligation to the whole polity to ensure the common good in urban areas is critical because of the limited experience and ability of the commoners. Their lack of sophistication means that they are ill-suited for public debate on questions of economic and commercial legislation. She warns her readers 'humble people do not commonly have great prudence in words or even in deeds that concern politics and so

---

45 Ibid., 110.
46 Ibid., 110–11.
47 Ibid., 111.
48 *Book of the Body Politic*, trans. Forhan, 99.
49 Ibid.

they should not meddle in the ordinances established by princes'.[50] But their anger at injustices or other problems can cause explosions of rage, and of course recent popular uprisings had revealed deep dissatisfaction with government and the economy, in Paris and the provinces. Thus it is in the bourgeoisie's own self-interest to act as a conduit for the legitimate claims of the common people:

> And so, if there is a case sometime when the common people seem to be aggrieved by some burden, the merchants ought to assemble and from among them choose the wisest and most discreet in action and in speech, and go before the prince or the council, and bring their claims for them in humility and state their case meekly for them, and not allow them to do anything, for that leads to the destruction of cities and of countries.[51]

It is only prudent for merchants to avoid the negative consequences of extremes of economic injustice by intervening or representing the common people's needs to the king: 'The reason is that these conspiracies and plots by the common people always come back to hurt those that have something to lose. It always was and always will be that the end result is not at all beneficial to them, but evil and detrimental.'[52]

Christine's view of the obligations of the merchant class to represent the needs of the poor is quite striking; in addition to representing their just demands, the bourgeoisie should also help 'to quiet the complaints of the people because of the evil that could come to all. They must restrain themselves this way as well as others.'[53]

As a prescription for social peace this may be effective, albeit inadequate and even culpable in the view of some scholars, such as Sheila Delany. Like Machiavelli, however, who was often criticized for immorality in politics, Christine's views are realistic, given the political climate in 1407:

> And if sometimes the laws of princes and their council seem to them to appear, according to their judgement, to be wrong, they must not interpret this as in bad faith, and there may be danger in foolishly complaining, but they ought to assume that they have good intentions in what they do, although the cause might not be apparent. It is wisdom to learn when to hold one's tongue.[54]

Thus, although social class is a given, it does not authorize greater worth and dignity, nor does it relieve higher ranks from social responsibility that is framed and imaged through the body politic.

50 Ibid.
51 Ibid., 99–100.
52 Ibid., 99.
53 Ibid., 100.
54 Ibid.

While it does not represent a concept of political or social equality, the idea of the body politic plays an important role in medieval political thought by providing an intellectual and moral justification or framework through which the value of the individual person can be affirmed. Perhaps nowhere else is the theoretical chasm between our world and medieval culture so deep; we define ourselves, according to Marvin Zetterbaum,[55] in opposition to society. In the medieval world, selves become most fully themselves within the community. It has been well established that there is a historical link between the concept of the self-evident equality of all citizens and the ideas of the early modern period that grew out of the radical Reformation claim of 'every man a priest'. But before the development of this innovation, political theorists developed other concepts that had a similar function of protecting the weak and establishing the essential dignity of all human persons. While Christine de Pizan has no understanding of the benefits of the egalitarian ideal, the metaphor of the body politic serves an analogous function of enjoining her readers both to respect the value of all human persons and to provide for the security of unequals, while simultaneously acknowledging socially expected and required differences of rank, of class and of gender. While not pretending to equality, the metaphor validates the dignity and worth of the individual person. The development of this metaphor may in fact have prepared the way for the evolution of the concept of equality as its modern equivalent.

Christine de Pizan and nationalism

The emphasis on virtue ethics and mutual obligation in Christine de Pizan's political thought is accompanied by a remarkable lack of interest in the institutional or structural elements of good politics. In order to understand this and its significance, a brief examination of institutional and constitutional development in France may be helpful.

Despite what was in many ways a shared political culture, certainly amongst the clerical classes in any case, the differences in institutional development and political experience between France and England were quite large. Especially after the mid-twelfth century, while England was enmeshed in building a centralized and bureaucratized administrative kingdom, France was far more fragmented. Like many European states, France emerged out of a system of overlapping and often competing jurisdictions with different customs, languages, institutions and rulers. Over several centuries a more centralized state gradually began to appear, but it did so only by default. Although there

[55] Marvin Zetterbaum, 'Self and Subjectivity in Political Theory', *Review of Politics*, 44/1 (Jan. 1982), 59–82.

emerged the idea in France that 'within fixed boundaries there is a definite superior who has the final decision regarding all political activities',[56] this idea was a polite fiction. French political writers were attempting to invent a centralized authority where none existed. The reality was a textbook case of fragmentation, comneting jurisdictions and decentralization, caused by a variety of factors. Competing regional rulers – dukes and counts in particular – had become progressively weaker. Owing to their excessively lavish lifestyles and incessant conflict among themselves, the nobility was haemorrhaging resources. By contrast, the relative wealth, influence and position of other social classes, most notably the bourgeoisie, was strengthened. The king was weak, the lower classes often in revolt. This is why political theorists in France, Christine de Pizan included, most commonly attempt to justify a strong monarchy to counterbalance the centrifugal forces of fragmentation. In essence, to paraphrase historian Charles Wood, while France consisted of the territory whose inhabitants a given ruler protected, that territory varied greatly with the strengths and weaknsses of its rulers, which is hardly a recipe either for political confidence or social stability.

As has been described by Joseph Strayer, Cary J. Nederman[57] and others, the growth in political theorizing about a strong centralized monarchy began first with the legalists, who in order to make judgements about the control of property within this system of competing jurisdictions needed to distinguish between the legislative and judicial functions of the monarchy. Early tracts by Philippe de Beaumanoir (d. 1296), Pierre du Bois (*c.*1250–*c.*1320) and the anonymous *Antequam essent clerici* (1297) work towards an early theory of royal sovereignty.

The extraordinarily close relationship between the University of Paris and the French monarchy represents a second, and perhaps slightly later, strand in this developing theory of royal power. Arising from the need to justify royal control over university-trained administrators – technically clerics and thus subject to Church authority – a series of treatises were written that established the importance of *regnum* over *sacerdotium* and justified royal rights. Works such as those by Jean Quidort and Giles of Rome gave rise to a tradition of scholastic political literature that attempted both to repel claims to world dominion by the Emperor or the Pope, and conversely, to strengthen royal powers as a means of mitigating and balancing competing claims to exclusive control over property. 'In particular, French authors shared a definite conception

56 Strayer, *Medieval Statecraft*, 261.

57 Ibid.; Cary J. Nederman, 'State and Political Theory in France and England, 1250–1350' (PhD diss., York University, 1984).

of lordship in terms of the wholly privatized and individualized application of power over property'.[58] Phrases like 'The king is emperor in his own kingdom' and 'the king acknowledges no superior power on earth' are not then early claims to some sort of absolutism – although they might later be used as fuel for that particular fire – they are defensive axioms, to support the very identity and existence of a French kingdom. In short, French political theorists were attempting to create a French nation.

The emergence of French nationalism and the creation of French national identity as a self-conscious project of both princes and poets is a facinating story.[59] Alain Chartier and Eustache Deschamps both invoked France's special identity as founded by divine command and the French people as God's elect. Charles V's library project was recognized by his contemporaries no less than modern scholars as a means of highlighting French language and culture. Nicole Oresme wrote of the significance of France. Christine de Pizan's own nationalism in particular has been the subject of some discussion. Several essays have appeared on Christine's attitudes and views of Jews and foreigners, most notably the English, and both Earl Jeffrey Richards and Angus Kennedy have made valuable contributions to a more theoretical understanding of her nationalism. Christine de Pizan's fervour for France is expressed passionately and intemperately. Any understanding of her political thought must examine whether she is expressing jingoistic fear and hatred or loyalty to a nascent nation-state.[60] Three different forms of nationalism are commonly recognized; first, cultural affinity or affection; second, political attachment; and third, an

58 Nederman, ibid., 193.

59 See the discussion in Deborah Fraioli, 'The Literary Image of Joan of Arc: Prior Influences', *Speculum*, **56** (1981), 811–30, at 820–21; Sherman, *Imaging Aristotle*, 3–11; Babbitt, *Oresme's Livre de politiques*, 127–46; Colette Beaune, *The Birth of an Ideology: Myth and Symbols of Nation in Late-Medieval France* (Berkeley, University of California Press, 1991).

60 There is an extensive literature on nationalism both in the contemporary world and with respect to Christine de Pizan. A recent cogent overview of the contemporary problem from the perspective of political theorists can be found in Margaret Canovan, *Nationhood and Political Theory* (Cheltenham: Edward Elgar, 1996). With respect to Christine de Pizan, Earl Jeffrey Richards has written extensively on nationalism. One of his most provocative essays is 'Why is Christine not Politically Correct? Reflections on Hermeneutics, Literary Politics and Difference', presented at CEMERS, SUNY Binghamton, 1995. Two other essays are quite important (Nadia Margolis, Earl Jeffrey Richards), as is the introduction (Jean Bethke Elshtain), in Brabant (ed.), *Politics, Gender, and Genre*. Angus Kennedy's introduction to Christine's *Ditié Jeanne d'Arc* is very insightful (Oxford: Society for the Study of Medieval Languages and Literature, 1977). On medieval nationalism, see Simon Forde, Lesley Johnson and Alan V. Murray, *Concepts of National Identity in the Middle Ages* (Leeds: University of Leeds, 1995). Other materials can be found in the Bibliography.

identity composed of language, religion and culture. All three elements are often blended together imperceptibly so that it may be difficult to differentiate mere preferences from hatred or loyalty from jingoism.

To begin this discussion of Christine's nationalism, it must be recognized that Christine's identity as French was a choice, despite her Italian birth. While her father's decision to bring his family to France in 1389 was not a determination to renounce his origins, and Christine was raised to respect her family and its cultural heritage, it is surprising how passionate her attachment to France was. After the death of both her father and her husband, a more conventional woman might have chosen to return to Italy and live under her brothers' 'protection' in Italy. Indeed, for those scholars who see Christine's mother as wholly conventional and thus a limiting influence, it should be noted that she too chose France, when as a widow she might have returned to Italy, where her sons controlled her husband's family's property, and where her own family, the Mondinos, had been influential. Thus, a literal preference for France as her home is one element of Christine's nationalism. A second is her fervour for France, enthusiastically and even passionately expressed both in her analysis of political systems and in her seemingly spontaneous outbursts of praise for all things French. Here too, we see a preference for the habits, institutions and values of France.

Throughout her life, there are three different stages that can be discerned in Christine de Pizan's expression of this partiality for France. A closer look at elements in this development may help us better to see and understand nationalism in the later Middle Ages. The first is so obvious that it is easily overlooked, but it is found in her early attachment, both financial and affective, to the royal family of France. This could be seen as merely self-interested or even mercenary; after all, for a 'professional' writer, that is someone who writes for pay or at least the hope of payment, it was important to please her patrons, and most of Christine's works were dedicated to or commissioned by members of the French royal families. Some of her early *ballades*, for example, were gifts of praise and good wishes for members of the royal houses for the New Year. For example, *Ballades* XVIII, XIX, XX were addressed to Isabeau of Bavaria, Louis of Orleans and Marie de Berry, respectively. To the queen, she wrote in 1402:

> High, excellent crowned Queen
> Of France, very redoubtable princess,
> Powerful lady, born at a lucky hour,
> To whom honour and valour address themselves,
> Of princesses, sovereign mistress,
> I pray that God, who wrongs no soul,

Send to you all joy,
This New Year's Day, my redoubtable Lady.[61]

The cynical may dismiss these anniversary poems as mere flattery. The fulsome quality of the language found in these *ballades* and in the dedicatory prologues to her works is certainly conventional for the time, but it would be consistent with Christine's general methodology that amongst the effusions there would be concrete political messages. And in fact, that is the case. In examining these poems, there is evidence of didactic purpose as well as flattery. In *Autres Balades*, no. L, Christine exhorts:

Noble sir, who desires to acquire prowess,
Listen to this; hear what you must do:
You must fight in many lands,
Be fair against your adversary.
Do not flee from battle, nor retreat
And fear God . . . [62]

Autres Balades, no. XLII (1404), addressing members of the royal family, the court and the people in turn, reminds the reader that the Duke of Burgundy's good judgement had saved them from many mistakes, difficulties and hardships. Thus, in mourning the death of Duke Phillippe she implores:

Weep, French! All, from a shared desire,
Great and humble, weep for this great loss![63]

---

61 Hault, excellent Roÿne couronnée
De France, trés redoubtée princece
Dame poissant, et de bonne heure née
A qui honneur et vaillance s'adrece
Des princeces souveraine maitresse,
Je pri cil Dieu, qui ne fault a nulle ame
Qu'il vous envoit de toute joye adrece,
Ce jour d'lan, ma redoubtée dame.

Christine de Pizan, *Œuvres poétiques de Christine de Pisan*, ed. Maurice Roy (Paris: Société des anciens textes français, 1886–96), i, *Autres Balades*, no. XVIII, pp. 227–8.

62 Gentil homme, qui veulx proesce aquerre,
Ecoutes ci, entens qu'il te faut faire:
Armes suivir t'estuet en maintes terre
Estre loyal contre ton adversaire.
De bataille ne fuir, n'en sus traire,
Et doubter Dieu . . .

Ibid., *Autres Balades*, no. L, pp. 264–5.

63 Plourez Francois! Tous, d'un commun vouloir,
Grans et petis, plourez ceste grant perte.

Ibid., *Autres Balades*, no. XLII, pp. 255–7.

The distinct political messages of these poems indicate that not only did she dare to counsel her social and political superiors on their behaviour but also thought it was appropriate to do so.

A greater measure of Christine's respect for France is probably indicated by her belief that particular members of the royal family were both able and willing to influence the political course of events by their intelligence and authority; otherwise addressing her exhortations or counsels to them would be fruitless. All of her political works were intended for royal recipients. Philippe of Burgundy certainly had both qualities, and Isabeau of Bavaria, by virtue of her status (after 1402) as regent during the king's incapacity, ought to have had them. Louis of Guyenne, dauphin and heir to the throne, was a particular object of her hopes in this regard. Yet, in summary, this first form of nationalism consists of little more than an affinity, combined with pragmatic advice, perhaps glued to the pleasures of observing the court.

A second and more political form of nationalism is found in her analyses and descriptions of the customs and beliefs of other societies, particularly as seen in her political treatises. In 1407, in a work with an entirely different purpose, audience, and of a genre of very different conventions from the *ballades*, Christine presented a preference for institutions and leaders in France as she described different forms of government in her discussion of the best regime in *Corps de policie*:

> Throughout the whole world, lands which are governed by humans are subject to different institutions according to the ancient customs of places. Some are governed by elected emperors, others by hereditary kings, and so on. Also there are cities and countries which are self governed and are ruled by princes which they choose among themselves.[64]

Her perspective on these other institutions was not uncritical:

> Often these make their choice more by will than by reason. And sometimes, having chosen them by caprice, they seem to depose them the same way. Such government is not beneficial where it is the custom, as in Italy in many places.
>
> Other cities are governed by certain families in the city that they call nobles, and they will allow no one not of their lineage to enter their counsels nor their discussions; this they do in Venice which has been governed thus since its foundation, which was very ancient. Others are governed by their elders who are called 'aldermen'. And in some places, the common people govern and every year a number of persons are installed from each trade. I believe that such governance is not profitable at all for the common good and also it does not last very long once begun, nor is there peace in and around it, and for good reason.[65]

---

64 *Book of the Body Politic*, trans. Forhan, 92.

65 Ibid. (translation modified).

Except in the case of Venice, Christine's criticisms seem to focus on the need for political stability, rather than criticism of alien ways.[66] This observation is buttressed by Christine's comments on the best regime, which distinctly privilege political stability and monarchy:

> I would have too much to do to speak of each people separately, but when it comes to choosing the most suitable institution to govern the polity and the community of people, Aristotle says in Book III of the *Politics*, that the polity of one is best, that is, governance and rule by one. Rule by a few is still good, he says, but rule by the many is too large to be good, because of the diversity of opinions and desires.[67]

Christine de Pizan plainly believes that while other institutions may be suited for other societies, the French are fortunate in their form of government; not only does it have the form of the Aristotelian ideal, but its stable monarchy explains the general prosperity and happiness of the French:

> On our subject, I consider the people of France very happy. From its foundation by the descendants of the Trojans, it has been governed, not by foreign princes, but by its own from heir to heir, as the ancient chronicles and histories tell. This rule by noble French princes has become natural to the people. And for this reason and the grace of God, of all the countries and kingdoms of the world, the people of France has the most natural and the best love and obedience for their prince, which is a singular and very special virtue and praiseworthy of them and they deserve great merit.[68]

Her preference for monarchy is in itself completely characteristic of her era, as will be discussed in the next chapter. Nevertheless it is evident from these passages that Christine's nationalism in this context is neither racist nor irrational. In her biography of Charles V, itself a mirror for princes 'tout familial', as Eric Hicks remarks in his introduction to the modern French edition, Christine's portrayal of the perfect prince is of one whose manners and courtesy to foreign princes – even Saracen – is gentle and sincere, with respect for their customs. This is presented not only as good policy, since the good ruler always cultivates allies, but as a virtue in princes:

> I was still a child when I saw a Saracen knight, richly dressed in the fashion of his country. Everyone knew why he had come. Our wise king, who always acted with diplomacy, knew the art of receiving and honoring, according to their customs, people of all ranks and from every country. Understanding the sincerity of the sultan who

66 The Venetian example may stem from her father's experience there since, according to Charity Cannon Willard, 'both her father and grandfather [were] "salaried counselors" there, which probably means that they belonged to the civil service'. Willard, *Life*, 18.

67 *Book of the Body Politic*, trans. Forhan, 92.

68 Ibid., 92–3.

> had sent a messenger so far, the king received this knight and his gifts with the dignity he deserved . . . He thanked the sultan and sent him handsome gifts.[69]

When Christine discusses the scandal of Don Pedro of Castile, which revolved around the fact that he was living with 'une Sarrasine', there is no racism in her tale; rather it is the murder of Pedro's wife, the sister of Jeanne de Bourbon, that labels him a 'bad Christian and apostate'.[70]

The third form of nationalism is exemplified by her 'violent and abusive'[71] language in discussing the English. This more exclusive (and not very attractive) kind of nationalism also appears in Christine's work, but, and perhaps not difficult to understand, it grows more virulent with age and the devastating experience of life in the early fifteenth century. In 1402, three *ballades* treat a conflict between seven French and seven English knights. The poet records:

> Well to offer them laurel and palms
> Of honour, as a sign of victory
> When they murdered and drove out
> The proud English, from which famous deed
> Stems their high worthiness.[72]

And

> . . . you have defeated, killed and seized
> The ambushed seven arrogant English.[73]

Nevertheless, the events of the subsequent years, especially the terrible years from 1415 to 1429, the siege of Paris, the disinheriting of the King's son by his own mother, the destruction of Paris and its occupation, forcing Christine among many others to flee the city and to seek refuge, no doubt left their toll. The *Ditié de Jeanne d'*Arc is nationalistic with a vengeance:

> And so, you English . . . You have been check-mated . . . You thought you had already conquered France and that she must remain yours. Things have turned out otherwise, you treacherous lot! Go and beat your drums elsewhere, unless you want to taste

69 *Charles V*, ed. Hicks, 247.

70 Ibid., 120.

71 Christine de Pizan, *Ditié de Jehanne d'Arc*, ed. and trans. Kennedy and Varty, 13.

72
> Bien leur affiert le lorier et les palmes
> De tout honneur, en signe de Vittoire,
> Quant ont occis et mené a oultrance
> L'orgueil Anglois, dont, com chose notoire,
> Sera retrait de leur haulte vaillance.

Autres Balades, no. XXX, 241–2.

73
> . . . vous avez desconfiz, mors et pris
> Les sept Anglois de grant orgueil surpris.

Autres Balades, no. XXXI, 243–4.

> death, like your companions, whom wolves may well devour, for their bodies lie dead amidst the furrows! And know that [Joan] will cast down the English for good.[74]

This 'concrete, violent, and abusive' language, in Kennedy's phrase, is not, however, merely a desire for vengeance, although certainly that element is strong. It also indicates a desire, even a passion, for justice and vindication, which becomes clearer when placed within the context of her own theory of just war: '[God] hears the prayer of the good whom they wanted to harm! . . . God will tolerate this no longer.'[75] Joan of Arc is revealed as the instrument of a just God:

> She will restore harmony in Christendom and the Church. She will destroy the unbelievers people talk about, and the heretics and their vile ways . . . Nor will she have mercy on any place which treats faith in God with disrespect. She will destroy the Saracens, by conquering the Holy Land. She will lead Charles there . . .[76]

Violent language indeed, this seems to be the stuff of which genocide is made. Yet the context is important in explaining, if not excusing, such passion. This is a nation torn apart by the evils of civil war, popular uprisings, economic chaos, papal schism and external aggressions for two generations. No political, social or economic institutions are functioning adequately. While the language is distasteful, given a sound concept of just war and the historical context, it is not irrational. The goal of this virulent anger is:

> That peace may be brought about through [Joan's] deeds. And yet destroying the English race is not [Joan's] main concern for her aspirations lie more elsewhere: it is her concern to ensure the survival of the Faith. As for the English, whether it be a matter for joy or sorrow, they are done for. In days to come scorn will be heaped on them.[77]

Thus Christine's discussions of foreigners in general are not always belittling or hostile; it is the English in particular who have earned her special venom. The impact of the war was not abstract or hypothetical for any French subject. One of Christine's earliest personal experiences had been the threat to the safety of her son, Jean du Castel. The boy had been companion to the son of John Montague, the earl of Salisbury. When the earl was killed in 1400 defending the ill-fated King Richard II, the 'usurper', Henry IV brought the 16-year-old into his own household and offered a position as court poet to his mother. Fearful for her son and of the political instability in England, and distrustful of a ruler whose character she believed questionable, Christine explained:

---

74 *Ditié*, ed. and trans. Kennedy and Varty, 46–7.

75 Ibid.

76 Ibid.

77 Ibid., 47–8.

> Under the circumstances, and as the prospect did not tempt me in the least, I feigned acquiescence in order to obtain my son's return. To get straight to the point, after laborious maneuvers on my part and the expedition of some of my works, my son received permission to come home so he could accompany me on a journey I have yet to make.[78]

The English were enemies who had caused great harm to France. From her perspective, not only had they made outrageous claims to the throne of France and manipulated French and Burgundians into civil war, they had destroyed the cream of French nobility through the war crimes at Agincourt, had murdered many innocents, had compelled her and others to flee their Paris homes, and had forced her only living son into exile, so that she would never see him again. Based on ugly experience, her detestation is reserved for the perfidious 'Englecherie', not for foreigners generally. Her hatred for the English is not nationalism *per se* since it does not demean or demonize all outsiders, only the English. It is a prejudice that was the result of dreadful experience and as such is both understandable and culpable, especially given Christine's earlier expressed views linking violent language with actual physical abuse.

In conclusion, the evolution of a concept of a French nation had required France's independence from the dominance of both the papacy and the imperial might of the Emperor as well as a degree of emotional attachment and commitment. A number of scholars have noted that jurisdictional independence was very clear by the reign of Charles V. Indeed, Christine's own tale of the visit of the Emperor to Paris in the biography of Charles V reinforces this, as she makes it quite clear that Charles's courtesies were designed to treat the Emperor as a guest rather than as overlord.[79]

The development of nationalistic sentiments, however, was also occurring. As Susan Babbitt remarks:

> As the war with England continued and the monarchy broadened its prerogatives, a combination of practical necessity and inherited notions . . . gave rise to popular expression (and public exactions) which would scarcely have been possible a few centuries before, and which make it possible to speak, not of nationalism perhaps, but of sentiment for, and even obligation toward, the nation.[80]

Pride in the French language went hand in hand with vilification and stereotyping of the English enemy. This process was one to which many French writers contributed, including Philippe de Mézières, Nicole Oresme and Jean Buridan from the previous generation. Christine's contemporaries, Alain

---

78 *Writings*, trans. Willard, 19.

79 *Charles V*, ed. Hicks, 250–57.

80 Babbitt, *Oresme*, 38.

Chartier, Jean Gerson and others also used passionate language both to extol the French and to excoriate the English, and the reverse was equally true.

Yet, in examining the evolution of the concept of nationalism, it must be acknowledged that the invention of the concept of the nation-state was extremely important to the growth of protections for ethnic and religious minorities living among a larger population. If a strong identity as a member of a nation helps us see members of other groups, such as Jews, Christians, Basques or Slavs, as fellow citizens, that is good. Conversely, a supranational identity may be too vague and nebulous to inspire feelings of attachment in humans, as Rousseau worried. Humans might then fall back on tribal or religious associations to help them mollify the need for emotional attachment, which could also reduce tolerance of others.

Given the situation, the individual's responsibility to the larger body politic is very clear for Christine. While she obviously prefers monarchy to the decentralized and fragmented examples of rule around her, that monarchy is far from a Leviathan of absolutism. In fact, Christine's vision of mediated monarchy comes closer to the mixed constitution of Cicero and Nicole Oresme. Although hierarchical in structure, at every level of society there is a constant and consistent web of intercession and intervention by groups and individuals. Recognition of this degree of interdependence is not only a moral or political obligation of a member of the body politic, but it is also prudential self-interest to acknowledge dependence within the fundamental structure of society.

CHAPTER FOUR

On Kingship

. . . it is necessary for the prince to be wise.

While other forms of political authority existed in medieval Europe, particularly in northern Italy, there can be no question that kingship was the preferred model of political structure. As Antony Black has pointed out, kingship in the Middle Ages had the kind of positive general associations that democracy does for us.[1] While in practice it differed in form, powers and effectiveness, the status of monarchy as the proof of Aristotle's dictum 'the rule of one is best' was virtually unassailable. In France, this was both a historical and a practical preference. French medieval society was highly fragmented as a consequence of both territorial and economic decentralization, rendering very attractive the ideal of a strong ruler who could administer justice impartially and ensure peace throughout the land. Yet the idea of kingship was not without its tensions. Like democracy today, its implementation was riddled with implications and fraught with contradictions.[2] The thought of Christine de Pizan illustrates this paradox: she was an Italian, born in the republic of Venice, and yet argues a strong case against republicanism and for monarchy.

Medieval political works rarely address the nature of kingship directly; rather, the central questions of rule are often buried in other contexts. The problems

---

1 Black, *Political Thought*, 136.

2 There is a substantial body of modern literature on medieval kingship. In part, this is the legacy of privileging elite classes and culture over popular culture. It also reflects the primacy of legal over social history. In any case, the field is dominated by important studies on the nature and origins of kingship. A century ago, the modern study of medieval political theory began with scholars like Otto Gierke, *Political Theories of the Middle Ages* (Cambridge: Cambridge University Press 1900). The Carlyles' master work, *A History of Mediæval Political Theory in the West* (New York: Barnes and Noble, 1903–36), was followed by such important contributors as Walter Ullmann, Brian Tierney, Ernst Kantowicz, and quite recently, but still in this traditional mode, K. Pennington, *The Prince and the Law, 1200–1600: Sovereignty and Rights in the Western Legal Tradition* (Berkeley: University of California Press, 1993).

of legitimacy, authority and tyranny – or, to put these standard terms more simply, the origins, purpose and limitations of kingship – are not theoretical questions typically found in medieval texts. While there are a few political treatises that explicitly articulate a theory of kingship, particular views of kingship are more typically discerned embedded within a variety of other forms. Coronation rituals, theological treatises and mirrors for princes illuminate attitudes towards kings. With the exception of the writings of Thomas Aquinas, medieval political treatises were rarely organized thematically, but almost always contextualized either with respect to some other question or a specific historical problem.

The problems of legitimacy, authority and tyranny

The theoretical justification for kingship as described by medieval authors often incorporated a variety of mythological elements conflated with historical events, not unlike American founding myths of cherry trees and tea parties. Ultimately, for the medieval writer, there is only one source for the legitimacy and authority of kings, and that is God; on this all political writers agree. God was imagined and imaged as a male ruler and since everyone in a hierarchical world was at least theoretically subject to an overlord, God's majesty was the pinnacle of a vertical structure throughout society. From God to king to lord to peasant, this perfect hierarchy required a king at its earthly apex.

The reciprocal relationship between metaphors and imagery in politics and theology further intertwined images of God as king, Christ in majesty, or the king mirroring Christ. This mirror imagery can be found not only in manuscript illuminations, but also in the language of ritual and ceremony. Kingship had a sacred aspect. The anointing and consecration of kings underlined their religious office, no matter how that power was considered to be transferred on a theoretical level. The images of Christ the King, or of God as Ruler of the Universe, played a dual role both in emphasizing the sacred character of the ruler's office, and in attributing to God ritualized ideas about the nature of princely and thus earthly rule. When a knight knelt in prayer he mimicked the act of homage to an overlord; the anointing of kings mirrored the consecration of bishops.

While God was the ultimate source of all legitimate power, the preference for monarchy as opposed to other forms of rule was explained by two common justifications. For some theorists, the need for monarchs was based on an inherent need for law and order that grew out of the essential sinfulness of human beings. The state was necessary to control naturally egotistical and selfish human behaviour. This need for order was grounded primarily in an Augustinian philosophical anthropology that saw human nature as corrupted by the first sin, and thereby no longer able to control itself, but buffeted by every impulse and desire. Rulers were placed over humans as a remedy for that internal disorderliness called sin. Good rulers or bad could be explained by the behaviour of the people who deserved either one or the other, and like a penance, they had to be endured. In an often quoted passage from the *City of God*, Augustine had claimed that the differences between a brigand and a king were in fact slight. The presence of justice alone differentiated them; thus, he asks: 'Without justice, what are kingdoms but great bands of robbers? What are robber bands but small kingdoms? The band itself is made up of men; it is ruled by the command of a leader, and is held together by a social pact. Plunder is divided in accordance with an agreed upon law.'[3] On this Augustinian view, an unjust kingdom is different only in scale and social acceptability from a band of brigands or pirates.

By contrast, some theorists justified kingship on the demand of the people rather than solely on an inherent human sinfulness. This second view was based on a reading of the Book of Kings. Discontented with governance by the prophets, despite the fact that prophets acted directly from God's inspiration, the ancient Israelites asked for a king to be set over them. John of Salisbury's account in the *Policraticus* weaves together the idea that rulers are set over us because of the demand of the people, with the view of kingship as sacramental. In his account, the people get the government they deserve:

> The first fathers and the patriarchs were in obedience to nature, the best guide to living. They were succeeded by leaders following the law of Moses and by judges who ruled the people according to the authority of God; and we read that these were priests. Finally against the wrath of God they were given kings, some good, yet others bad. For Samuel had become old and when his sons did not walk in his path but pursued avarice and impurity, the people who had perhaps deserved that such priests should preside over them, had extorted a king for themselves from God, whose will was disregarded. Therefore Saul was selected . . . who would take away their sons in order that they might be made into charioteers, and their daughters in order that they might be made bakers and cooks, and their lands and estates in order that they might be distributed to his servants according to his will, and who would oppress all people with the yoke of servitude. Yet the same man was called the anointed of the Lord, and exercising tyranny, he did not lose the honour of kingship . . . they venerated Saul like a minister of God, whose image he would in a certain measure display.[4]

While this view of kingship implied a certain justification for election (to which John alludes elsewhere), in a sense it was also justified by human weakness. These two very different but not incompatible theories of political authority

---

3 Augustine, *De civitate dei*, 4. 4, in *Political Writings*, trans. Michael Tkacz and Douglas Kries (Indianapolis, Ind.: Hackett 1994), 30.

4 John of Salisbury, *Policraticus*, trans. Nederman, 201–2.

had considerable consequences for ideas about tyranny.[5] Since all rule was ultimately established and ordained by God, in the Augustinian tradition, bad rulers constituted a punishment for sin and their cruelties and injustices were not to be resisted. As Augustine wrote, 'Nevertheless, the power to dominate is not given even to [tyrants] except by the providence of the most high God, when he judges that the condition of human affairs is worthy of such masters.'[6] While it is important to remember Augustine's purpose in writing the *City of God* was not to justify tyranny but to explain the success of the pre-Christian Roman Empire, his words were certainly used later to justify acquiescence to despotic government. By contrast, for John of Salisbury, anyone could become a tyrant. The abuse of authority is the defining characteristic of tyranny, thus one could be a tyrant in any walk of life, whether domestic, ecclesiastical or political:

> All power is good since it exists only from him from whom everything is good and only good exists. Yet occasionally power is not good but bad for the person who uses it or suffers under it . . . Therefore even the power of tyrants is in a certain sense good, yet nothing is worse than tyranny . . . It is therefore evident that tyranny exists not among princes alone, but that everyone is a tyrant who abuses any power over those subject to him.[7]

The remedy depended on the nature of the tyranny. Those subject to despotic behaviour from fathers, husbands, masters or overlords had recourse to the law. Despotic churchmen could be reproved and sanctions imposed, although physically harming them was illegitimate. Political tyrants ran the risk of assassination, and if handled honourably, this indeed might not be inappropriate. But one must be very careful in attempting to reprove, control or remove tyrants because in some sense they are executing God's will. As John stipulated, 'Yet I do not deny that tyrants are ministers of God, who by his just judgement has willed them to be preeminent over both soul and body. By means of tyrants the evil are punished and the good are corrected and trained.'[8]

However, a third element coloured the entire debate. Long before the conventional 'recovery of Aristotle', medieval writers had inherited the classical notion that humans are essentially political and that participation in civic life

5 Medieval views of tyranny are discussed by John D. Lewis, 'Medieval Theories of Resistance,' in Oszkár Jászi and John D. Lewis, *Against the Tyrant: The Tradition and Theory of Tyrannicide* (Glencoe: Free Press, 1957), 17–34.

6 Augustine, *Political Writings*, 43.

7 *Policraticus*, trans. Nederman, 202. Kate L. Forhan and Cary J. Nederman debate the meaning and significance of John of Salisbury's theory of tyrannicide in two articles. See Nederman, 'A Duty to Kill', *Review of Politics*, **50** (1988), 365–89 and a counterargument by Forhan in 'Salisburian Stakes', *History of Political Thought*, **11** (1990), 397–407.

8 *Policraticus*, trans. Nederman, 201.

is a meaningful component of happiness. The claim that human beings are essentially political or social implies that living in communities is good for us. This classical view that only in communities are humans integrated into their humanity and that living together can in fact lead us to our true end in the good life had been transmitted primarily through Cicero. The amalgamation of Christianity and classical political thought extended human purpose to include not only a natural good life but also a supernatural one of the vision of God after death. Political life has not only a coercive function because of our intrinsic sinfulness, but also a positive and liberating one: living in civil societies can bring happiness as well. While the early Augustinian pessimism about human society was very strong, the twelfth-century renaissance brought a change of tone. Descriptions of kingship began to be far more positive, in particular the idea that kingship brought unity, justice and safety within the kingdom.

This idealized, even romanticized, view of the importance of kingship played an important role in the development of courtly literature. If a king is essential to the well-ordered society, if he carries this heavy symbolic as well as political burden, then it is important what kind of person the king is. And if dynastic laws of succession limit the selection to the nearest male heir, despite his talents or inclinations, then the formation of prince into king is of vital importance. The process of socialization into this rôle was composed of a number of elements. Religious rituals were believed to shape human behaviour through God's grace. The quasi-sacramental process of anointing and coronation was intended to impart special gifts to the king. The king's regular participation in the Church's sacraments was considered important to good rule. But ultimately, only his own character ultimately determined a king's desire and ability to rule in his people's interest. This could be shaped by the mirror for princes, to educate the prince so that he is transformed into a model king. Providing the prince with political role models was believed effective, either through historical accounts of great kings, or of mythological forebears, such as the Trojan House of Priam, or through the lives and liturgies of canonized kings like Charlemagne or Louis IX (r. 1226–70). Together these components of socialization were to give rise to literary and artistic genres designed to educate the prince, such as vernacular hagiography and royal chronicles. Indeed, it could be argued that the whole concept of courtliness was a mechanism of socialization intended to shape and direct the energies of young men. Courtliness or chivalry as a model of behaviour was also a way of moulding a king's value system when there were only limited institutional constraints.

In her appreciation and even adulation of kingship, Christine de Pizan was well within these norms. Despite her familiarity with Italian republicanism, her clearly expressed preference was the French monarchy. All her political treatises extol its virtues even when her sentiments vis-à-vis its incumbents are more muted. In part, this is a reflection of both the culture of patronage and her nationalism, but it is nonetheless a real preference. In this regard, her most important political mentor is Giles of Rome, although she may also have had knowledge of Dante's *De monarchia* via Nicole Oresme, and through him some sense of Dante's arguments in favour of a universal monarch.[9] This preference for monarchy and a hierarchical system has formed the basis for some of the modern criticism of Christine de Pizan. Her best-known contemporary critic has undoubtedly been Sheila Delany, who in two essays has criticized Christine's politics as conventional, sycophantic and unprogressive.[10] While sometimes it seems that some of this criticism is deliberately provocative and anachronistic, perhaps directed more at Christine scholars than the writer herself, nevertheless those looking for an early champion of democracy or even of constitutional monarchy will not find it in Christine's books. Although both her contemporaries Jean Gerson and Nicole Oresme contributed theories of representation and in Gerson's case conciliarist theories to their intellectual heirs, Christine was consistent in her preference for a strong monarchy, albeit a mediated one. While she was critical of the society of her day, her solutions to the problems she saw were not to be found in new institutions, but in appealing to political virtues, primarily to self-interest.

The ideal king

The ideal king as he was understood in the Middle Ages has been described by Dora Bell in a pithy summation that bears repeating: 'The Middle Ages drew the portrait of a wise and virtuous king surrounded by an elite group of counsellors ready to second his efforts in the cause of justice and of peace.'[11] In a sense this statement says it all; the prince was perfect, the magnificent man of Aristotle, a courageous military leader, wise and prudent, concerned only with the welfare of his people and crowned with every virtue. The wonderful illuminations of the later medieval period, showing a king seated on the throne who is strong and handsome, 'inclining neither to the right nor to the left, but dispensing justice to all', present powerful images that are evocative even today. The image of Christ the King indicates the high standards of virtue, self sacrifice and sheer physical presence and majesty that kings were expected

9 Christine often quotes from the translation of Giles of Rome's *De regimine*. We know that she was familiar with Dante's *Divine Comedy*, and she had access to Nicole Oresme's translation of the *Politics*.

10 Delany, 'History, Politics, and Christine Studies', and 'Mothers to Think Back Through'.

11 Dora Bell, *L'Idéal éthique*, 183.

to uphold. The reality of kingship is more complex. Political writers in the medieval period were neither naive nor particularly optimistic. Rather, they understood that appearances shape perceptions, and they shrewdly appreciated the power that high expectations and social pressures can exercise on individuals in the public spotlight.

A closer look, however, reveals differences in the typologies of virtues to which kings were expected to conform. In general, the virtues of kings included the Christian virtues of faith, hope and love; the cardinal virtues of justice, temperance, courage and prudence, and the classical princely virtues of clemency, magnanimity, glory and fame. While the first two sets of virtues are well known to modern audiences, the virtues termed 'princely' in this volume are less well recognized and at first glance seem quite odd to cultures that have been profoundly influenced by Puritan virtues of thrift and sobriety. But these princely virtues are classical in origin, and in their medieval expression was a direct result of the great prominence of the *Somnium Scipionis*. Cicero's dialogue is modelled on Plato's *Republic* and like Plato's work it ends with one of the characters recounting a significant dream. In Cicero's work, the dreamer is Scipio Africanus Minor, who tells of being transported into heaven, led by his famous grandfather, Scipio Africanus Major. There Scipio is shown the cosmos: the sun and stars as enormous globes in the heavens. The earth itself is spherical and two of its five zones, the Arctic and Antarctic, are too cold for habitation. Between the two temperate zones is a region too hot for occupation. These descriptions, transmitted through the commentary of Macrobius, were the basis for the earliest maps of the world, the famous *mappa mundi* or T-O maps of the Middle Ages. From commentaries on Cicero, as well as other sources drawn together over the centuries by encyclopedists as varied as Isidore of Seville and Bartholomaeus Anglicus, developed an entire cosmology that placed every creature in the universe in an intimate and intricate association, macrocosm to microcosm. At the centre of the universe was the sun, the *mens mundi*, or the world's mind, and Cicero's heaven is populated by public men, who had served in life as politicians and generals:

> But, Africanus, be assured of this, so that you may be even more eager to defend the commonwealth: all those who have preserved, aided or enlarged their fatherland have a special place prepared for them in the heavens, where they may enjoy an eternal life of happiness. For nothing of all that is done on earth is more pleasing to that supreme God who rules the whole universe than the assemblies and gatherings of men associated in justice, which are called states. Their rulers and preservers come from that place, and to that place they return.[12]

12 Cicero, *De Re publica; De legibus*, trans. Clinton Walker Keyes (London: Heineman, 1928), Bk. 6, ch. 13, l. 13.

There Scipio is taught the virtues of statesmen: to despise the talk of the rabble, to seek honour and glory, and to be generous with gifts. These virtues, after centuries of commentary and explanation, particularly when they later became joined with the Aristotelian tradition of the virtue of great-souledness – magnanimity – were the hallmark of princes. 'Virtue, herself, must attract you by her beauty to true honor.'[13]

The virtues were varied, taking on different shapes and emphases as their audiences changed – a reminder that political theory was almost always applied to a particular problem in a particular set of circumstances. By the later Middle Ages, however, there is an increased awareness that just 'to govern oneself is manifestly no longer sufficient for governing others', as Jacques Krynen notes.[14] More is necessary for good government beyond the exercise of individual virtue. This enlargement of perspective focused attention on two virtues in particular, which were increasingly emphasized. Wisdom and prudence become the royal virtues par excellence, and in fact 'prudence (*prudentia*) never ceased being closely linked with *sapientia*, and even confused with it'.[15] For Thomas Aquinas, prudence is the particular virtue of princes because the ability to judge among different choices and to anticipate consequences was particularly necessary in rulers. For Nicole Oresme, 'However much the prince must have contemplation, nonetheless active prudence concerns more the office of the prince.'[16] For Giles of Rome, 'Just as an archer could not direct his arrow without seeing the target, so without prudence no prince could orient his actions nor conduct his subjects to their good. Without prudence the king is king in name only.'[17]

By the late fourteenth century, the melding together of all human knowledge, which included the personification of the virtues as characters in a cosmology as interconnected and complex as modern physics, reached a peak of expression in the encyclopedias of the court of Charles V. Jean Corbechon's *Livre des propriétés des choses* (1372) influenced Nicole Oresme's *Le Livre du ciel et du monde* (1377) as much visually as textually, and both were available to Christine de Pizan.[18] Although Bernard Ribémont does not believe that

13 Ibid., 214.

14 Krynen, *L'Empire*, 207.

15 Ibid.

16 Oresme, *Politiques*, ed. Menut, 286.

17 Krynen, *L'Empire*, 218.

18 Jean Corbechon's work is a translation – in the medieval sense – of Bartholomaeus Anglicus' *De proprietatibus rerum*. Oremes's is a translation of Aristotle's *On the heavens*. See Sherman, *Imaging Aristotle*. The website of the Bibliothèque Nationale de France has a wonderful virtual tour of the era of Charles V that includes illuminations from Corbechon's vernacular version of Bartholomaeus Anglicus. It can be found as of this writing at http://www.bnf.fr.

Christine read Corbechon's work with any great depth, but tended to pluck morsels from these works as she did others,[19] their visual impact is extraordinary and may have influenced her more than is readily apparent. Emphasis on prudence as a character as well as as the essential virtue of princes would later become a hallmark of Christine de Pizan's own political theory, but the phrase from Giles brings us full circle, for the common good is the chief end of the prince's conduct in political life. Both prudence and wisdom are essential for its conduct. The other virtues, however critical for salvation or even public esteem, are less necessary, for it is by his adherence to the common good that any king will be judged.

Tyranny and misrule

The classic formulation of the good king, as one who puts his people's good above his own, clearly provides a benchmark for the evaluation of rulers. Before the fourteenth century, the standard view was that the king should conserve the law. Indeed, this was how the idea of tyranny was made operative. A king who obeyed the law was good; a king who changed the law was not. When the law and the king were in conflict it was a grave enough offence to be a significant infraction, and was considered to be an assault on just rule and a harbinger of tyranny.[20] Although the legalists generally regarded the prince's power to be unlimited, since the purpose of the law is the common good, if the law cannot fulfil its function, then it is not really a law. A king who does not fulfil his purpose is not a king but a tyrant. In practical terms, the question of the common good, or the social utility of a law, was not so easily determined, and the legalists saw gradations of interpretation. Gross malfeasance would be necessary before an argument could be made that a ruler was a tyrant. The removal of the tyrant through assassination was complicated by an increasing emphasis on the sacred character of the king's physical body. The multiplication of national images increasingly invested the king's person with religious significance: 'The king, our sire, has not only temporality, but also divinity.'[21] In his prologue to the

19 B. Ribémont, 'Christine de Pizan et l'encyclopédisme scientifique', in Zimmermann and De Rentiis (eds), *City of Scholars*, 174–8; and B. Ribémont, *De natura rerum* (Orléans: Paradigme, 1995), esp. ch. 8.

20 This was still a major component of tyranny in the seventeenth and eighteenth centuries. One of John Locke's indicators of tyranny in the *Second Treatise* was the 'altering of the legislative', which also appears in Thomas Jefferson's Declaration of Independence in 1775.

21 As quoted in Marc Léopold Benjamin Bloch, *Les Rois thaumaturges: étude sur le caractère surnaturel attribué à la puissance royale, particulièrement en France et en Angleterre* (Publications de la Faculté des lettres de l'Université de Strasbourg, 19; Strasbourg: Librairie Istra; London: H. Milford, Oxford University Press, 1924), 212.

translation of Augustine's *City of God*, Raoul de Presles told Charles V: 'You have such virtue and power given and attributed to you by God, that you do miracles in your life.'[22]

Conversely, the continuing political crises of the fourteenth century had spurred debate about tyranny and the legitimacy of tyrannicide. The assassination of the royal duke, Louis of Orleans,[23] generated a great deal of discussion of the nature of tyranny. The defence of Jean sans Peur, mounted by Master Jean Petit, was that this particular act of tyrannicide was justifiable and justified. In the case he constructed, Jean Petit assembled citations from a variety of sources, including a verbatim quotation from John of Salisbury: 'it is lawful for any subject, without any order or command, according to moral, divine, and natural law, to kill or cause to be killed a traitor and a disloyal tyrant. It is not only lawful, but honorable and meritorious especially when he is in such power that justice cannot be done by the sovereign.'[24]

Where Petit's argument misses the mark is that Louis could not have been a political tyrant, since he was not sovereign, and thus anyone tyrannized by him had recourse to other remedies, most notably the king's own justice, and the reality of a weak king does not obviate that aspect of the argument as it had been articulated in his source.[25] By contrast, it was on exactly this point that Jean Gerson condemned Petit's defence[26] and argued for a condemnation of tyrannicide at the Council of Constance in 1414. It was not that Gerson did not see the possibility of true tyranny, nor that he saw tyranny as something merely to be endured. In his sermon before the king, 'Vivat Rex', preached well before the assassination, Gerson made arguments about the legitimacy of tyrannicide, and he included the close analysis of circumstance and exhaustion of other remedies that marked his major source, which was also the *Policraticus*.[27] Consistent with his preference for consultation, and the position he would take at the Council, Gerson argued that a council of prudent and learned experts ought to discuss whether or not tyranny had reached such a degree that measures needed to be taken to remove the tyrant.

---

22 Quoted in P. S. Lewis, *Essays in Later Medieval French History* (London: Hambledon Press 1985), 170.

23 By agents of his cousin, John of Burgundy, who would himself be assassinated in 1419. See Ch. 1.

24 As quoted in J. D. Lewis, 'Resistance', 29. See also A. Coville, *Jean Petit: la question du tyrannicide au commencement du XVe siècle* (Paris: A. Picard, 1932), 220 and *Policraticus*, trans. Nederman, 25.

25 See Forhan, 'Salisburian Stakes', 402.

26 Jean Gerson, 'Discours au roi contre Jean Petit', in *Œuvres complètes*, ed. P. Glorieux (Paris: Desclée, 1960), vii, 1005–30.

27 Linder, 'Knowledge of John of Salisbury'.

In the case of Christine de Pizan, her preference for the rule of law, for the fair administration of justice, and for strong monarchy are the source of her apprehensions about misrule. In the late fourteenth century, bad governments together with misguided, egocentric and foolish kings were much in evidence. In Christine's view, therefore, the stereotypical portrait of an all-powerful and despotic ruler was less of a possibility than weak government and ineffective rule. Usurpation of power by the king's brother, uncles and nephews was a far more serious threat to the kingdom's population. Christine de Pizan was voiced her criticisms openly, albeit judiciously:

> Let these things be a mirror for the prince, in which to look at himself, and all others should do so as well. For let us suppose that there was one of these vices to which one were naturally inclined. If the person does not learn how to master himself, and conquer it, it is a sign that he is not virtuous, and a person without virtue is not worthy of honor.[28]

Because of the culture of patronage and her own social and economic vulnerability, Christine de Pizan's critiques of misrule were generally oblique. In her earlier works her primary method both of criticizing rulers and of signalling the consequences of misrule are found in her *exempla*; some of her most pointed examples are found in *Corps de policie*. The following is a subtle criticism of the spoiled behaviour seen at court:

> Valerius tells more of this Fabricius: It was recounted in his presence that there was a philosopher in Athens who followed a sect and way of life which taught that humans should do nothing except for delight and bodily ease. These ideas and words greatly displeased this worthy man who believed them vain, foolish, and dishonorable, and that all pleasure, not only of the body but of the soul as well, if not earned in virtue ought to be despised. But for those that are good, delight in doing well is their reward. And this saying is true, says Valerius, and appears certain. Because the city of Athens which was governed by great labor and the study of wisdom and virtue was conquered by pleasures and lust, losing its supremacy. The city of Rome, as long as it was obsessed by the exercise of virtue, conquered, won and overcame all other rulers, and how Athens lost its virtue will be told below.[29]

She did not limit herself to verbal criticism. Sandra Hindman has argued that Christine's warnings have also been presented to her readers through the programme of illuminations of her lavishly designed manuscripts. In *Epistre d'Othéa* in particular, Hindman provides evidence that after the assassination of Louis of Orleans, who was the work's original recipient, the book was repackaged in such a way that the illuminations underscore Louis's own demise as a warning to other princes:

28 *Book of the Body Politic*, trans. Forhan, 54.

29 Ibid., 24.

> The miniature becomes a kind of counter-example to the message of the text, which dwells on the virtues of family ties. By engaging in internecine quarrels, neither cousin took the advice of Christine's gloss. Moreover, in his defense of Louis's murder, John [of Burgundy] had been accused of bearing false witness and perjury. That is, he violated the second commandment referred to in the allegory.[30]

In fact, the entire *Epistre d'Othéa* is a warning for princes, concealed within this deceptively light allegorical poem, as Hindman demonstrates in her analysis of the illuminations. Later in her career, Christine's warnings to princes became less oblique and allegorical and more explicit. By 1412, in her letter to the Duke of Berry on civil war, she confronts the royal reader with a strong criticism of the conduct of the political leadership of France. 'For Heaven's sake! For Heaven's sake! Mighty princes open your eyes . . . Thus you will see cities in ruins, towns and castles destroyed, fortresses thrown to the ground! And where? In the very midst of France.'[31]

Even a poet can criticize a prince. However, despite the tremendous theoretical power given to kings by theorists of the Middle Ages, we must not assume that there were no boundaries to control or at least shape a king's behaviour. There were three important institutional constraints on rulers: the Church, the king's council and the law. Both the Church and the king's council will be discussed below. Consideration of the law as a restraint on the king will be deferred to the next chapter.

Limits on kingship: the Church

That the political and spiritual power of the Church was a significant constraint on the king's authoritative exercise of power is well known. Since the king's power was fundamentally from God, then God's vicar on earth, the pope, ought, at least in principle, to have something to say about how that power is to be exercised. Independent of any potential conflict with the papacy, the king expected that his authority would be very much buttressed and strengthened by religious norms, primarily biblical precepts. Both Pauline and dominical passages emphasized obedience to authority and the sacred role of the king. Models like David and Solomon coupled with strictures about 'rendering unto Caesar' emphasized the legitimacy of royal authority.

Despite this support, the relationship between king and pope, *regnum* and *sacerdotium*, was much more ambiguous and complex than may appear. It was a major task of theorists for centuries to try to justify and explain the often tense connection between the two swords of power. In brief, the Church had a

30 Sandra Hindman, *Christine de Pizan's 'Epistre d'Othéa': Painting and Politics at the Court of Charles VI* (Toronto: Pontifical Institute of Mediaeval Studies, 1986), 120.

31 'Lamentation', in *Writings*, trans. Willard, 304.

variety of means, including interdict or at least the threat of excommunication, powers of episcopal and archiepiscopal appointment, control over marital alliances and moral authority, by which it could and did discipline kings. All of these methods were used with frequency and exacted compliance on the part of kings to an remarkable degree. Celebrated confrontations such as those between Frederick Barbarossa and Pope Alexander III, Henry II of England and his archbishop Thomas Becket, Ludwig of Bavaria and Pope John XXII are three notable exceptions that proved the rule, at least until the Great Schism of 1378–1417. All three conflicts generated a great deal of political theorizing about what we would call church–state relations.[32]

To understand Christine de Pizan's views of the Church's power and its role as either a support or a constraint on France's monarchy, it is helpful to look first at the broader picture of her religious beliefs. All too often medieval historians assume as a given a conventional and orthodox Catholicism in lay persons, unless the individual in question was the subject or object of some religious controversy. The scrutiny becomes intense for a Joan of Arc or a Peter Waldo; but lay piety in general is taken for granted. Yet the relationship between theology, or an intellectual understanding of God and church, and its lived expression or application in a practical world is critical. Politics is, after all, the expression of our most deeply held ideas and beliefs about human nature and society.

Despite having written a number of religious works and having made her choice to spend her retirement in a convent, Christine de Pizan's religious beliefs are virtually unexplored, and yet hold enormous potential for scholars, provoking us to a better understanding of late medieval piety. Charity Cannon Willard points out that Christine de Pizan's religious beliefs are exactly what one would expect of a woman of her social class and circumstances.[33] That she was devout and appears conventionally pious is evidenced by her equally customary appeals to God in her works. But convention yields to complexity and even paradox when we examine her works more closely.

Christine wrote several religious works, all of them within the well-defined limits of their respective genres. Her allegorized penitential psalms, *Les Septs psaumes allegorisés,* were orthodox in both form and content, as comparison with other works shows. Her meditation on the Passion, *Les Heures de*

32 See, for example, Brian Tierney, *The Crisis of Church and State, 1050–1300* (Englewood Cliffs, NJ: Prentice-Hall, 1964); and *Foundations of the Conciliar Theory: The Contribution of the Medieval Canonists from Gratian to the Great Schism* (enl. new edn; Studies in the History of Christian Thought, 81; Leiden and New York: Brill, 1998); Babbitt, *Oresme*; Black, *Political Thought*, 42–84.

33 *Writings*, trans. Willard, 318.

contemplacion sur la passion de Nostre Seigneur, is an example of the *vita Christi* tradition, a then relatively recent literary development that grew directly out of the Franciscan spirituality of affective and highly imaged piety. Christine's prayer to the Virgin, *Une Oroison Nostre Dame*, is interesting because it reveals not personal but political piety, since each stanza pleads for a particular public figure.

> . . . To you I pray that our Queen
> Of France will never know infernal punishment . . .
> Give to the Lord the Dauphin,
> Give him the wisdom to govern . . .
> For the noble duke of Orleans
> I pray for protection from the enemies
> Within, who watch him constantly . . .[34]

However, she also uses very unexpected and non-traditional language in theological contexts. For example in *L'Avision* she refers twice to the nature of God in quite original language. Addressing Dame Philosophy, she says: 'God who is properly you, and you who are properly God, know that I speak the truth in these matters!'[35] And: 'You see, when man has happiness, he is blessed. And if Happiness is God, then man is god when he has happiness.'[36] Finally in the conclusion of that work, she praises Lady Philosophy as both the sum of all knowledge and the *summum bonum* itself:

> Oh Philosophy, the repository and substance of all the other sciences . . . you show yourself to those you love in any guise you please, depending on how they wish to search for you. To me, a simple woman, you have shown yourself by your noble grace in the form of holy theology to nourish my ignorant spirit. . . . have you not treated me as your handmaiden . . . served me from your most advantageous and worthy dishes that come from the table of God the Father for which I thank you (which is to say God which is you) . . .? Truly you are all sciences . . . the true physics . . . you are ethics . . . you are logic, you are the study of politics.[37]

These are extraordinary statements from someone who is thought to be merely conventionally pious and they deserve considerable further textual examination. While fascinating, this is not the place for that particular analysis.[38] The proper question to address is whether or not Christine de Pizan sees the Church as having any role as a countervailing power vis-à-vis the monarchy. The answer,

34 'Prayers to Our Lady', ibid., 323–4.

35 *Christine's Vision*, trans. McLeod, 124.

36 Ibid., 140.

37 Ibid., 142–3.

38 Christine may have been influenced in her religious beliefs by the mystical theology of Jean Gerson, for whom soul and God became identical (not just unified) in prayer. See Jean Gerson, *Early Works*, trans. Brian Patrick McGuire (New York: Paulist Press, 1998).

in brief, is that her view is highly unconventional: the king's role is to limit or control the Church rather than for the Church to constrain the king. Two significant discussions of the relationship between king and Church will illustrate this. The first is found in *Charles V*, where in hindsight she must deal with the fact that Charles apparently miscalculated in the events of the Great Schism. Indeed, Charles the Wise could be criticized as a major cause of the division in the Church over the papacy. Christine recounts the circumstances of the election of Bartolomeo Prignano, archbishop of Bari, which took place while the cardinals were pressured by the threat of riots and the demands of the Roman populace for a Roman pope. According to Christine, Charles V received word of the circumstances of the election from his cardinals and from other sources, presumably spies. 'Le dit Barthélemy', now Pope Urban VI, had been elected by the cardinals under duress, they had been pressured by Roman mobs, and thus, the French bishops argued, his claim to the papacy was an usurpation. The king called together a council of 'prelates, the archbishops and bishops of his kingdom, all the best clerks, doctors of theology, and other savants of the Universities of Paris, Orleans, Angers, and elsewhere; he made them come from everywhere he could find competent persons, and brought them to Paris'.[39]

These canon lawyers, theologians and the wisest lay members of his own council discussed the matter, and after long and careful deliberation, Charles refused to recognize the election and encouraged the election of a new pope, who became Clement VII. Christine's account stresses the king's concern for the Church and for thoughtful consideration and widely based consultation in making his decision. Despite appearances, however, the decision was a disaster. Ultimately, the resulting schism in the Church caused by the installation of rival popes was to continue until 1417, to the great distress of many, including Christine. Unlike the majority of political theorists of the Middle Ages, however, it is apparent that Christine believes that it may be necessary for a king to curb what he sees as the Church's impolitic conduct. This is proper if handled with consultation and concern for the greater good. It is clear that Christine does not see the papacy as providing a check on the excesses of temporal power – rather the opposite, that kings may need to constrain the Church.

Obviously, Christine was uneasy about the wise king having been the cause of such divisive and potentially iniquitous events. She added a further comment to preserve Charles's reputation as defender of the Church, telling her reader that despite his confidence that Clement was the true pope, the division of the

39 *Charles V*, ed. Hicks, 286. The full account of these events can be found in *Charles V*, Book 3, chs 51–62 in the edition by Suzanne Solente (Paris: H. Champion, 1936–40), or pp. 284–95 in the modern French edition by Eric Hicks.

church was so dreadful and disgraceful that Charles intended shortly before his death to 'persuade all Christian princes to bring together all the prelates in a general council' of the Church, have the rival popes resign and 'under the guidance of the holy spirit' elect a new pope.[40] Significantly, she never questions the right of the king to convene such a council.[41] Unfortunately, the premature death of the king halted this possibility.

A second illustration of Christine's view of the institutional role of the Church can be found in *Corps de policie*, where she places responsibility for the church into the hands of the good prince: 'This good prince, as vicar of God on earth, will care with all his heart for the welfare of the Church, so that his Creator can be served as his reason demands. And if there is any discord through the instigation of the enemy, he will bring peace whatever the difficulty.'[42] This vicariate includes ecclesiastical appointments: 'He should examine carefully the promotions of the ministers, that he does not grant a request for a prebend, no matter how much affection he has for the individual who requests it, unless he knows him to be a good and prudent cleric and fit to serve God and his service.'[43]

The concern evinced about scandalous and worldly behaviour on the part of clerics leads her to explicit criticism of both the behaviour and self-exculpatory justification offered by the offenders: 'But there are enough of our bishops and priests who can be publicly seen in horrible faults. There is no prince nor other person who will reprove them, but they excuse themselves from what they are accused, by saying that they are human beings, not angels, and that it is human nature to sin.'[44] On a theoretical level, Christine does argue for the good prince to use his moral authority to check the misadventures of clerics. Practically speaking, clerics are as responsive to public disapprobation, she argues, as anyone else. This provides a weapon that a ruler may use. But the authority to correct clerics is moral only; she explicitly excludes princes from the right to control clerical conduct:

> So the good prince ought to take care of all these things, because despite the fact that correction of people in the Church is not his to undertake, nonetheless what prelate, priest, or cleric is so great that he will dare withstand or complain about the prince who reproves him for his manifest vice or sin? Moreover the king or the good prince

40 *Charles V*, ed. Hicks, 294–5.

41 The Council of Constance, organized under the leadership of Jean Gerson and Emperor-elect Sigismund of Luxembourg was exactly the sort of council Christine envisioned. Perhaps she was influenced in this by Gerson, or perhaps the contrary was the case. See Black, *Political Thought*, 170.

42 *Book of the Body Politic*, trans. Forhan, 12.

43 Ibid.

44 Ibid., 13.

> takes care that the temple and the house of God is not polluted nor profaned by the many sins committed there by many of our Christians nowadays; nobles, merchants, and people of every rank who are not ashamed to hold their meetings in churches, to have assemblies on their worldly affairs. They and God know what false contracts are made here.[45]

Despite the exalted status of the Church, clerics themselves are found among the 'ordinary people' of the body politic, a very significant claim in this work, which lays so much stress on the importance of interdependence in all parts of society. 'In the community of people are found three estates, which means, especially in the city of Paris and other cities, the clergy, the burghers and merchants, and the common people, such as artisans and laborers.'[46] Her view of the priesthood is entirely functional, as has been noted elsewhere.[47] The well-ordered kingdom is dependent on each member functioning as obligated by his or her role, just as a baker is to bake bread, and a merchant to take part in commerce, so a priest is to dispense the sacraments. The king, even though he is only a layman, has the responsibility to see to it that each person performs in his or her role for the good of the whole, even the cleric:

> [The king] ought to desire that his subjects perform their best in whatever office God has placed them. The nobles ought to do what they ought to do, the clerics attend to their studies, and to the divine service, the merchants to their merchandise, the artisans to their craft, the laborers to the cultivation of the earth, and thus each one whatever his rank, ought to live by good policy, without extortion nor over-charging, so that each may live properly under him, and that they love him as a good prince ought to be loved by his people, and that he have from them the legal revenue that is reasonable to collect and take from his country, without gnawing to the bone his poor commoners.[48]

Passing remarks in other works underscore this minor role for the church and clergy in general; in *Le Livre de la paix*, the clergy are third in her hierarchical listing, the 'flanks' of the body politic: 'the head which is the king, the shoulders and upper body which represent princes and lords, the arms which are knights, the sides which are the clergy, the lower back and belly are the bourgeois, the thighs which are the merchants, the legs and feet which are the common people.'[49]

The role of guardian of the Church is even properly undertaken by a laywoman. In *Le Ditié de Jeanne d'Arc*, it is the heroic figure of Joan who is

45 Ibid., 13–14.

46 Ibid., 95.

47 K. L. Forhan, 'Respect, Independence, Virtue: A Medieval Theory of Toleration in the Works of Christine de Pizan', in C. J. Nederman and John C. Laursen (eds), *Difference and Dissent* (Lanham: Roman & Littlefield, 1996), 67–82, at 75.

48 *Book of the Body Politic*, trans. Forhan, 19.

49 *Livre de la paix*, ed. Willard, 124.

the knightly sword that saves the Church and the faith. 'She will restore harmony in Christendom and the Church. She will destroy the unbelievers people talk about, and the heretics and their vile ways . . . Nor will she have mercy on any place which treats faith in God with disrespect.'[50]

Given the common presupposition that medieval writers gave unqualified support to the institutional Church as a check on excessive secular power, Christine de Pizan's view that the Church is to be corrected and cajoled by royal and lay authority is remarkable. Her conviction is directly related to her functional theory of politics, and provides a fine example of the increasing secularization and laicization of political life, a process which began in the twelfth century.

Limits on kingship: the king in his council

The second type of institutional constraint described by medieval theorists was the king's council. Despite its often informal origins, stemming from remnants of imperial office, traditions of personal service and gatherings of tribal or clan leaders, royal councils later evolved into the parliaments, cabinets and legislative assemblies central to governance in France and England. That a king's advisers play a crucial role is obvious, but the presence of councils generated significant discussion in mirrors for princes and in political treatises, particularly in the later Middle Ages. The *Policraticus* places the 'senate' in the heart of the body, seat of wisdom and the will. Giles of Rome said that 'If the king loves the good of his people and his kingdom he will have himself often counselled by wise men in order to have and procure the well-being of his kingdom and to withstand the evils and perils that might arrive.'[51]

But counsel, however welcomed, is not the same as a council, a political institution with its own purpose and authority as a representative institution. In the words of P. S. Lewis, 'the failure of the French to develop an adequate system of representation in the later Middle Ages has long been seen as an essential element in the making of the Ancien Regime'.[52] The historically decentralized and fragmented power in France discussed earlier is reflected in the development of those institutions; where England had one Parliament, France had dozens of general and regional 'estates', with quite fluid forms of representation. Although they met fairly actively during the reign of Philippe IV, by the late fourteenth century the estates met less and less, despite advice to the contrary, until well into the fifteenth century. Contemporary scholars

50 *Ditié*, ed. and trans. Kennedy and Varty, 47.

51 Giles of Rome, *De regimine*, 1. 36–40, p. 327.

52 P. S. Lewis, *Essays*, 105.

see a number of factors in this devolution. Not all of it had to do with the unwillingness of kings to listen, especially to unpleasant advice about taxes, although that certainly played a role. Rather, it stems from the decentralized nature of the French polity and its overlapping political institutions:

> Unlike England, France was a country in which the king had only recently in the early fourteenth century extended a precarious authority over domains from the beginning divided by those geographical, ethnographical and linguistic barriers. Regional economy, law, custom, politics and sentiment had had time to harden under regional rulers effectively independent of the crown . . . The structure of politics was essentially a regional one.[53]

The fragmentation of the French political system profoundly affected political theorists, even those not French. Dante Aligheri (1265–1321), whose *De Monarchia* (*c.*1317) stresses the importance of strong and independent monarchies, spent formative years of exile in France. Marsiglio of Padua (*c.*1275–1342) wrote the *Defensor pacis* (1324) after a long residence in France, from perhaps as early as 1310 until 1316, and then again from about 1319 until 1326. Marsiglio left Paris in 1326, fearful for his life after his authorship of the *Defensor* became generally known. His generalized dissatisfaction with the papacy's tendency to usurp power in weakened or fragmented political systems like the Italian city-states led him to underline the need for an emperor whose authority comes from the people, and for a completely dismantled Roman ecclesiastical hierarchy. While Philippe IV was a strong monarch, perhaps Marsiglio saw France as potentially a kingdom that could become 'divided and wounded in virtually all its parts' and thus ripe for usurpation and oppression.[54] Yet the devastating years of the early fifteenth century inspired a number of political writers to develop theories of representation, most notably Christine's contemporary and friend Jean Gerson. In the generations preceding theirs, only one other French political theorist dealt explicitly with representative systems in a theoretical way. This was Nicole Oresme and his primary vehicle was his commentary on Aristotle's *Politics*.

Oresme's use of *policie* to translate Aristotle's *politeia*, an elastic and potentially revolutionary addition to medieval political thought, serves as an excellent example of his creativity. *Politeia* is used by Aristotle to signify the characteristics – or constitution – of the *polis* in a general sense, but he also

53 Ibid., 112.

54 Nederman, *Community and Consent: The Secular Political Theory of Marsiglio of Padua's Defensor pacis* (Lanham, Md: Rowman & Littlefield, 1995), 15. To my knowledge, the question of the influence of the 'French experience' on Marsiglio has not been addressed by any scholar except Cary Nederman in his doctoral dissertation, 'State and Political Theory in France and England, 1250–1350'.

used it to denote the third good form of government in his sixfold schema, called by modern translators 'polity' or 'republic'. Aristotle's definition of *politeia* in this sense is 'when the masses govern the state with a view to the common interest, the name used for this species is the generic name common to all constitutions (or polities), the name Polity'.[55]

Clarified and elaborated by a century of commentary before him, the term was translated by Oresme with two of his own: *politiques* – already part of the French language – and the neologism *policie*.[56] Oresme's intention to use his new term *policie* to signify Aristotle's *politeia* is clear not only from his extensive discussions of this term in general but also from his care in defining for his readers the differences between *policie* in the general sense, and its specific narrower meaning as the name of the third form of good regime, depending on the context in his source. He emphasizes his point by interpreting Aristotle through the Ciceronian tradition. The Latin term *res publica*, usually translated 'republic' or 'commonwealth', had been used by Cicero to explain Aristotle's term *politeia*. Naturally the intervening millennium had allowed the Latin expression to acquire its own rich meanings via Augustine, John of Salisbury and many others. Oresme used a literal translation of *res publica, chose publique*, and commented on its usage in Cicero, here called Tully, and Aristotle:[57]

> Item, Aristotle distinguishes these governments under the name polity, and Tully distinguishes them under the name republic for [in] the republic, [the end] is the common good and that is the end to which the good polity is directed. And thus the republic is not among the bad polities.[58]

In his analysis of the medieval understanding of Aristotle's typology of regimes, *democratie*, *politie* and *politic royale*, Antony Black claims that Oresme's is the first systematic statement of the 'strong presumption that

55 Aristotle, *The Politics*, ed. and trans. E. Barker (Oxford: Oxford University Press, 1946), 120. Constitution is another term that is easily misunderstood in a medieval or classical context by modern readers, since for us 'constitution' has lost most of its meaning of attributes, make-up or characteristics and has come to mean a set of laws governing a state. In considering the organic metaphor and its meaning one does well to remember that classical and medieval thinkers often wrote about the constitution of the human body as well.

56 *Politiques* did not originate with Oresme. Brunetto Latini used the term in 1265 in *Li Livres dou tresor*.

57 By contrast, in Denis Foulechat's 1372 translation of the *Policraticus*, *res publica* is rendered as *bien commun*. But he means it to be understood as synonymous with the state in the sense of the commonwealth. I would argue that Oresme's translation is better since it is more faithful to the text and less misleading than the more context-dependent *bien commun*.

58 'Item, Aristote distingue ces gouvernemens sous le nom de policie, et Tulle les distingue sous le nom de chose publique . . . car la chose publique ce est le bien commun et est la fin a quoy tent bonne policie. Et donc la chose publique est nulle en malveses policies'. *Politiques*, ed. Menut, 128.

parliament acts as the people as a whole would wish'.[59] James Blythe concurs with this assessment of Oresme's 'progressive' views, noting that Oresme alone understood Aristotle's doctrine of the mean as applying to constitutions as well as to virtues, and thus explaining Oresme's preference for limited monarchy and mixed constitutions.[60] Susan Babbitt also sees elements implying the significance of representation and of consent in Oresme, particularly with respect to taxation. Since Christine de Pizan had access to Oresme's commentaries, her neglect of representation and constitutionalism underlines her affinity for monarchy and perhaps signals a deliberate unwillingness to explore these topics, given her fears of mob violence.

Theories of representation were evolving in France during this period in great part because of the importance of the ecclesiastical conflict, discussed above, which was fostered by the Great Schism of 1378. Already in a period of decline, by the time of the schism the papacy had clearly lost both moral and political credibility as a form of monarchy. Over the thirty years that followed, the election of rival popes supported by different – and nationalistic factions – brought the crisis of authority and legitimacy to a head. Long after the death of Charles V and his abortive attempt at a council, political and ecclesiastical rulers ultimately attempted to resolve the crisis by convening a general council of the Church that would have the authority to elect a 'true' pope. Jean Gerson argued that God had intended the Church to be governed by council. When the Council of Constance was finally convened in 1414 under his leadership and that of the Emperor Sigismund of Luxembourg, strong arguments for the council as a representative body – conciliarism – were articulated. Resultant reforms requiring regular conciliar meetings made the council into the first 'constituent assembly of Christendom',[61] with powers of administration and taxation as well as legislation. Although the papacy had re-established itself as an absolute monarchy by the end of the fifteenth century, the seeds of constitutionalism were sown and a theory of representation had been established. Sadly, French politics profited little from this and French representative institutions continued to weaken during the reigns of Charles VI and Charles VII. As Lewis remarks, many of the late medieval assemblies in France 'appeared wraith-like and faded quickly away'.[62]

59 Black, *Political Thought*, 166–7.

60 See Blythe, *Ideal Government*, ch. 12. Blythe perhaps states the case too baldly. Limits on kingship and a preference for the economic mean – that is, a strong middle class – do not of themselves make a democratic theorist. But the evidence of Oresme's originality and substance as a political thinker is very strong and this much ignored political thinker deserves much more analysis. See also Babbitt, *Oresme*, ch. 4.

61 Black, *Political Thought*, 170.

62 P. S. Lewis, *Essays*, 113.

It is within this context that we must situate Christine's views of counsel as an institutional check on monarchical power. For Christine de Pizan, while the king is certainly supreme in authority for a well-regulated France, and representative government or republicanism dangerously factional, counsel is an essential component of a strong and healthy monarchy. All of her political writings discuss counsel at disproportionate length in both anecdote and *exempla*.

Even in her most oblique and earliest mirror for princes, *Epistre d'Othéa*, Christine makes references to obtaining advice before action. In *Othéa*, where advice is both spiritual and political, she recounts the story of Helenus, brother of both Hector and Paris, who when asked by Paris if he should pursue Helen, advised against it. Christine's text reads:

> Despise not the counsel
> Of Helenus; I counsel you,
> For often many injuries take place
> Because of not wanting to believe the wise.[63]

Consistent with the book as a whole, the text is interpreted on both political and spiritual levels as an exhortation to listen to the wisdom of others and to have the humility to be taught. The lesson in *Othéa* is underlined by the fact that the reader knows the ultimate consequences of the fact that Paris did not listen to his brother – warfare, the destruction of Troy and the loss of an entire civilization.

By contrast, for Christine the ability to listen graciously to advice is a hallmark of greatness, and thus marks a heroic king, like Charles V. In Part One of the biography, Christine discusses the characteristics that demonstrate the youthful king's wisdom. Along with stories of his intellectual qualities and his self-discipline, she points out that:

> The king desired to fill his court and his council with just and wise men, understanding government affairs and conducting themselves according to moral order, capable of administering the royal house and of enriching the common good. Just as, for the good conduct of his wars, he made men come from every country, seasoned knights wise and expert in the ways of war . . .[64]

Although she demonstrates a preference in some of her works for 'wise old men', who despite bodily weakness have the wisdom of experience, her

---

63 Christine de Pizan, *Epistre Othea*, ed. Gabriella Parussa (Geneva: Droz, 1999), 308.
Ne deprises pas le conseil
Helenus, je le te conseil,
Car souvent avient maint dommages
Par non vouloir croire les sages.

64 *Charles V*, ed. Hicks, 64.

predilection for older advisers may have to do with the specific audience of each mirror. *Corps de policie* was written for the very young dauphin, Louis de Guyenne, whose incapacitated father was unable to advise him. By the time *Le Livre de la paix* was written, Louis was an adult, and the mirror emphasizes expertise and virtue rather than the age of the ideal counsellors. 'Since there is nothing more despicable than a dissolute old age, ignorant and without virtue, [aged advisers] must be understood as meaning worthy, loyal, of a virtuous and good conscience.'[65] Some of the images accompanying her texts also reveal the importance of the type of counsellors that a ruler chooses. In *Othéa,* the chapter on Saturn describes wisdom. The illumination in the manuscript for the planet Saturn portrays those governed by this planet as bearded 'saturnine' scholars.[66] Although she clearly emphasizes age as bringing 'learning as well as long experience',[67] age is tangential in advisers in comparison to expertise. In all of Christine's political treatises, expertise is explicitly made their most important quality, as this, from *Corps de policie*, demonstrates:

> And on the subject of believing the wise and following their advice, [Aristotle's] great *Dialectic* says that one ought to believe each expert in his art. This means that the good prince ought to consult a variety of people according to the variety of things to do. For the governance of justice and the diverse important cases which he hears, he ought not to take advice from his soldiers nor his knights, but from jurists and clerks of this science. The same with warfare; not from clerks but from knights, and similarly in other matters.[68]

In *Le Livre de la paix*, written five years later, there is candid discussion of types and roles of political officials and how to recognize them, how to keep them honest and trustworthy, and how to identify some of the stratagems of dishonest public officials. In this work, which is more direct, pragmatic and less bound by the traditional formulae than Christine's earlier mirrors, the most important characteristic of advisers is that they be chosen not by rank, but by talent and probity: 'Because of the fact that government of an empire, kingdom or country faces a diversity of states or difficulties, the counselors of the prince should also come from different ranks and not all from the same estate; they

65 *Livre de la paix*, ed. Willard, 74. 'Mais neantmois, se avons loué en conseilz les veillars sages, n'est à entendre, pourtant, que tous les vieulx aient sens ni dignes soient que on use de leur conseil, comme il en soit assez de tres nices et folz où n'a vertu ne quelconques autre bien. Si n'est riens plus desprisable que veillece dissolue, nice et sans vertu, mais doit estre entendu des preudesommes loyaulx, de conscience vertueulx et bons.'

66 See, for example, L'Epistre d'Othéa, Paris, BNF fr. 606, fol. 6^{v}. This illumination has been reproduced and analysed in Sandra Hindman, *Christine de Pizan's 'Epistre Othéa'*, pl. 12.

67 *Livre de la paix*, ed. Willard, 73, 'tant science comme par longue experience'.

68 *Book of the Body Politic*, trans. Forhan, 39.

should be the same in one thing alone and that is in prudence and good judgement.'[69]

Since advisers provide a critical restraint on rulers, the qualities and attributes of those in a king's retinue are obviously important, as she makes very clear. By contrast, the role of the king's council as a formal institution is scarcely visible in Christine's theory. Not even the great attribute of French legislative bodies, the esteemed principle of taxation, 'what touches all should be approved by all', attracts her attention. Christine has apparently little contribution to make concerning the development of other and more representative political institutions. While the context in Christine's works sometimes indicates that she is speaking specifically of members of the king's council and at other times more generally of advisers, she has little to say about representative institutions at all. From her familiarity with Italian writers like Brunetto Latini and with Italian government in general, city councils were well within her awareness. Indeed, her father is believed to have been a counsellor in Venice, yet she does not see these institutions as having a contribution to make to good government. This apparent paradox stems from her interest in adapting existing ideas to the situation of her time. A weak king with a council of regents had demonstrated itself to be too fragmented a form of political authority to be welcome. A strong ruler in a centralized kingdom advised by a panel of experts is something else. Anything that would tend to further fragment the monarchy and the country could be viewed as an evil to be avoided. Rather than a formal institution that might weaken the process of centralization, Christine preferred an interlocking interdependence of social groupings that could intercede with each other as needed.

This presents a paradox. The whole of modern political thought, until recently,[70] has been directed against a political system that relies on personal virtues in favour of those that rely on institutions. The separation of person and office, which grew out of the Donatist heresy of early Christianity and began to be applied to political offices and their incumbents in about the twelfth century, is usually regarded as a progressive development. In general, citizens in liberal democracies believe that it is better to rely on political institutions to

---

69 *Livre de la paix*, ed. Willard, 75–6. See also *Charles V*, ed. Hicks, 64. 'Item, quant au fait de ce que au gouvernement de l'empire, royaume, ou pays appartient pour ce que diverses choses ou difficiles y sont comprises, appartient que de divers estas soient autressi les conseilliers du prince et non mie tous d'un mesmes estat, ne pareulx ce n'est en une seulle choses, c'est assavoir en preudommie et en bonne conscience . . .'

70 The recent revival of interest in virtue ethics is seen on both a theoretical level, beginning with Alasdair MacIntyre's influential *After Virtue* (Notre Dame: University of Notre Dame Press, 1981) and in practical politics, as is seen in William J. Bennett's *The Book of Virtues* (New York: Simon & Schuster, 1993).

restrain public officials in their office rather than to rely on a private and necessarily personal virtue. Moral suasion and disapprobation are considered not only insufficient practically as a constraint but inadequate theoretically as well. Yet the case of Christine is interesting for precisely this reason. At her time, the distinction between person and office was after all fairly well established, but the institutions were in disarray and their restraining influence sadly inadequate. Given disintegrating institutions, good government comes from a sense of virtue that can restore political life, especially stability and order. However, it is an odd set of virtues indeed.

Virtue

Despite acquiescence in the conventions and to the conventionalized virtues of princes, Christine de Pizan's desperate and ultimately futile effort to save the French monarchy causes her to conflate all the other virtues of the tradition – whether liberality, generosity and glory of the Roman tradition or the cardinal virtues of the Greco-Christian tradition – into one, the pragmatic self-interest that she calls prudence. Ultimately, even the quintessential virtue of justice is subsumed under prudence. This pragmatic view of the virtues articulates a significant shift away from both the classical view, as understood in the Middle Ages, and even the conventional medieval view, in the understanding of good rule and the just ruler. Prior to Christine's work, only two solutions to the problem of good government had been proposed: the modified classical view in which the cultivation of idealized virtues would culminate in the good prince, or philosopher-king; or the medieval view that ordered institutions well administered by a virtuous and often clerical caste would ensure a just government.[71]

Christine de Pizan rejects both of these views. Through her writings, she attempts to motivate the prince to consider pragmatic self-interest in governance so that his kingdom will be administered by non-clerics who are experts in their own fields, respected for their specialized knowledge, and rewarded appropriately, even if they are foreigners or women. Depending on her audience, she characterizes this self-interest differently. In each of Christine's mirrors for princes, there is a taxonomy of virtues that she calls upon the prince to develop. These come from a variety of sources, including Brunetto Latini's *Li Livres dou tresor* and Henri Gauchi's translation of Giles of Rome's *De regimine*, both of which include paraphrases of Aristotle's *Nicomachean Ethics*, as well as Nicole Oresme's translation and glosses on the *Ethics*. Martin of Braga's

71 Most medieval writers followed John of Salisbury in using both approaches. Some, like Thomas Aquinas and Giles of Rome, emphasized the virtues. Others, especially later writers, like Brunetto Latini, took a more 'institutional' approach.

Formula for an Honest Life, which at the time was believed to be a work by Seneca, provides a significant Ciceronian flavour enriched by Christine's direct knowledge of Cicero through *De senectute*, which she mentions by name, and perhaps others of Cicero's works, such as *Somnium Scipionis*. She may also have absorbed Ciceronian views through important intermediaries like Boethius, with which she was very familiar, and various compendia.[72]

These taxonomies of virtues vary, presumably with differences in the audience for the work, but also because of the *crise du jour* aspect of French political life. In *Epistre d'Othéa*, Christine discusses the cardinal virtues: justice, prudence, temperance and fortitude as well as glory, and faith, hope and charity from the Christian tradition, to which she adds humility. Wisdom, an essential virtue both in this work and in the biography of Charles the Wise, is not part of any established taxonomy, but is consistently recognized and identified in the mirror tradition. In *Prod'homie/Prudence*, we find the cardinal virtues of *Formulae honestae vitae*; justice, fortitude, temperance and prudence. The biography of Charles V articulates the Ciceronian and Christian virtues: justice, wisdom, clemency and generosity, as well as humility. In *Corps de policie*, justice, humanity, clemency, and generosity are part of the Ciceronian tradition and in *Livre de la paix*, justice, magnanimity, fortitude, clemency, liberality and truthfulness also have classical echoes. Each of these clusters of virtues can be examined with an eye to the ideals of kingship they represent.

The princely virtues of humanity, generosity and liberality are essential to the conventional mirror for princes, since these are aspects of the prince's personality that reflect his noble character and cause his people to love him. In *Corps de policie*, however, generosity and liberality consist in rewarding those who have served or might serve the prince. Rewards are to be appropriate to rank and the nature of the service. The worst vice in a prince is to be miserly in rewarding his servitors, not because it is ignoble, but because it is neither just nor prudent. Liberality, as a form of generosity both of the purse and of the spirit, is the key to the virtue of justice in the prince, but because it is expedient rather than because it is noble: 'There is no doubt that nothing profits a prince

72 Significant scholarly work has been accomplished by scholars in identifying Christine's sources through the study of individual manuscripts, many of which were compilations of favourite texts. This borrowing, although frustrating for scholars, typifies much of medieval writing. Christine scholars have identified various compendia, like Guillaume de Tignonville's *Les Ditz des philosphes*; some specific texts, like the translation of Valerius Maximus, and other contemporaneous works. We know Christine had access to the library of Charles V. Charity Willard believes that Christine could read Latin, although I suspect that she preferred translated texts. Many modern readers erroneously assume that this 'borrowing' on the part of all medieval writers is a sign of the lack of originality in medieval culture. See the conclusion of this work, below.

as much as discreet generosity.'[73] Generosity is a virtue both because it is a form of distributive justice and because it is prudent.

In a medieval advice book one would quite naturally expect to see the triumvirate of theological virtues, that is, faith, hope and charity, as part of a program for inculcating the virtues in a prince. On this expectation, Christine presents another paradox. Despite alleging their importance, she explicitly abbreviates her discussion of their significance. The theological virtues appear as a taxonomy only in *Othéa*, and are given very little attention even there. Faith, a belief in God and in the teachings of the Church, is named in all of Christine's mirrors, yet it often appears to be a standard component that interests her very little. In *Corps de policie*, princes are told of the importance of faith, but in a way that reveals her own lack of interest in this convention: 'And so, the good prince who loves God will carefully observe and keep the divine law and holy institutions in everything that is worthy and devout (which I will not discuss for reasons of brevity, and also because most people would prefer to hear of less boring things).'[74] From her perspective, the point is that if the prince respects the religious conventions, it will improve his lot:

> But the good prince that keeps and observes these things ought to firmly believe that God will guard, defend, and increase him in virtue of soul and body. And why should he not have faith in God, the living, all powerful, and just; when the pagans trusted that their needs would be met generously, because of the worship that they gave to their gods and their idols?[75]

It is the prudential or self-interested component of the exercise of religious duty that she enjoins upon her readers. Whatever her own religious convictions and spirituality, in these advice books it is quite clear that a conventional piety is what she has in mind for the prince. This is a part of her functional view of religion. A prince simply does not have the same responsibilities as a priest: 'The virtues of a prince are seen in three things, without which he will not achieve this crown of reputation, good name, and consequently, honor. The first and most important, is to love, fear, and serve God without dishonesty, but with good deeds rather than spending time withdrawn in long prayers.'[76] This view, it should be noted, is also seen in *Trésor*, where the princess who has chosen the active life shows her love of God 'by her dutiful labor in her exalted occupation', while her contemplative sisters spend their lives in prayer.[77]

---

73 *Book of the Body Politic*, trans. Forhan, 26.

74 Ibid., 15.

75 Ibid.

76 Ibid., 11.

77 *Medieval Woman's Mirror of Honor*, trans. Willard, 71.

Hope, the second of the traditional theological virtues, 'ought to be joined with the virtues of a chivalrous spirit without which he may not prevail'.[78] The significance of hope is merely that it provides psychological compensation for suffering, and thus is important to knights, presumably because of the physical risk of death or injury. But it appears to be another religious virtue to which Christine gives little attention. Nor does she address the question of false hope or redress of grievances. This superficial treatment of one of the great Christian virtues is the more surprising, given Christine's own experience of suffering. Charity is treated with similar superficiality, described as 'patient in adversity, temperate in prosperity, powerful in humility, joyous in affliction; willing the good to her enemies and friends alike'.[79]

Perhaps Christine's confession was truthful; she herself found these virtues too commonplace and boring to develop; perhaps her consciousness of the enormous literature on them made her see their discussion as less important to her purpose. In any case, it is only in this very early work that she discusses the theological virtues as part of kingship. This does not mean that she considered them unimportant, but rather they are virtues for all Christians, not particularly for rulers, and it is to princely guidance that her mirrors were directed.

By contrast, prudence is the noble virtue by which a prince can become a great king, like Charles the Wise, and can overcome the turn of Fortune's wheel. The importance of prudence to kingship is confirmed by Christine, and given the blessing of Aristotle himself: 'And as the virtue of prudence is much to be recommended, said the prince of philosophers, Aristotle: "In that knowledge is the most noble of all other things, it must be demonstrated by the best reasoning and in the most appropriate manner."'[80] Thus, Othéa's true identity is revealed in the opening chapter:

> Othéa, goddess of prudence,
> Who addresses hearts great in valour,
> To you, Hector, noble puissant prince, . . .
> Salutation.[81]

Personified as Hector's teacher and warning the prince of the dangers that

---

[78] *Othéa*, ed. Parussa, 223 'doit estre la vertu d'esperance adjouxtee aux bonnes vertus de l'esperit chevalereux, sans la quelle il ne pourroit prouffitter'.

[79] Ibid., 225. 'Elle est paciente en adversité, attrempee en prosperité, poissant en humilité, joyeuse en affliction, bien vueillant a ses ennemis et amis mesmement.'

[80] Ibid., 200. 'et comme le vertu de prudence face tres a recommander, dist le prince des philosophes, Aristote: "Pour ce que sapience est la plus noble de toutes autres choses, doit elle etre monstree par la meilleur raison et la plus couvenable maniere".'

[81] Ibid., 197. 'Othea, deesse de prudence, qui adrece les bons cuers en vaillance, a toy Hector, noble prince poissant, . . . salutacïon.'

surround him, Othéa is explicitly revealed by Christine to be a wise woman:

> Othéa, according to Greek, can be understood as the wisdom of women; and as the ancients, not yet having the light of true faith, adored many gods . . . and as they had the custom of embellishing everything out of the common course of things . . . many wise women in those times were called goddesses, and it was true, according to the histories, that during the time of great Troy's flourishing in its fame, there [was] a most wise woman, named Othéa.[82]

As title character, Prudence is given the opportunity to warn the prince of the devasting consequences of neglecting her advice. Othéa confronts Hector directly and warns him of his impending death:

> Hector, it was necessary to announce your death,
> For which a great heartfelt sorrow kills me.
> That will occur when you do not believe
> King Priam . . .[83]

In Christine's political commentary, found in the gloss, she states that Hector's death was a consequence of disobedience to his father and sovereign: 'And because he had never disobeyed his father except on that day, she could say that the day he would disobey his father he would then die. And it may be understood that no one ought to disobey his superior in reason, nor his good friends when they are wise.'[84] An astute reader might understand this cautionary tale. Louis of Orleans, named in the work's prologue, is advised not to disregard his brother Charles VI, who despite his illness is nevertheless his sovereign. The dauphin, too, might read and see the warning to princes who ignore a king. An act of defiance to king and father led Hector to his death. The text reminds us of the consequence of that form of princely disobedience – rebellion – that could embroil France in civil war. Secondly, a prudent prince is also

---

82 Ibid., 199–200. 'Othea, selon grec, peut estre pris pour sagece de femme; et comme les ancians, non ayans ancore lumiere de vraye foy, adourassent plusieurs dieux . . . et comme yceulz coustume de toutes choses aourer qui oultre le commun cours des choses . . . plusieurs femmes sages qui furent en leur temps apellerent deesses. Et fu vraye chose, selon l'istore, que, ou temps que Troye la grant flourissoit en sa haute renommee, une moult sage dame, [fut] Othea nommee . . .'

83 Ibid., 327. 'Hector noncier m'esteut ta mort, Dont grand douleur au cuer me mort; Ce sera quant le roy Priant Ne croiras . . .'

84 Ibid., 327–8. 'Et pour ce que onques n'avoit desobeÿ a son pere, fors a cellui jour, pouoit dire que le jour que il desobeÿroit a son pere adont mourroit. Et peut estre entendu que nul ne doit desobeïr son souverain en raison ne ses bons amis quant ilz sont sages.' The citation includes a pun. 'Superior in reason' could also be translated as 'sovereign [ruler] in reason'. Christine often emphasizes choosing advisers who are experts in their areas. Thus the warning may be directed towards those who contemplate rebellion against an overlord, or who disregard the advice and warnings of those who are more intelligent and experienced.

wise to heed his counsellors: those 'wise men' with the practical wisdom and foresight to make them his superiors despite his rank. Finally, the message of the allegory is one of spiritual preparation – also prudent, since fortune is no respecter of social status. This is explicit in another part of *L'Epistre Othéa*:

> In Fortune, the great goddess,
> Do not trust her nor her promises,
> For in a short time she changes;
> She often throws the most exalted into the gutter.[85]

Thus, for Christine, the remedy to Fortune's unpredictability is Prudence, found in the guise of Othéa: 'And because [Fortune] promises to many people much prosperity, and indeed gives it to some and takes it back quickly as it pleases her, [Othea, i.e. Prudence] says to the good knight that he should not trust [Fortune's] promises nor despair in adversity.'[86]

This warning was certainly appropriate for a prince involved in conspiracy and intrigue at the court of a disabled king. *L'Epistre*'s royal recipient, Louis of Orleans, was assassinated in 1407 by agents of his cousin and rival, Duke Jean of Burgundy (himself later murdered by agents of the dauphin). As Sandra Hindman has shown, Christine then used that fact to reiterate her warning with double force to other factions of the royal family.[87] Having been designed first for Louis of Orleans, after his death the work was reformulated with new illuminations, so that Louis himself became an exemplar for those who do not heed Prudence's warning. The importance of prudence was thus underscored; the prince himself became a metaphor for imprudence in the hands of an author who delivered more than one warning to princes in her works for them.[88]

Another example of the centrality of prudence in Christine de Pizan's political thought can be found in *Prod'homie/Prudence*. Not only is the work glossed, but it concludes with a helpful lexicon of terms, very like that which Nicole Oresme added to his translation of Aristotle's *Politics*.[89] Of prudence she writes:

---

85 Ibid., 304. 'En Fortune, la grant deesse, Ne te fies n'en sa promesse, Car en pou d'eure elle se change, Le plus hault souvent gette en fange.'

86 Ibid., 304–5. 'elle promet a maint assez prosperitez et de fait en donne a aucuns et les retolt en petit d'eure quant il li plast, dit au bon chevalier il ne se doit fyer en ses promesses ne se desconforter en ses adversitez.'

87 Sandra Hindman, *Christine de Pizan's 'Epistre Othéa'*. A second manuscript was prepared for Duke John of Berry shortly after the assassination, and a third, executed about the same time, was presented to Isabeau of Bavaria between 1410 and 1415.

88 See the introduction to *The Book of the Body Politic*, pp. xvi–xvii.

89 In my view this adds evidence to my belief that Christine was well acquainted with Oresme's translation. Oresme was the first to add a glossary and other scholarly apparatus to a vernacular work, although such innovations were fairly common in Latin scholastic texts. See Forhan, 'Reading Backward'.

Prudence is the discernment of good and evil things, in the flight from evil and the choice of the good. For it is not sufficient merely to divide and discern one from the other, if the choice of the good is not made in putting aside and rejecting evil. And [prudence] is divided into the following categories: Understanding, Foresight, Circumspection, Prudence in Meekness, Caution, Intelligence, Memory.

Understanding is judgement, examination, and comprehension of the things one ought to do.

Foresight is [that] by which one assesses and anticipates things to come according to the past and the signs one sees.

Circumspection is shrewedness in recognizing opposing things and those that can harm, and also to see those [things] which could have value and which teach the way to flee the vice of avarice and also prodigality and foolish largesse.

Meekness is the power to educate and instruct oneself and others in true doctrine.

Caution is to perceive the vices that hide under the appearance of virtue. Of which Saint Gregory said that sometimes the vices manifest themselves as virtues, as when Vengeance and Cruelty would like to be seen as Justice, Equity and Reason; and also as when Negligence feigns being Pity. Thus in diverse ways, evils and vices disguise themselves beneath the shadow of good and virtue.

Intelligence is only the clear knowledge of first principles and their causes, that is, of God and of Ideas and of Prime Matter and of spiritual and incorporeal substances. Memory is a natural virtue ordained to retain firmly things seen and understood. And it is called memory for it remains long in thought.[90]

---

90 'Ces quatre sont dictes "cardinales" ou "commençales" ou "principales", car ce sont les principes des autres vertus, et d'elles ont commencement. La premiere d'icelles est Prudence: sy parlerons premierement d'icelle, en voiant quele chose est Prudence; secondement en queles choses elle se consiste et extent; tiercement, en quantes especes elle est divisee.

Prudence est disceptacion de bonnes et de mauvaises choses en la fuite du mal et en l'election du bien. Car il ne souffist mie les biens et les maulz diviser et dicerner les uns des autres, se l'election des bons n'est prise en deboutant et laissant les maulz. Et est divisee es especes qui s'ensuivent: Entendement, Providence, Circonspection, Prudence en Docilité, Caucion, Intelligence, Memoire.

Entendement est jugement, advis et comprehension des choses que on doit faire.

Providence est par laquele on conjecture et extime les choses a venir selon les passees, et les signes que on voit.

Circonspection est cautele a cognoistre les choses contraires et qui peuent nuire; et aussi advisier celles qui peuent valoir et qui enseignent la voie de fuir le vice d'avarice, et aussi prodigalité ou fole largesce.

Docilité est pouoir d'informer et introduire soy et autrui par vraie doctrine.

Caucion est appercevoir les vices qui se cueuvrent soubz umbre de vertu. De quoy dist saint Gregoire que aucunefois les vices se vueulent monstrer estre vertus, quant Vengence et Crudelité vueulent estre reputees Justice, Equité et Raison; et aussi quant Negligence se feint estre Pitié. Et ainsi en diverses manieres se cueuvrent maulz et vices soubz umbre de biens et de vertus.

Intelligence est seulement clere cognoissance des premiers principes et de leurs causes (c'est a dire de Dieu et des Ydees et de la Premiere Matere, et des substances esperitueles et incorporeles).

As a cumulative lesson in the meaning of Prudence, this is a very powerful assortment of characteristics, much more shrewd, intelligent, self-interested and bold than our contemporary and much diminished view. On this account, prudence is not simply a pusillanimus kind of caution; our moral vocabulary has been depleted of the rich significance prudence held for its fifteenth-century audience, and thus we fail to appreciate the impact of Christine's privileging of this most political of virtues. 'Prudence' is of course the French translation of the Latin *prudentia*, itself a translation of the Greek *phronesis*, which might better be translated as 'moral wisdom'. To Christine there are no modern connotations of prudishness.

Aristotle places prudence in the rational part of the soul and treats it as an aspect of practical wisdom. Moreover, in the *Politics* he argues that 'Prudence is the only form of goodness which is peculiar to the ruler. The other forms [temperance, justice and courage] must, it would seem, belong equally to subjects and rulers.'[91]

By the late Middle Ages, Christine was able to draw much more into the term than the classical Greek or Roman virtue denoted since the classical root had been considerably enriched by medieval theories of interpretation and centuries of writing and reflection, which had created a concept that was both Christianized and given female gender, based on its Latin root. In Macrobius' commentary on Cicero's *Somnium Scipionis*, the interpretation of prudence is layered to include contemplation of the divine and indifference to the temporal. Prudentius' fifth-century poem *Psychomachia* had allegorized the virtues as warriors against the vices and was very influential in presenting virtues as powerful. Pseudo-Dionysius included the virtues in the celestial hierarchy of angels, rulers themselves of other-worldy realms.

Prudence as the capacity to see past, present and future and to act in accordance with that assessment is emphasized in illuminations, to which Christine was extraordinarily attuned. Claire Richter Sherman, Sandra Hindman and Sylvie Jeanneret[92] have shown that illuminations of the image of Prudence both commissioned by Christine and in libraries to which she had access, reveal Prudence as a multivalent concept whose application was essential to overcoming Fortune. The representation of Prudence in the translation of Aristotle's *Ethics* shows a nun-like figure topped by a death's head with three

Memoire est une vertu naturele, ordenee pour retenir fermement les choses veues et comprises. Et est dicte memoire, car elle demeure longuement en la pensee.'

91 Aristotle, *Politics*, trans. Barker, 106 (1277^{b}25).

92 Sherman, *Imaging Aristotle*; Hindman, *Christine de Pizan's 'Epistre Othéa'*; Sylvie Jeanneret, 'Texte et enluminures dans l'Epistre d'Othea', in Hicks (ed.), *Au champ des escriptures*, 723–849.

faces looking in different directions. Sherman writes that these faces 'refer both to past, present, and future aspects of time and to Prudence's three psychological faculties associated with them: memory, intelligence, foresight'.[93] This is a conception of prudence that is found in both Seneca and Cicero, and is also alluded to in the French translation of Giles of Rome's *Regimen principum*. Literary examples of this view are found in Dante and in Chaucer as well. Christine has taken this tradition and expanded it to give Prudence a new richness as a means of overcoming Fortune.

Ideals of kingship

Many works in the mirror tradition focus on love of glory and of honour as virtues that spur a prince to govern well. Justice, too, is a central concern for all political writers. But Christine's choice of virtues to emphasize, and her preference for prudence as the essential quality in rulers, represent a significant departure in emphasis that separates her work from others within the tradition of mirrors for princes. Hers is a practical vision designed to appeal, not to a ruler's vision of the good life, but to his self-interest. Perhaps her experience of a court filled with intrigue and deception, and her dependence on a livelihood based upon the favour of her patrons, encouraged her to see rulers as also vulnerable to the vicissitudes of life and fortune and thus to hope that they might be motivated by self-interest as well as (or instead of) the public good, and in this they would be no different from any other mortal, herself included. The subversion of the idealized virtues of the prince into something less glorious, whether termed prudence, expediency or self-interest, has often been remarked on in the work of that other Italian political writer and courtier Niccolò Machiavelli. Christine's subversion is less naked, perhaps because of her greater social, economic and personal vulnerability, but is nonetheless real. The significance of this appeal to self-interest in her political thought cannot be overstated. By contrast, two of the most important medieval sources on politics, John of Salisbury and Giles of Rome, stress that governing out of self-interest is one of the hallmarks of the tyrant, not the good prince.

At the height of the twelfth century, political writers could hope that institutional restraints on rulers prescribed by law, buttressed by custom, and constrained by competition with the clergy and papacy, might control the behaviour of the unjust prince. By the early fifteenth century, in the absence of institutional restraints caused by civil war, weakened authority, external threats and a papacy divided between two contending powers, movement towards continuity, stability and peace could perhaps be found in the personal qualities

93 Sherman, *Imaging Aristotle*, 127.

and leadership of the prince, as classical writers had argued, despite their very different era. A wise prince, like Charles V, might be willing to search for new models of good government, in classical studies like Aristotle's *Politics*, or medieval ones like John of Salisbury's *Policraticus* and Giles of Rome's *De regimine principum*, or even in newly commissioned works, like Christine's multiple mirrors for princes. By contrast, a weak or self-interested prince, like Charles VI, his brother, sons, nephews and other family members, might need to be exhorted, cajoled or frightened into good government out of fear or self-interest. A self-interested but intelligent monarch could serve the needs of a government moving away from a clerical hierarchy towards a more secular and secularized state. A prudent monarch could discover that advice and wisdom can come from any direction, whether a foreigner, a middle-class person or even a woman.

CHAPTER FIVE

Justice and the Law

I have a special place among the Virtues, for they are all based on me.

This chapter begins an examination of Christine de Pizan's approach to a pivotal conceptual question: the idea of justice. Since justice is the central problem of any political theory and is intimately connected with one's sense of the fairness of life, the analysis will begin with an overview of the concept of justice in general and some of its major contributing threads before turning to Christine de Pizan's own views. By thus situating Christine's views in her intellectual world, the nature of her contributions to medieval political ideas can be better appreciated.

The late medieval understanding of justice was a complex and rich construct of Aristotelian ideas about virtue and equity, mediated by the process of adapting Roman and canon legal codes to the realities of medieval life. Discourse on law and jusice was enriched by commentators as varied as Thomas Aquinas, Giles of Rome and Brunetto Latini. It was deepened and complicated by allegorists, poets and artists, and infused with biblical, patristic and Roman ideas about law. This spicy stew resulted in an understanding of justice that is so rich and complex that it is difficult fully to savour and digest its impact.

The traditional textbook distinction between procedural and substantive justice is very useful in this regard. The substantive idea of justice refers to objective norms that are thought to exist independently of human thought or will. Many religious traditions provide their adherents with substantive codes of justice, for example, the Ten Commandments of the Judaeo-Christian tradition are one such objective standard. The virtues of temperance, courage, prudence and justice are also objective norms of behaviour originating in classical Greek texts. Justice can even encompass privileges that belong to particular communities or guilds or classes. In the medieval view, both the sin of envy and the act of revoking chartered liberties were offences against substantive justice. What these illustrations share is that each provides a standard content by which justice can be measured.

Substantive theories of justice have the major drawback of incommensurability. While presumably we all support justice in the abstract, on a closer examination we discover that we have quite different understandings of the meaning and application of justice. The justice that is essential to one person turns out to be the epitome of injustice for another. Depending on the complexity of a particular society, there may be a variety of notions called by the same name competing with each other.[1]

It is the recognition of this problem of incommensurability and an awareness of mutually contradictory ideas in views about justice that has led to the preference for formal-procedural theories of justice, inherited from nineteenth-century utilitarianism. Contemporary theorists hope that a substantively empty formula can provide an impartial, scientifically neutral equation that, because it is not substantive, can lead to results all can recognize as just. Into the equation, the variables can be inserted – e.g. handicapped from birth, rich father, white skin, female sex – and the proper formula applied. The result would be justice. This calculus has been a particularly beguiling endeavour since the nineteenth century.[2] The allure of the formulation is that it aids in the toleration of differences in many substantative codes of behaviour arising from religious and cultural diversity, and yields quantifiable results. Two contemporary – and quite different – theories of justice provide examples: the eminent contemporary political theorist John Rawls has attempted to develop, elaborate, modify and revise an equation that will yield justice. So, too, do today's practitioners of the rational-choice model of judicial decision-making.

The most common and acceptable equation of this type is found in the idea that justice is due process in the legal system. No matter what the social status, economic position, political or religious credo, sex or race of the accused, he or she will undergo the same legal procedures, such as trial by jury, the right to confront the accuser, the right to legal counsel, and the right against self-incrimination. According to the norms of procedural justice, the only legitimate

---

1 The incommensurability of ideas or partial ideas about justice seems to be a particular problem for political philosophers. Our training and habits of mind teach us that each theory of justice succeeds another, from Plato to Aristotle, to Stoicism, to Augustine, to Aquinas *ad infinitum*. We can put each theorist into a box and isolate him on the grounds that his ideas about justice were superseded by the next thinker. Yet if we would, in Wittgenstein's phase, not think, but look, we would probably find that the Italian Catholic American's view of justice includes elements of Aristotle and Aquinas as well as 'justice as fairness'. The Yorkshire farmer may see justice as 'keeping promises' as well as having ideas about merit in her view of justicc.

2 The efforts of early utilitarians such as Bentham and Mill are one example. John Rawls's monumental *A Theory of Justice* is another.

variable in the equation is the offence itself; thus, at least in theory, all rapists are subject to the same process, as are all speeding offenders and embezzlers.

In the medieval culture of the West, both procedural and substantive aspects of justice were considered fundamental. Substantive justice was conceptualized as a virtue, and included among the powerfully evocative cardinal virtues. Procedural justice developed more slowly, as a consequence of the institutionalization of judicial administration and legal codification that began in the twelfth century. The study of civil and canon law and the incorporation of custom gave the medieval European world its first written norms of criminal and civil procedure, enshrined in codes like Magna Carta and the Customs of the Beauvaisis.

Justice and the law

The *Corpus iuris civilis* was one of the most important and significant contributions to civilization made during the medieval period. Not only was the development of law and legal theory important in tempering the behaviour of kings, it was also the single most significant institutional political advancement that today links us directly to our medieval past.

In AD 533 the Byzantine Emperor Justinian had ordered the entire body of existing law to be organized. The legal codes included in this effort were the *Digest* or *Pandectae*, fifty books of excerpts from Roman legal authorities; the *Institutiones*, an elementary textbook on the law; the *Codex Justinianus*, the then newly revised legal code of legislation and decisions; and the *Novellae*, new laws that had been added to the collection over the succeeding years. These works, commonly referred to as the *Institutes*, the *Digest*, the *Code* and the *Novels*, together constitute the *Corpus iuris civilis*. Beginning with the *Digest* in the eleventh century, these collections of Roman statutes were the focus of a revival of interest in the academic study of civil law that began at the University of Bologna and flourished in the twelfth and thirteenth centuries at major university centres, including Orleans and Toulouse (but interestingly, not Paris). Glossators, like Azo and Accursius, provided an important textual contribution, and by the fourteenth century most legal writers were focusing primarily on the study of these influential glosses, rather than the corpus of texts themselves, which had begun to retreat into the background.

The revival of legal scholarship also encouraged the study of canon law, for which Paris was an important centre. This began in the twelfth century, with Gratian's monumental effort to make sense of extant canon law by organizing the *Concordance of Discordant Canons*, commonly referred to as Gratian's *Decretum*. The revival of interest in these two very different legal codes in the twelfth century also encouraged the academic study of other surviving legal codes, including customary law. The development in the thirteenth and early fourteenth centuries of ideas about the law, particularly from the law schools of France and Italy, contributed significantly to the development of political theory during this period.

Two important caveats must be noted in examining the effect of legal study on legal practice in the evolution of Western law. First, although the legalists were always writing about what they saw as a living legal code, the very age of the core documents meant that they were responding to texts that had developed under very different institutions, where precedents and analogues could rarely be exact. Secondly, they were glossing specific texts, not writing political theory. Answers to particular legal conundrums were always tied to particular points in the law. Yet the theoretical impact of these discussions was considerable. The *Digest* and the *Institutes* both open with a foundational definition of justice that resonated throughout the Middle Ages: 'the perpetual and constant will to render to each one his due'.[3] And, 'Justice is the firm and constant resolve which gives to each their due. Jurisprudence is the knowledge of things divine and human, the science of the just and the unjust . . .'.[4] So esteemed was this definition that it was often associated with Aristotle's concept of distributive justice and even attributed to him, especially in the case of Christine de Pizan. This famous formulation of justice – 'giving to each his due' – was understood to incorporate both substantive and procedural aspects of justice.[5]

In the medieval world, as in the modern, distributive justice – giving to equals equally and to unequals unequally – exists when things or qualities considered good are distributed fairly. The theoretical and practical problem that follows is, first, to find what qualities or goods are to be distributed, economic, political or social. These might include access to job opportunities, to education, or to medical care in the modern world. For medieval society, they might include luxuries. Societal concern for their fair distribution is in part the purpose of the ubiquitous sumptuary laws of the fourteenth and fifteenth centuries. Fair distribution might also pertain to individual rights or liberties that one has as a member of a particular guild or inhabitant of a particular city.

3 *Digest*, 1. 1. 10.

4 *The Institutes of Justinian*, trans. B. Moyle (Oxford: Oxford University Press, 1896), 3–5. 'Iustitia est constans et perpetua voluntas ius suum cuique tribuens. 1 Iuris prudentia est divinarum atque humanarum rerum notitia, iusti atque iniusti scientia' (*Institutes* 1. 1. 1).

5 On the tendency to conflate what Roman law and Aristotle had to say about justice, see Ernst Hartwig Kantorowicz, *The King's Two Bodies: A Study in Mediaeval Political Theology* (Princeton: Princeton University Press, 1957), 132 ff. He argues that once the *Ethics* and *Politics* began to circulate, Roman law ideas were read into Aristotle fairly indiscriminately; also vice versa. See Forhan, 'Reading Backwards'.

The second problem is what constitutes fairness, which is dependent on who is considered equal to whom. 'Giving to equals, equally' encompassed not only substantive and procedural understandings of justice, but could be applied to a wide variety of situations, such as the preservation of rights or privileges, the punishment of malefactors, the submission of king to law, as well as to due process. Surprisingly, given modern popular misconceptions that associate medieval jurisprudence uniquely with trial by ordeal, the process by which wrongs were righted, that is, procedural justice, was very important and generally highly regarded in medieval society.

Another consequence of the general revival of interest in legal study was a more positive and commodious view of the state. As M. H. Keen writes:

> The role of the law, and thus of the ruler who frames it, is to do justice, and justice means, in Ulpian's words, a *voluntas constans et perpetua ius suum cuique tribuere*. It is concerned that the legitimate interest of every individual be protected, for it is in the well-being of its component members that the well-being of the whole, the *res publica*, consists.[6]

In France, this emerging respect for law and its conflation with the concept of justice provided a restraint on royal wilfulness, especially in cases involving the monarch. In particular, the law provided that 'no one could be a judge in his own case', which meant that a case against the king would be heard by the Parlement of Paris, rather than by the king himself.[7] Evolving theories of kingship emphasized that the king's major function was not merely order, and therefore his most important duty was not the exercise of coercive power but rather the responsibility to provide for the well-being of the whole. Accordingly, the function of law and government was to promote the common good. In this role, the king acted as a representative of the people, not of course in the modern sense, but as a kind of collective person. In principle, the law could serve as an important institutional constraint on monarchical power, framing both the legitimate end of government and the means by which to achieve it. The common good would be reached by obedience and fair administration of the ancient laws of the kingdom.

Most of the most important twelfth-century contributors to the development of ideas about procedural or legal justice were the canonists and the legalists, but as sources they would have had little direct impact on lay persons such as Christine de Pizan. Indeed she shows little knowledge of legal theory, despite

6 M. H. Keen, 'The Political Thought of the Fourteenth-Century Civilians', in Beryl Smalley and P. R. L. Brown (eds), *Trends in Medieval Political Thought* (Oxford: Blackwell, 1965), 109–10. See also P. G. Stein, 'Roman Law', in J. H. Burns (ed.), *Medieval Political Thought* (Cambridge: Cambridge University Press, 1988), 37–50.

7 Black, *Political Thought in Europe*, 153.

considerable experience with its practice in the courts of Charles VI. Far more important to her as written sources were 'popularizers' like Brunetto Latini and other mirror writers and translators/commentators such as Nicole Oresme. Some of Christine's own contemporaries, most notably Jean Gerson, also influenced her ideas. Many traditionally highly esteemed classical political authors also provided sources for Christine's ideas about ethical behaviour, particularly justice as a virtue. Here, pseudo-Seneca's *Formulae honestae vitae* must be considered an important inspiration.

Brunetto Latini's contribution to the question of justice in *Li Livres dou trésor* (*c*.1260) is especially engaging. A marvellous medieval encyclopedia, as is reflected in its name, *Trésor* is a warehouse of enchanting mythologies, fractured histories and imaginative etymologies, coupled with pragmatic lessons in etiquette and rhetoric for rulers. The first part of *Trésor* is dedicated to wisdom, the second to ethics, the third to rhetoric and the last to politics, and thus the work contains the essentials of knowledge for a member of the ruling classes. Like many works of its type, it was frequently mined for nuggets of wisdom. Its usefulness as a vernacular source of classical thought rested primarily on its synopses of Cicero's *De inventione* and Aristotle's *Ethics*. It includes a discussion of justice as a virtue combined with justice as fairness that Christine may have read: 'Justice is a laudable state of character through which man is just and does works of justice and does just things . . . man is just in three ways: one is that he behaves according to the law, the second is that he is fair, and the third is that he strives to judge well and justly . . . Justice is not just a part of virtue, rather it is all virtues.'[8]

Even today, justice as a virtue means treating others fairly; it is esteemed as an important personal characteristic because of its comprehensive impact on social life. In both the Aristotelian and Christian traditions, all of the other virtues are actions or states of character intrinsic to the individual, and as such might conceivably exist even in a hermit's cell. Thus, prudence allows one to overcome the vicissitudes of fortune; temperance teaches self-control; and courage gives the energy to do what we have to do despite enemies both internal and external. Justice alone requires the presence of other beings and therefore justice is the most socially embedded of all the virtues. As a personal quality,

[8] Latini, *The Book of the Treasure*, trans. Barrette and Baldwin, 166–67. Brunetto also stresses justice as the mean, that is, a moderate position between extremes, a well-known aspect of Aristotle's moral philosophy. While not particularly significant to Christine's ethical theory, the idea of the Aristotelian mean was very important to Nicole Oresme, who used the idea of the virtuous mean to apply to the best political constitution, a fascinating and under-regarded innovation in late medieval understandings of politics. See Blythe, *Ideal Government*, 203–42, and Forhan, 'Reading Backward'.

justice requires judgement because it means treating others fairly. It requires understanding and evaluating others and what is appropriate for them. As the mean between two extremes, justice requires restraint from being overly beneficent with some or too parsimonious with others. While it is certainly an important characteristic of princes, as one of the cardinal Christian virtues, justice is necessarily enjoined upon all individuals regardless of their rank.[9]

Christine de Pizan on law

By the early fifteenth century, the fragility of representative institutions in France, coupled with a weak and incompetent monarchy and a wilful and predatory aristocracy, meant that the law was often the only visible governmental constraint on behaviour, and even that, as Christine's complaints show, was largely inadequate because of judicial dishonesty, greed and corruption. As she commented in *Corps de policie*:

> Anacharsis the philosopher compared law to spider webs, and said that the spider webs never caught fat flies nor wasps, but catch little flies and frail butterflies, while letting strong birds go, which often destroy them when they fly through. So it is with the law, because the great and powerful often break it and pass through without fear, but the little flies are caught and trapped. This commonly happens to the poor and humble people because of the avarice of ministers of justice.[10]

Christine de Pizan's knowledge of the law as a political institution was neither professional nor scholarly. She rarely refers to specific law codes on a theoretical level. By contrast, her legal knowledge came from considerable personal experience with the law and the judicial process. As a widow attempting to clear up the muddled affairs left at her young husband's premature death, she recounts her experiences waiting in cold and drafty antechambers for justice to be done:

> Now came the tedious pursuit that I often and most painfully had to make, constrained by necessity and pursued by the many responses pro and con . . . I had to run after them according to procedure, and then sit and wait in their courts or antechambers with my file and summons, most days without accomplishing anything or receiving, after long delays, ambiguous replies and false hopes.[11]

---

9 Cicero considers generosity a part of justice, just as magnanimity is a part of courage and decorum an aspect of temperance. These are the premier virtues of princes. In determining the appropriate gift or reward, that is, exercising the virtue of generosity or *liberalitas*, it is necessary to know how much, to whom, and when it is appropriate to give. Cf. Cicero, *De officiis*, 1. 42–60; Neal Wood, *Cicero's Social and Political Thought* (Berkeley: University of California Press, 1988), 100.

10 *Book of the Body Politic*, trans. Forhan, 40.

11 *Christine's Vision*, trans. McLeod, 115.

In a picture worthy of Dickens's *Bleak House*, she describes her attempts at vindication through the legal system:

> I saw the time when I was a defendress in lawsuits at four Parisian courts, and I swear to you on my soul that I was wrongly injured by wicked parties. For this reason, if I wanted to have peace, I finally had to give in to them, thus forfeiting my rights at great cost and expense . . . And so that leech Fortune did not finish sucking away my meager possessions until she had finished them all and I had nothing to lose, and then my lawsuits stopped.[12]

These damaging experiences coloured her advice to others. She advises widows who are not from privileged classes to be well informed, to pay for good advice, but, most emphatically, to pursue their rights:

> [A widow] must be constant, strong and wise in judging and pursuing her advantage, not crouching in tears, defenseless like some simple woman or like a poor dog who retreats into a corner while all the other dogs jump on him. If you do that, dear woman, you will find most people so lacking in pity that they would take the bread from your hand, because they consider you either ignorant or simple minded . . . [H]ire always the best advice, particularly on important matters you do not understand.[13]

Her anger at injustice that comes from abuse of the legal system is undisguised. She laments the situation of poor widows in particular:

> The judges do not ward off injustice
> The magistrates do not award them two pence
> In most cases, the strong ones harass them . . .
> And the princes do not deign to hear them.[14]

Similar accounts of her experiences, expressing both frustration at injustice and at the magnitude of the difficulties faced by the ordinary person in dealing with the legal system, can be found in *Le Livre du chemin de longue estude* and in *Trésor*. Of particular interest and significance, these powerful and often moving descriptions stem from personal knowledge and even desperation, giving us tremendous insight into her passion and respect for the potential of law as the protector of the vulnerable. Christine's disgust with the legal process is all the deeper because of her view of the rule of law as normative in a chaotic society. In her biography of the deceased king, her ideal prince, Charles the Wise, is portrayed as an exemplar because of his respect for law:

> [Charles's] recognition of the rights of Jews shows that without exception, he demanded from all a perfect respect for the law, and if he learned that one of his

12 Ibid., 113.

13 *Medieval Woman's Mirror of Honor*, trans. Willard, 199–200.

14 *Christine's Vision*, trans. McLeod, 115–16.

> judicial officers had behaved otherwise, he demanded on the spot that such a one be demoted and punished as he merited, to the goal of showing other officials how they ought to serve justice and respect the law.[15]

She also reveals a more theoretical understanding of legal principle. In a chapter on the wise king's prudence and expertise in kingship, she raises the question of whether the laws should ever be changed. In answering it, she refers to the four arguments against changing the law found in the French translation of Giles of Rome's *De regimine*, giving guidelines for the evaluation of legal codes:

> If the law, whether customary or written, is just and good, that is, it is founded on natural law, it is then just as it regulates different acts in human life. But a law can be deficient for the following reason: it can be in effect contrary to nature, in which case it is a perversion and not a law. If in some place there is a law of this kind, one must not observe it, but abrogate it and make a new one, because written law must not be contrary to natural law, as was the case of the [ancient] Jewish law authorizing men to sell their wives. Nonetheless, it is necessary to know that even if a law is deficient, and it does not apply for example to all the conditions and circumstances of cases to be judged, it must not be abrogated even if one can write a new and more adequate [one], because that will induce bad habits.[16]

In an unstable world, change in the laws should be considered very conservatively:

> For it is good that the law endure a long time and it is in this that it is different from other sciences; laws get their strength from the long duration of a habitual practice, whereas other sciences come from the intellect. This is why, we say in conclusion, that kings and princes ought to observe the ancient laws of their country, and ought not to abrogate them, at least if they are not contrary to natural law. They can, however, amend them with careful study in the interest of the common good.[17]

An Aristotelian ethical principle has been extended by Christine to society as a whole. Customary obedience to long-established laws provides for a virtuous, that is, just, society, a process that is analogous to the development of habitually virtuous behaviour of individual persons. Not only does conformity to firmly instituted legal codes contribute to a more just society, it also provides a way to curb, or at least judge, the worth of kings. While natural law provides a yardstick for legal statutes, rulers can be evaluated by their compliance with it. The immutability of laws provides a plumb line for assessing rulers, and thus furnishes a kind of restraint on a king's power. Significantly, there is no indication that the king is superior to the law in Christine's view. Indeed, it is apparent that the king is to approach changes in the law with the utmost caution.

---

15 *Charles V*, ed. Hicks, 79.

16 Ibid., 207.

17 Ibid.

The conservatism of Christine's political ideas is exemplified by this preference for incremental change. The real issue for Christine is not the nature of the law, but the lawlessness of every member of the society in which she lives, from peasant to town dweller, to members of the royal houses. The sharp contrast with the present is the source of her general predilection for the reign of Charles V. Her primary concern, therefore, is the fair execution and administration of the law, which to her is the major ingredient of justice, and which reveals the fundamental character of the king. In *Le Livre de la paix*, she underscores due process as the primary function of the king's ministers: they mirror the king's justice. She concludes: 'as the common proverb says, by his ministers one recognizes the lord, so let us see each one proclaimed just'.[18]

Christine de Pizan on justice

While modern readers tend to evaluate medieval political theorists by categories that reflect contemporary concerns and issues, the separation of moral from political philosophy stems back to Aristotle's own categories of practical wisdom: ethics, as the government of the person; economics, as that of the household; and finally, politics, as rule over the *polis*. If one were to divide Christine de Pizan's works into political and moral ones, then it would be sensible to assume that her discussions of justice in the former group of works would focus on justice as fair administration of the law, and on justice as a personal virtue in the latter. This commonsense expectation is valid in three of her political works. Justice presented as following procedural and administrative norms is the primary focus in *Corps de policie*, *Charles V* and *Livre de la paix*, as might be expected. But three of the works that are most ostensibly focused on the moral virtues in rulers, *Othéa*, *Prod'homie/Prudence*, and *Cité des dames*, present us with a paradox. The presentation of justice in *Cité de dames* is especially puzzling. *Exempla* are to model and illustrate the lessons a particular author is teaching, yet the *exempla* of justice found in Part III of the work are virgin saints and martyrs, which one might assume would better demonstrate virtues of obedience, or filial piety, or chastity. A critical aspect of medieval justice and of Christine's understanding of justice as virtue may be missed if one fails to comprehend her choice. Significantly, if unexpectedly, Christine de Pizan's view is that justice is never an exclusively personal virtue; moreover, she does not have a truly substantive view of justice. Justice, whether presented as a virtue in her ostensibly moral works or as a legal process in her political works, always refers to procedural justice. In short, for Christine, justice is the

18 *Livre de la paix*, ed. Willard, 96. '. . . car si que dit le proverbe commun, aux menistres congnoist on lc seigneur, si le clamera chascun juste.'

maintenance of law and order. The virtue of justice is entirely conflated with and subsumed by justice as process. To illustrate, let us look at these three didactic moral treatises in turn.

As was discussed earlier, *L'Epistre d'Othéa* is a remarkable work and has been much studied for its uses of iconography and mythology. Its verse *texte* is followed by a *glose* based on a classical quotation and an *allégorie* citing Scriptures, accompanied by sumptuous illustrations that illuminate – in every sense – the whole. One of its fascinating characteristics is that in each chapter, the gloss emphasizes what one could call the public or political interpretation of the text, and the allegory emphasizes the spiritual concept associated with it, hence the inclusion of scriptural quotations. Willard describes the work as designed 'to reconcile ancient wisdom with Christian teachings' for the young prince, providing an education 'both social and spiritual',[19] a fairly typical goal in the mirror-for-princes genre. The spiritual component includes 'the Cardinal Virtues, the Theological Virtues, the Seven Gifts of the Holy Spirit, and the Seven Deadly Sins, all basic to the religious training of the day'.[20] This is one work where the reader expects to find justice presented as a virtue in the traditional and religious sense. Yet, the *texte* for the chapter on the cardinal virtue, Justice, presents the figure of a king sitting in judgement, Minos, King of the Underworld:

> It behoves you to resemble Minos,
> Though he be judge and master
> Of hell and of all its beings,
> For if you would advance
> It is necessary for you to be a judge.
> Otherwise you are not worthy
> To wear a helmet or govern a realm.[21]

In this ethical work, only one image of justice is presented, that of the just judge. This firmly links the responsibility of kingship to the administration of justice, and provides a measure of a king's competence. Furthermore, this is an interesting example of Christine's role in the general transmutation of this

---

19 *Writings*, ed. Willard, 90.

20 Ibid.

21 *Othéa*, ed. Parussa, 207.

> Ressembler te couvient Minos,
> Tout soit il justicier et maistres,
> D<e>nfer de tous li estres,
> Car se tu te veulz avancier,
> Estre te couvient justicier,
> Autrement de porter hëaume
> N'es digne ne tenir royaume.

concept of justice from the twelfth century to the fourteenth. According to an argument by Ernst Kantorwicz, the earlier period saw justice as a virtue, a *habitus* that might be 'triumphant over all the other virtues'.[22] By the later period, Kantorwicz argues, 'justice acquires a religious patina that is closely linked to the person of the king. Righteousness of judgement is seated like a king on his throne.'[23] Christine's image is architectonic of kingship. Whether Kantowicz's position on ascending and descending concepts of kingship is completely valid or not, Christine's text provides a telling example of the conflation of Aristotelian ideas about justice with Christian authority, which is characteristic of the period. While Christine credits Aristotle in the gloss for the statement, 'He who is a righteous judge ought first to judge himself, for he who would be not be judged is not worthy of judging another', she says that the quotation means that one should be able to correct one's own faults, and only then ought to correct others'.[24] Self-reflection is the personal and spiritual form of the virtue of justice, and it is the cornerstone of the character of a prince who will become a just judge. By contrast, in the allegory for this chapter, she cites St Bernard of Clairvaux for the idea that justice is to render to each that which is his:

> Render, therefore, says he, to the three kinds of people that which is theirs: to your sovereign, reverence and obedience, reverence of heart and obedience of body; to your peer, counsel and aid, counsel in instructing his ignorance and aid in comforting his weakness; to your subject you ought to give protection and discipline, protection in keeping him from wrongdoing and discipline in chastising him if he has done wrong.[25]

This citation is striking since in other works she attributes the fundamental definition of justice to Aristotle, and in actuality it comes from Roman law, as we have seen. No doubt her choice is governed by the constraints she has imposed on herself in her choice of formats. To be consistent, she was obligated to choose a Christian citation for the *allégorie* on the virtue of justice, but of all the quotations on justice from Christian sources available to her, it is significant that she chose a definition that stresses the web of mutual obligation

22 Kantorwicz, *The King's Two Bodies*, 137.

23 Ibid., 139.

24 *Othéa*, ed. Parussa, 207. 'Cellui qui est droiturier justicier doit premierement soy meismes justicier, car cellui qui faudroit a soy meismes seroit non digne d'autruy justicier.'

25 Ibid., 208. 'Rens, dist il, doncques, a .iij. paire de gens ce qui est leur: a ton souverain reverence et obeyssance, reverence de cuer et obeyssance de corps; a ton pareil tu dois rendre conseil et ayde, conseil en enscignant son ignorence et ayde en confortant sa non puissance; et a ton subget tu dois rendre garde et discipline, garde en le gardent de mal faire et discipline en le chastiant se il a mal fait.'

between social classes, an idea she more fully developed later in *Corps de policie*. Bernard's elaboration of the legal dictum was a choice made because it reinforced one of her most consistent values; in fact, she was to use it again in a later work. The very nature of *Othéa* as an allegory is to allude and to suggest; it is not meant to be a didactic treatise; thus the discussion of justice is quite short, awaiting more theoretical depth in later works.

For an explicit discussion of justice as an ethical concept, we can turn to one of Christine's early didactic works, *Prod'homie/Prudence,* which also has a structure of text, in this case from Martin of Braga, followed by Christine's own gloss. In its presentation, particularly the prologue, it resembles a mirror for princes, but its content reflects strong classical influence and an explicit avoidance of scriptural authority. Nor does the text itself offer specific guidance for rulers; rather its overall theme is the ethical behaviour of any person in ordinary life. These circumstances make it easy to understand why, once separated from its prologue, the text could have been believed to be by Seneca. Its modern editor, Claude Barlow, assumes that it may in fact have been adapted from an authentic work of Seneca's, since apparently Martin had already adapted Seneca's *De ira* in the same way.[26] In Christine's treatment, the transformation of justice as a moral virtue into a political one is very clear. In her introductory remarks to the section on justice, she writes: 'Even though it is necessary to all for their salvation to be just, still the application of this virtue, properly speaking, is especially significant to princes by whom others are governed, or for those who are responsible for administering justice, than it is for others.'[27]

The purpose of justice is the common good, primarily in the protection of the prince's subjects from harm. Thus, the punishment of malefactors is essential: 'True justice is to protect people from harm, which is to say from criminals and others who would do them harm.'[28] Justice means the apt administration of the law. Any moral component attached to justice is entirely instrumental to the administration of public justice as a social good. A political leader is to be restrained from misbehaviour, not because it is moral but because such restraint serves an important function. The vices such as greed that would cause the prince to behave unlawfully himself must be controlled: 'Do not allow sensuality or vice . . . and take care that your judgement is not corrupted by undue greed which might undermine the effect of reason and propriety.'[29] In other words, the other virtues of continence and wisdom are to be exercised

26 Claude W. Barlow, *Iberian Fathers* (Washington, DC: Catholic University of America Press, 1969), i, 12.

27 'The Book of Man's Integrity', in *Writings*, trans. Willard, 261.

28 Ibid.

29 Ibid., 261–2.

in order that public justice may be duly administered. They are instrumental to the public weal and functional rather than objective norms of behaviour.

The concern for due process shapes the choice of judges and their character as well, and the passages once again reflect Christine's own experience with legal injustice:

> And as for judges, if they impose unreasonable and unjustified fines and other expenses, or if they take gifts that are intended to corrupt them, whereby justice becomes fraudulent, or if they charge the poor and simple by a different system from others and fail to punish their officials who do this sort of thing . . . such people are not ministers of justice but of the devil himself.[30]

Christine argues that restitution is essential for true justice and reminds her readers of her personal experience, when the powerful and well-connected escaped from both punishment and restitution: 'It is not enough as the authority says to avoid taking from another; it is necessary for the prince or dispenser of justice to make criminals give back what they have taken and punish them.'[31] She is concerned not only for the protection of the weak, but for the consequences of corruption in high places, of which she had bitter experience: 'I refer to a true situation and to many who know that favor often misleads both princes and judges in such cases, for if the thief is powerful and well connected, or perhaps even the one who has himself made the judgement concerning the restitution and punishment, God knows how it will turn out.'[32]

Finally, justice is threatened by ambiguity of language on the part of the powerful. Law needs to be clear and readily understood; and its fair administration requires that there be no pretense or hypocrisy from those in authority. Yet Christine is very much aware of the dangers of straightforward speech on the part of the supplicant, and argues that 'one can practice licit pretense to guard one's honor'.[33]

Given our discussion of the king's role in limiting the excesses and misbehaviour in the Church in an earlier chapter, it is interesting to note that Christine includes church courts in her criticisms, as though they, too, were under a king's jurisdiction:

> In many church courts, there are the high and mighty, and it is a great wonder what tricks they have found at the devil's instigation to deceive and devour the ordinary people without conscience . . . And such people, in spite of calling themselves servants of the Church, are certainly not, indeed quite the opposite.[34]

---

30 Ibid., 263.
31 Ibid., 265.
32 Ibid., 263.
33 Ibid., 264.
34 Ibid., 263.

The third moral work where Christine ostensibly addresses the quality of justice as virtue is in the *Cité des dames*. In this, which many would consider Christine's masterwork, Justice is personified as a beautiful lady carrying a measuring cup, the better to mete out to each his or her due. The queen of this city is the Virgin Mary, who will be 'defender, protector and guard against all assaults of enemies and the world . . .'.[35] The exempla, Christine herself tells us, are chosen 'to demonstrate God's approval of the feminine sex'[36] and to serve as examples for other women. St Margaret, who was martyred for resisting both the sexual and religious advances of her captor, Olybrius; St Lucy, who resisted her king's attempt to make her a goddess; St Martina, who so exhausted her torturers that they converted; and St Justine, who vanquished the devil with her preaching: all earned their martyrdom because, as Christine writes of St Catherine of Alexandria, who was punished for her philosophical arguments against idolatry, each was 'upholding [God's] holy law'. They are models of justice because when unjust kings, fathers and husbands desired them to break the law – divine or human – each of them refused. Those in authority, whether domestic or political, were unjust, not only in encouraging or forcing others to break the law, but because they did not defend the innocent through the impartial administration of justice. The saints' holiness was not in charity or chastity alone, but rather in the respect for the law.

All of the presentations of justice discussed thus far were the products of Christine's earliest and most productive years of writing, the period from 1400 to 1405. In each of them, justice has been called a virtue but has been presented as the equitable administration or execution of the law. It is therefore not surprising that in her more explicitly and pragmatically political works, the rule of law as paradigmatic of true justice is unequivocal, and presented as the *sine qua non* of good rule. As with all of Christine's works, the context is critical; her audience is always foremost in her approach. In each of these works, *Corps de policie*, *Charles V* and *Le Livre de la paix*, it is important to remember that her primary goals are to end destruction, civil war and weak government. In her view, those evils will disappear if all members of the body politic obey the law. Justice entails the protection of all members of society against injustice. Rulers and magistrates are to administer legal codes impartially and justly. Justice as virtue and as due process are one; justice consists in giving to each his due, particularly those who have fewer resources, such as Jews, the poor, widows and orphans.

In the biography of Charles V, for example, while the concept of justice in the abstract is not addressed by Christine, personal virtue is found among the

35 *Book of the City of Ladies*, trans. Richards, 218.

36 Ibid., 219.

qualities of the king. Prudence, wisdom, justice, clemency, generosity, humility, religious devotion and charity inform this character. Charles V was the pillar of justice on the model of the Emperor Trajan: 'In fact, he made justice so respected in the kingdom that no one had the temerity to dare to offend the most humble of his subjects, whether [the perpetrator] was the greatest prince of the kingdom or [Charles's] most beloved servant.'[37] Several stories are told to illustrate the king's justice. A knight who struck his servant in the course of his duties was spared punishment only after the pleading of his friends, and he was never able to recover the king's favour. A Jew who had been the object of an 'outrageous theft' by a Christian had his rights respected.

> There was no doubt that he exacted from all a perfect respect for the law; and if he came to learn that one of his judicial officers behaved otherwise, he ordered that he be demoted and punished on the spot, as he merited, in order to show the other officials how they ought to serve justice and respect the law.[38]

The parallel with the virtuous Trajan and the widow of legend was perpetuated by a similar story told about Charles:

> Similarly, one day, when the king was at his château at Saint-Germaine-en-Laye, a widow came to him with cries and tears, demanding justice, because one of the servants of the court who had been billeted in her home in the exercise of his duties had violated her only daughter. Outraged by an action so shameful and perverse, the king had him arrested, and since the accused confessed his fault, he was hung without delay from one of the trees in the forest.[39]

The king also was a model for the more formal process of justice, seated magisterially on his throne, surrounded by his advisers. As exigent for the form as well as the spirit of justice, he also decided the cases that were under royal jurisdiction 'according to the proper ceremony of ancient tradition'. Following some remarks on the king's opposition to trial by combat, Christine concludes her discussion of virtue with some remarks on justice more generally:

> To keep us to the essential, it is without doubt that it is thanks to his concern for justice that our king came to surmount his difficulties – which were not small – and to dam the tide of evils that had submerged him for a long time. For as St Bernard said, justice is to render to each his due in everything, following its order, its measure, and due weight . . . We can say of our king, to conclude, what was said in the *Book of Proverbs*: the happiness of the just is that justice be done.[40]

Corps de policie, completed in 1407, introduces Christine's most lengthy portrayal of justice thus far, one that is, not surprisingly, well embedded in the

37 *Charles V*, ed. Hicks, 79.

38 Ibid.

39 Ibid., 80.

40 Ibid.

organic metaphor. The significance of this image for Christine is evident not only in the name of this work, but also, as was discussed earlier, in her indebtedness to the metaphor to emphasize the importance of interdependence in the polity. Yet, in *Corps de policie*, her discussion of the virtues is most diffuse and the most unlike her previous works. She underscores her usual tripartite structure by assigning three essential virtues to the king; love of God, love of his people and love of justice. His reward for the exercise of those virtues is the princely honour of the Ciceronian tradition joined to the celestial prize of Christianity:

> The virtues of a prince are seen in three things, without which he will not achieve this crown of reputation, good name, and consequently, honor. The first and foremost is to love, fear and serve God without dishonesty, but with good deeds rather than spending time withdrawn in long prayers. Another is this: he ought solely to love the good and benefit of his country and his people. All his ability, power, and the study of his free time ought to be for this, rather than his own benefit. The third is that he must love justice above all, guarding it and keeping it without restraint, and must do equity to all people. By keeping these three points well, the prince will be crowned with glory in heaven and on earth.[41]

Given the tradition as well as the political climate of 1407, it is not surprising that the bulk of Christine's discussion centres on love of justice, but her use of the concept is Procrustean. On the one hand, Christine's view of the good or just society is derived from John of Salisbury's *Policraticus*. When each member of the body politic performs his or her functions virtuously, there is justice in the whole kingdom:

> For just as the human body is not whole, but defective and deformed when it lacks any of its members, so the body politic cannot be perfect, whole, nor healthy if all the estates of which we speak are not well joined and united together. Thus, they can help and aid each other, each exercising the office which it has to, which diverse offices ought to serve only for the conservation of the whole community, just as the members of a human body aid to guide and nourish the whole body. And in so far as one of them fails, the whole feels it and is deprived by it.[42]

Although interdependence is stressed as a major component of this conception of justice, so too is the dependence of rulers on the ruled. The moral of the story of the revolt of the members of the body against the belly is that all are harmed if the prince makes unreasonable demands: 'Likewise, when prince requires more than a people can bear, then the people complain against their prince and rebel by disobedience. In such discord they all perish together.'[43]

41 *Book of the Body Politic*, trans. Forhan, 11.

42 Ibid., 90.

43 Ibid., 91.

This notion of justice is grafted onto Aristotle, whose categorizations of justice as universal and particular, remedial and distributive, had catalysed discussion for generations of political writers, as we have seen. Yet despite the availability of both the texts and the commentaries on Aristotle's concept of justice, Christine ignored the conceptual language of Aristotle's categories; nor did she address the problem of remedial justice, that is, punishment – surely a practice of concern to rulers – except in very general ways. Rather, the discussion of justice is pragmatic in *Corps de policie*, showing concern primarily for what Aristotle would call distributive justice and we have termed procedural justice. Once again, Christine defines the justice that a prince is to love as a measure that renders to each his due.[44] This takes the form of reminders that enforcement of obedience to the law is a critical component. In the introductory description of the image of justice, Christine writes: 'Felicity is a very beautiful and refined queen seated on a royal throne, and the virtues are seated around her and look at her, waiting to hear her commands, to serve her, and to obey. . . And she commands Justice to do everything that she should and to keep the laws so that there will be peace.'[45]

Enforcement is important, but rewarding those who serve the ruler is a major constituent of the practice of justice on the part of the prince. The reward is utilitarian, prescribed in order to strengthen the bonds of interdependence for the purposes of bringing about the common good as perceived by the prince: 'he will attract the hearts of his own subjects as well as those of strangers to himself. There is no doubt that nothing profits a prince as much as discreet generosity.'[46] Thus rewards ought to be given to a person of low rank or even of no rank:

> The prince or the giver, must understand his own power and authority, and also the power and rank of him to whom he would give, so as not to give a lesser gift than is appropriate, nor to give more than appropriate. The prince or the donor ought to consider to whom and why he gives the gift, because there is a difference between giving for merit, as a reward for something well done, and giving out of the frank generosity of pure courtesy . . . [A]lthough it is the role of a prince or powerful person to give as great a gift as appropriate, nonetheless they can also give small ones to poor and indigent persons.[47]

The purpose justice has in this regard is almost entirely prudential. Since all the members of the body politic must contribute to make the polity function well, all contributions must be rewarded to encourage them to continue. The

44 Ibid., 35.
45 Ibid., 5.
46 Ibid., 26.
47 Ibid., 35.

reward is practical, even to 'poor and indigent persons'.[48] The theme of compensation as a component of justice, repeated in other works, includes 'honoring foreigners'[49] as well as subject peoples, lower classes and even women. This is in marked contrast to the traditional Ciceronian view, where liberality is seen as a reflection of a prince's glory and nobility, to be practised for its own sake as part of his aura of greatness.

Justice is the duty of a prince, but it is functional in that it serves his interests to be just, to render to each his due, rather than from *noblesse oblige* in some abstract sense. This functional and procedural aspect of justice is so vital to Christine that she departs from two of her most influential intellectual mentors on a related but essential point. Both Brunetto Latini and Giles of Rome had discussed whether it is better for the king to be loved or to be feared. Brunetto Latini maintained that it is wisest to steer a middle course between these extremes.[50] Giles of Rome preferred that subjects act 'out of goodness and virtue rather than acting out of fear of punishment'.[51] In her work, Christine argues the contrary:

> The nature of justice and what it serves and to what extent is well known and understood; it is appropriate for the good prince to punish (or have punished) evildoers. And so I will pass by this for a time and proceed to that which also befits the good prince: The virtue of justice, which renders to each that which is his due, according to his power. If he keeps this rule, which is just, he will not fail to do equity in everything, and thus, he will render to himself his due. For it is rational that he has the same right he gives to everyone, which means that he would be obeyed and feared by right and by reason, as is appropriate to the majesty of a prince. For in whatever land or place where a prince is not feared, there is no true justice.[52]

The certainty of procedural justice causes a people to fear to break the law, ensures the punishment of malefactors, maintains peace and stability and leads to the common good.

Lastly, we turn to an examination of Christine's discussion of justice as it is found in *Le Livre de la paix*, a work of political thought that develops some of the ideas that Christine first presented in *Corps de policie* in 1405–7, but in much more direct and less conventional way. Written in 1412, *Le Livre de la paix* was the product of the worsening political situation in the aftermath of the assassination of Louis of Orleans in 1407. By 1411 the Burgundians were

48 Ibid., 27.

49 *Le Livre de la paix*, ed. Willard, 159.

50 Latini, *Li Livres dou tresor*, 3. 96. Translation from Nederman and Forhan, *Medieval Political Theory*, 90–91.

51 Giles of Rome, *De regimine*, 3. 36. Translation from Nederman and Forhan, *Medieval Political Theory*, 151–2.

52 *Book of the Body Politic*, trans. Forhan, 38.

conducting both marital and commercial negotiations with the English, and Jean sans Peur was able to make Charles VI condemn both the dukes of Bourbon and Orleans as outlaws. On the other hand, the young dauphin, Louis of Guyenne, who for years had been nominally in charge when his father was disabled and had thus been a vital pawn in the ducal machinations, was now 18 and beginning to exercise his own initiative. As a consequence of the desperate situation, exacerbated according to some observers by financial exhaustion and the summer's heat,[53] a treaty was concluded between the warring factions, ostensibly because of the efforts of the young prince. Christine, always optimistic in the education of this young man, wrote *Le Livre de la paix* both to encourage and guide him in these promising steps. This mirror for princes is very explicit and direct and less reliant on the *exempla* of *Corps de policie* that might have entertained him as a fourteen-year-old. It focuses on princely virtues of course, but also on pragmatic strategies for ensuring good rule and honest administrators, through a fair and appropriate system of rewards: '[justice] is like a trustworthy dispenser who distributes and disperses to each the part and portion that is his due according to his deeds, whether good or evil'.[54] The traditional idea of distributive justice, alluded to previously in *Corps de policie*, is explicitly directed to rewards and punishments for behaviour in *Le Livre de la paix*. In a lawless kingdom, where the king's deputies and enemies alike behave without restraint and where even a prince can be assassinated or abducted, there can be no return to order until all are forced to obey the law and punishments and rewards are determined on the basis of behaviour: 'Nothing is more appropriate for a king or a prince. Oh, what good will come to you who keep [justice] well!'[55] Lawful justice will constrain evildoers, which in turn will lead to the internal peace, glory and benefit of the whole kingdom; regardless of rank, economic condition or nationality, no one will fear justice. The result will be 'the glory and increase of the country, for merchants and all people will willingly restrain themselves, because they will fear being found in the wrong. From this will flow all riches and goodness and joy.'[56]

In her earlier works, Christine invokes and defines justice, citing examples of its correct administration. In the *Livre de la paix* she writes more theoretically,

---

53 *Journal d'un bourgeois de Paris*, 53. See also Willard, *Life*, 188.

54 *Le Livre de la paix*, ed. Willard, 95. '. . . c'est si comme une loyalle despensiere qui distribue et depart à un chascun tel part et porcion qui lui est due par ses faiz, soit de bien ou de mal . . .'

55 Ibid. '. . . comme riens ne soit plus partinant à roy ou prince. O quel bien t'ensuivra se tu bien la garder!'

56 Ibid., 97. 'ITEM, la gloire et augmentacion de la contrée, car marchans et toutes gens voulentiers s'y trairont pour ce que paour n'aront que on leur face tort. Et ainsi y affleura toute richece et bien et joye.'

addressing judicial policy as well. The concept of justice has four principles that the king ought to observe in its administration: first, the wrongdoer ought to be punished so that the good are not harmed or general peace disturbed; secondly, the innocent and their rights ought to be protected from harm; thirdly, if justly administered, further crimes will be deterred; and finally, the good ought to be rewarded. If these principles of justice are used to guide the administration of the legal system, both the country and the ruler will benefit enormously, but since the king cannot be everywhere [or, as in the case of Charles VI, he may be incapacitated] the ministers and judges that are entrusted with this responsibility are absolutely essential.[57] The characteristics they ought to share are clear: '[They are] to be wise so that they see clearly in all cases, that there be no errors in their judgements, that they fear God in order that they cannot be corrupted by any greed for favor or flattery . . . gentle and humane so that the poor and simple dare to come to them when they have been wronged.'[58]

Christine gives us real insight into the decay and degeneracy of the political system in her discussions of the evils that ensue when justice is not properly administered, particularly the problem of political corruption from the greed and covetousness of judges and other judicial officers: 'O! Greed, root of all evils and vices . . . nothing is more insatiable than the heart of the covetous which commits and perpetuates all evils.'[59]

Although Christine relies on some of the traditional exhortations to virtue and warnings about flattery of the mirror tradition, she also has some more institutional controls in mind. Although she stresses recruitment of properly trained officials, a theme, as we have seen, whenever she discusses court offices and advisers, she constantly emphasizes the importance of rewarding the meritorious. In her view, the king's weakness has resulted in two general problems in the political administration of the kingdom: misdeeds are not punished and good deeds go unrewarded. This must be changed so that 'the bad are to be punished without sparing them through favoritism; and that it be according to the specifics of their offenses and not at all from hatred, but in righteous justice . . .'.[60]

---

57 Ibid., 95–7.

58 Ibid., 96. '. . . estre sages afin que cler voyant en toutes causes et que erreur ne soit en leurs jugemens, qu'ilz craignent Dieu afin que convoitise par faveur ou flaterie ne puissent estre corrumpus . . . doulx et humains afin que les povres et simples s'osent tirer vers eulx quant tort est leur fait.'

59 Ibid., 97. 'O! convoitise, racine de tous maulx et de tous vices . . . riens ne soit plus insaciable que le cuer du convoiteux auquel faire et perpetuer tous maulx . . .'

60 Ibid., 101. '. . . que les mauvais fussent punis sans nulle espargne de faveur qui que ilz fussent selon le cas de leurs deliz et non par hayne nullement, mais en droituriere justice . . .'

Christine's philosophical anthropology grounded her idea that providing incentives to reinforce good behaviour and to deter misconduct is an essential part of a king's role. It is also evident, however, that she was not advocating particular institutional reforms to governmental problems, rather she counselled what one might call a combination of management techniques and exhortations to virtue. This situation is, however, more complex than appears. In the twelfth century, there was a general optimism about the possibility of good political administration through fairly simple expedients such as an organized and orderly process of tax collection, as in Richard Fitznigel's *Dialogus de scaccario* or in the administration of justice, as suggested in John of Salisbury's *Policraticus*. The earlier emphasis on bureaucratic organization can be seen in part as a result of the training in categorization that was such an important element in the twelfth-century University of Paris. By the fourteenth century, however, a weak king, a prolonged war and a divided papacy had encouraged the growth of outlaw bands, marauding soldiers, peasant uprisings and an avaricious and dissolute nobility, many of whom were members of the king's own family. For a theorist to advocate a strong king was to attempt to ensure law and order to mitigate the fracturing effects of lawlessness within the kingdom. But central authority in the form of a strong king is not a licence for tyranny, and in Christine's view may actually counteract despotic and selfish tendencies amongst lesser, but dangerously powerful, rulers, such as the warring dukes. With institutions in disarray, Christine argued for the recruitment and compensation of wise counsellors, justiciars and other officials to ensure the better functioning of institutions rather than replacing them with untried or alien alternatives. In *Le Livre de la paix*, Christine emphasized recruitment, using Charles V as her exemplar:

> Thus, in order to govern the policy of his kingdom well, [Charles] wanted to have noted jurists around him, so that, with their advice based on legal principles, everything could be well planned, with the result that as long as he reigned . . . he governed his kingdom with great magnificence and it more and more increased in prosperity, through the perfect administration of justice.[61]

Judges themselves should have no special privileges of rank or civil status and Justice herself will guard those who rightfully and lawfully administer justice. Those who do so will be protected by God. The wicked should be

---

61 Ibid., 68. 'Item, et pour bien gouverner le fait de la policie de son royaume, [Charles] voult avoir notables clercs legistes expers afin que par leur consaulx selon ordre de droit peust toutes choses bien disposer dont lui en ensuivi que tant il regna . . . tint son royaume en grant magnificence et croissement de felicité de mieulx en mieulx, c'est assavoir par tenir justice tres parfaictement . . .'

punished whatever their rank, not just rigorously, but lawfully, through proper procedures.[62]

In conclusion, the paradox of Christine de Pizan is that despite being characterized as a *moraliste*, that is, a moral rather than political philosopher, politics consistently takes precedence in her moral theory. Her emphasis on procedural justice is conspicuous and provides a strong and urgent theme throughout her political works. In apparent accord with other medieval thinkers, Christine emphasized the virtues. Yet her stress on advisers and judges being chosen by talent and integrity rather than by rank is an institutional solution to the problem of judicial corruption, and it was a significant contribution to the generally reformist aspirations of other intellectuals of the era. The problems caused by the royal dukes, particularly during periods of the king's incapacity, were intractable, expensive and violent. It is worth stressing Christine's strong emphasis in all of her political works on the crucial importance of sure and impartial administration of justice in a lawless world.

Le Livre de la paix is the most theoretical of all Christine de Pizan's mirrors for princes and the least dependent either on exhortations or, ironically, on *exempla* of good behaviour. It is also perhaps the least dependent on wholesale copying from other sources, except from her own *Charles V*. Ultimately, Christine's vision of the just society is well-ordered in the Augustinian sense. In *Le Livre de la paix*, good institutions, advisers, offices, legal experts and a well-disciplined army will lead to a well-defined and well-ordered kingdom where justice is understood as the protection of rights and privileges and civil order can be accomplished. The name of the work reveals its purpose, a purpose that went unfulfilled, however, with the early death of Louis de Guyenne.

Christine's emphasis on procedural justice as a virtue, her conflation of the moral with the political, and her awareness that the appearance of virtue is essential in kings are all themes on which later political writers will build.

62 Ibid., 99.

CHAPTER SIX

Peace and Just War

. . . bitter and endless tears flow like streams . . .

The fifteenth century and ours have at least one melancholy aspect in common: war and the rumour of war as a fact of life. North Americans and Europeans are by and large shielded from the worst aspects of war, yet for many in the world, war does not seem terribly more civilized today than during the later Middle Ages. War as a fact of life, as the normal condition of things, does not diminish the desire for peace, indeed it may augment our sense of how precious peace is. In the Middle Ages, the destructiveness and devastation of conflict was so much a part of life that ensuring peace often meant controlling war, or at least some of the negative and destructive by-products of the seemingly interminable hostilities. The longing for peace was intimately connected to the development of the concept of the just war.[1]

This chapter addresses Christine de Pizan's most significant and yet paradoxical contribution to political theory. As a writer who dedicated her career to attempting to persuade French political leaders to choose peace, Christine's most influential and original offering to later thinkers was her just war theory, and yet, as we shall see, she had grave reservations about its efficacy. Following a brief description of the classic elements of just war theory, attention will be given to both Christine's lifelong campaign for peace and her theory of just war.

---

1 For a general overview of just war theory, see Michael Walzer, *Just and Unjust Wars: A Moral Argument with Historical Illustrations* (New York: Basic Books, 1992) and James Turner Johnson, *Just War Tradition and the Restraint of War: A Moral and Historical Inquiry* (Princeton: Princeton University Press, 1981), or id., *The Quest for Peace: Three Moral Traditions in Western Cultural History* (Princeton: Princeton University Press, 1987). For the medieval period, see Frederick H. Russell, *The Just War in the Middle Ages* (Cambridge: Cambridge University Press, 1975) and M. H. Keen, *The Laws of War in the Late Middle Ages* (London: Routledge & Kegan Paul, 1965).

Christianity and war

The problem of warfare for a Christian state and for Christianity in general stems from ambiguity about violence and governmental authority in some of the earliest Christian sources, which derived at least in part from the marginality and powerlessness of the community. While the pacifism of some early Christians is well established, the pacifism of early Christianity as a whole is more controversial, and has inspired considerable debate. To summarize the controversy: many have believed that the earliest Christians were exclusively pacifist. On this view, the legitimization of Christianity by the Edict of Milan in 313 corrupted authentic Christian belief and Apostolic teaching. By becoming respectable, the Church attracted ambitious persons seeking power and influence, which resulted in engaging the early church too much with the state. In the words of Frederick Russell, this exerted 'a subtle but powerful influence on Christian theologians to accommodate Christian citizenship to Roman wars'.[2] By contrast, others have reasoned that the early church was more heterogeneous in belief than this account allows. James Turner Johnson has suggested that the claim of a pre-Constantinian pacifism is a partisan position primarily held by pacifist and Protestant scholars desiring to use the argument for early Christian pacifism polemically. The historical record, he argues, is more ambiguous than they allow.[3] In any case, despite a Roman just war tradition, the concept of just war becomes an object of discussion in the Christian world with St Augustine, whose reflections on warfare and the human condition created a space for a morality of war with a distinctively Christian cast. Augustine's comments were fragmentary and based on a Roman, especially Ciceronian, understanding of the rules of warfare.

These citations, later collected in the twelfth century as part of Gratian's *Decretum*, led to the gradual development of a theory of war through written commentaries on Augustine by both decretalists and theologians. Two weighty issues were addressed: first, what constitutes a legitimate and moral reason to go to war? Secondly, what constitutes the proper conduct of war itself? These two themes are referred to in the literature as *ius ad bellum* and *ius in bello* respectively and are very useful distinctions even today. The development of *ius ad bellum* relied initially on concerns by canon lawyers to control the bellicosity of still largely tribal feuds within an elastic power structure that had only fairly sketchy lines of authority. In a sense the canonists could be seen as part of the overarching centralization and Romanizing influence of the Gregorian reformers.

2 Russell, *Just War*, 12.

3 Johnson, *Just War Tradition*, p. xxvii, also 330–38.

Ius in bello developed with the generation of a particularly Christian ethical system, including an intentionalist ethics via Peter Abelard. Together with the development of a theory of penance as a sacrament, intentionalist ethics encouraged more reflection on the proper conduct of the soldiers' participation in warfare. Without an ethics based on the interior condition or intention of the soldier, the ethical distinction between murder, manslaughter, or even accident, including causing a death in battle, had been very imprecise. Before the twelfth century, sin had often been treated as though it were entirely dependent on the nature of the act, regardless of the reason why the offence was committed.[4] The elaborate taxonomies of sins and their assigned penances listed in pastoral manuals are witnesses to this mechanistic view of sin. Philippe Contamine points out that punishments were assigned to all soldiers who had killed in war, regardless of the individual circumstances. Thus, Bede's penitential required all soldiers who had killed in battle to fast for forty days without distinction. By contrast, penances levied for other sins that were not in war but resulted in death were differentiated according to what we might call the motive for the killing. The penitent might receive three years' penance for murder in anger, one year for an accidental death, seven years for death by poisoning, or ten years if the murder followed a quarrel.[5]

Peter Abelard's brilliant and revolutionary twelfth-century work, *Scito te ipsum*, argues that the interior intention of an individual is essential for determining the moral guilt or innocence of a person: 'In fact we say that an intention is good, that is right in itself, but that an action does not bear anything good in itself but proceeds from a good intention. When the same thing is done by the same man at different times, by the diversity of his intention, his action is now said to be good, now bad . . .'.[6] While interior condition clearly plays an important role in Augustinian moral philosophy, Abelard takes a giant leap by arguing that even Judas, the betrayer of Christ, may not have sinned by his act of betrayal, if his intention had been to save others from what he saw as Jesus' foolhardiness:

> However, if one asks whether those persecutors of the martyrs or of Christ sinned in what they believed to be pleasing to God, or whether they could without sin have

4 Augustine's view of the importance of intention had not entirely disappeared, but emphasis on the use of penitentials in counselling sinners was perhaps another aspect of the general bureaucratization of ecclesiastical life that was part of the Gregorian reform. For a study of the development of virtue ethics, see Bonnie Kent, *The Virtues of the Will* (Washington, DC: Catholic University Press, 1998).

5 P. Contamine, *War in the Middle Ages* (New York: Blackwell, 1984), 266–7.

6 Peter Abelard, *Peter Abelard's Ethics*, ed. and trans. D. E. Luscombe (Oxford: Clarendon Press, 1971), 53.

> forsaken what they thought should definitely not be forsaken, assuredly according to our earlier description of sin as contempt of God or consenting to what one believes should not be consented to, we cannot say that they have sinned in this, nor is anyone's ignorance a sin or even the unbelief with which no one can be saved.[7]

This emphasis on intention grounded just war theory in two fundamental principles: first, that the person of conscience cannot engage in a war unless it is just, and secondly, that once it is engaged, the war must be fought according to certain rules. A war can be considered just when it meets the necessary criteria as legitimate, honourable and lawful, or as the Middle Ages framed it, with *auctoritas*, *recta intentio* and *causa*. Briefly, these criteria establish a framework that covers the persons, their intentions in fighting, and the causes and conditions of war. Over the centuries, different terminologies were developed by different authors, and discussions of just war included minds as varied as those of scholastics such as Thomas Aquinas, Aristotelian popularizers such as Brunetto Latini, as well as jurists, most notably John of Legnano and Baldus de Ubaldis.[8]

The first criterion, *auctoritas*, or the authority to fight a war, was an absolutely essential consideration. A major social and political problem throughout the Middle Ages was the existence of marauding gangs of unemployed soldiers. Sometimes fighting as mercenaries, sometimes for a rebellious lord, they presented an obstacle to social order that had reached serious proportions by the fourteenth century. In response to this endemic concern, theorists had stipulated that only the head of state had the authority to fight a war. 'It is not the business of a private individual to declare war',[9] wrote Thomas Aquinas, because an individual who is not a head of state has other solutions available to him to rectify an injustice. He may appeal to an overlord or search for justice through a lawsuit. For some theorists, perhaps even the majority,[10] the emperor alone had the right to wage war, since he was the head of a single unified Christendom. Theoretically, any other prince faced with an injustice or wronged by an enemy could apply directly to the emperor for redress. The emperor himself could consider his cause just if he waged war either against the infidel or against rebellion within his empire. According to Jonathan Barnes, a few

7 Ibid., 55–6; see also 67.

8 The various terminologies are discussed by Jonathan Barnes, 'The Just War', in *Cambridge History of Later Medieval Philosophy* (Cambridge: Cambridge University Press, 1982), 771–84. For the contribution of the jurists, see Russell, *Just War in the Middle Ages*. For Thomas Aquinas, see John Finnis, *Aquinas: Moral, Political, and Legal Theory* (Oxford: Oxford University Press, 1998).

9 Thomas Aquinas, *Summa theologica*, Part II, Question 40 (New York: Bensinger Bros., 1947). Found at http://ethics.acusd.edu/texts/JustWar/html. See also Finnis, *Aquinas*, 264.

10 Barnes, 'Just War', 776.

more 'liberal' theorists allowed the authority to wage war to other princes within the empire as well. For Thomas Aquinas, one of that minority, justification for this was based on analogy between the prince's duty to ensure justice both internally and externally to his territory: 'Just as the rulers of a city-state, kingdom or province rightly defend its public order against internal disturbance, by using the physical sword in punishing criminals . . . so too rulers have the right to initiate a war.'[11] Once conceded the authority to wage war, a ruler could only do so for the appropriate reasons, which were routinely described by theorists as either to promote good or to avoid evil, although in reality those could be fairly inclusive categories. For Brunetto Latini, for example, 'the good' included being able to live in peace without harm. For St Bernard of Clairvaux, promoting the good meant to defend the Church. Significantly, Cicero's *De officiis* (1. 11. 36) had argued that the recovery of material goods was a just cause, a point elaborated by Aquinas:

> A just cause is required, viz. that those who are to be warred upon should deserve to be warred upon because of some fault. Hence Augustine says, 'just wars are customarily determined as those which avenge injuries, if a nation or a state which is to be warred upon has neglected to punish crimes committed by its people or to restore what has been unjustly taken away'.[12]

Notice that Thomas's view of just cause includes both the idea that there is an actionable injury, and that the injured person or ruler has the right to rectification. The enemy therefore deserves or merits punishment, which is as justly inflicted as on a criminal. He draws a very powerful and persuasive analogy between the right to punish the criminal within the civil community and the right to wage war against him, thus conflating the terms 'criminal' with 'an enemy from outside the community'.

Thomas also includes invasion by another among just causes. When attacked by an enemy, the prince acts in self defence and he needs no other justification to go to war. This seems self-evident, but Thomas Aquinas draws a conclusion from this that can trouble modern political theorists because of its wide-reaching implications. Aquinas, like other post-Augustinian writers, envisages the pre-emptive strike: 'it is permissible to attack enemies to restrain them from their wrongdoing'.[13] Yet this is a phrase so vague and open-ended that it could encompass a wide variety of offences, in both the moral and sporting senses of the word.

---

11 Hereafter, the quotations are as cited in Finnis, *Aquinas*, 284–5.

12 Finnis apparently accepts the attribution to Augustine. The quotation cited by Aquinas as Augustine is found in *Summa theologica*, Can. Apud Caus. xxiii, qu. 1.

13 Aquinas, *Summa theologica*, Part II, Question 40. See also Johnson, *Just War Tradition*, 30.

The third element in establishing a just war was the intention of the combatants. The *causa* or purpose of the war involved the intentions of the war leaders. By contrast, *intentio* referred to the state of mind and heart of the combatants, even ordinary foot soldiers. Social status and rank were partial determinants of whether fighting in war was appropriate and just for a particular individual or not. In fact, James Turner Johnson argues, rather than truly providing a restraint on war and protecting innocent bystanders, these exclusions were a way of privileging ecclesiastic and knightly classes in maintaining their stranglehold on political and social power. In any case, most medieval theorists addressed social class. Honoré Bouvet believed that clerics could fight, but only in self-defence. The more bellicose Bernard of Clairvaux saw clerics as legitimately engaging in crusades. In the view of most thinkers, peasants were not to be combatants at all: their social status forbade it, and excluding them was clearly a way of reinforcing social norms about their natural inferiority as the 'cowardly peasant'. Some writers stressed the mental and spiritual dispositions of those who fought; soldiers could not fight for booty or out of greed, although it was certainly considered moral for them to be paid as mercenaries. In John of Salisbury's view, soldiers, the armed hand of the body politic, ought to be paid, since he believed it would lessen the temptation of theft or pillage. Brunetto Latini thought that the soldier should act with 'right conduct'. For Thomas Aquinas, *recta intentio* included the behaviour and disposition of every individual involved, from highest prince to lowest foot soldier, from the highest goals of preserving the common good and the protection of the people, to the individual soldier's methods and purpose. He enjoins soldiers to exclude cruelty, fraud and certain states of mind, such as lust for domination.[14]

Clearly the idea of *recta intentio* spills over into the category of the conduct of war, *ius in bello*. Failure to abide by the rules of war or to have a *recta intentio* could vitiate the status of a war as just; by contrast the combatant in a just war was participating in something 'not merely permissible but meritorious'.[15] These rules of war were elaborated over the centuries, and constrained the conduct of war, at least in principle. For example, war was technically forbidden – at least among Christians – against non-combatants and 'innocents', on fast days and feast days, at plowing and at harvest. In fact, there are so many exclusions that one could reasonably wonder if war were ever truly legitimate.[16]

14 Finnis, *Aquinas*, 285.

15 Ibid.

16 The Peace of God is discussed by Contamine, *War in the Middle Ages*, 270–80 and by Johnson, *Just War Tradition*, 124–36.

While developments in just war theory in the twelfth and thirteenth centuries were primarily from the pens of canon lawyers and theologians, several profound changes in the life of the later Middle Ages led to passionate interest in the conduct of war. Some of these were intellectual and spiritual challenges to the status quo. There was an increasingly diverse body of literature responding to Aristotle's political writings to be sure, but also individuals, even lay individuals, were responding to the radical gospel preaching of the Franciscans. Theorists were also forced to reconsider traditional views by political changes, such as the capture of Jerusalem, the papal schism, the growing power of both monarchies and empire, and finally, the Hundred Years War. The concerns of writers in this later period focused more on conduct *ius in bello*, and less on justification. And so Giles of Rome comments, not on the technical aspects of justification for war, but merely on discretion as the better part of valour, and military practicalities. Once war has been decided upon as a matter of policy, Giles provides a catalogue of issues into which the prince should enquire before engaging in a war. Brunetto Latini and Honoré Bouvet both stress preparation and consultation with advisers. Latini also advises respecting truces and sparing prisoners of war who fought fairly.

Lay and even vernacular works in both prose and verse on the fair conduct of war and the behaviour of the military class exploded in the fourteenth century, as courtly literature developed new forms and expression. The evolution of the chivalric code and the concept of courtliness can be seen as an attempt to wrestle with the conduct of combatants. The medieval romance could even be read as a lay and vernacular expression of just war theory. Historically, chivalry was a way of authorizing and legitimating the control of power by the warrior castes of Europe while simultaneously regulating and civilizing their behaviour. The concept of chivalry itself grew out of the confluence of two quite separate codes: the first was the warrior code of medieval Europe, a code of blood feud and bride-snatching that prided itself on military efficiency, loyalty and prowess. The resulting behaviour was hardly the flower of chivalry in our modern understanding of the term. As Georges Duby describes them, 'Such was the aristocratic youth of France in the twelfth century; a mob of young men let loose, in search of glory, profit and female prey, by the great noble houses in order to relieve the pressure on their expanding power.' [17]

This warrior code was tamed by the second code, the competing and very different values of the *curiales*, the clerical bureaucrats who, beginning in the eleventh century, had to reconcile their clerical training, centred on contemplation of God, with the values of the courts in which they served. Encouraged

[17] Georges Duby, *The Chivalrous Society* (Berkeley: University of California Press, 1977), 122.

by the presence of powerful women at court, such as Eleanor of Aquitaine and Marie de Champagne, this ethic of courtliness involved not only behaviour – elegance, politeness and the proper manners – but also qualities of generosity, nobility, compassion and protection of the weak. During the twelfth through fourteenth centuries, these two very different codes became one; the aristocratic ethic of the successful knight was that he had earned his rank through his merit as a warrior. 'Courtliness', the behaviour expected of a noble person – courtesy and generosity[18] – had been merged with 'chivalry'. The chivalrous knight was first and foremost a mighty warrior whose merit was confirmed by his courtesy and his wealth. Also beginning in the twelfth century, this process was fostered and transmitted by the literary development of the romance, particularly *Le Conte du Graal*, *La Mort le Roi Artu* and the rest of the Matter of Britain, including *Tristan*, as well as the *Roman de la Rose*, the *Roman de Troie* and other later courtly romances. The primary literary justification for knighthood was the defence of the population, a notion that was underlined by the king's pre-eminent role as war leader. Alexander the Great was the quintessential king because of his ability as a general. While wars of expansion were frowned upon in the concept of just war, Alexander as an aggressor seems to have been overlooked in the mirror for princes tradition, where his magnificence and his responsiveness to his tutelage by Aristotle that are the stock images evoked.

By the fourteenth century, the military class or caste dominated life, at least in its own imagination, and its 'virtues' or characteristics began to be imitated by newly emergent ranks of merchants and burghers, as the evidence of sumptuary laws reminds us. But that adaptation did not go uncriticized. Geoffrey Chaucer, in particular, satirized the values emphasized in this tradition, and made his own commentary on just war in 'The Tale of Melibee'.[19] The generalization of the code of chivalry from behaviour in wartime to a set of values applicable to other persons and classes was extremely important,[20] and one to which Christine de Pizan contributed directly.

18 Some historians, most notably Stephen C. Jaeger, *The Origins of Courtliness: Civilizing Trends and the Formation of Courtly Ideals, 939–1210* (Philadelphia: University of Pennsylvania Press, 1985) and Aldo Scaglione, *Knights at Court: Courtliness, Chivalry and Courtesy from Ottonian Germany to the Italian Renaissance* (Berkeley: University of California Press, 1991), underline the Ciceronian component in the concept of chivalry, a view with which I strongly agree. The *Somnium Scipionis* was a very influential source in this regard, as were *De officiis* and *De senectute*. See also Wood, *Cicero's Social and Political Thought*, 100–104.

19 This is discussed in 'Poets and Politics: Geoffrey Chaucer and Christine de Pizan on Just War', presented at the annual meeting of the American Political Science Association, Washington, DC, August 2000.

20 Its repercussions have been felt as far away as the antebellum south of the United States and in the romantic films of Hollywood.

In closing these remarks on the background of just war theory, it is well to remember that there is something ineffably poignant about it. The history of warfare teaches that the reality of medieval war was far less civilized and elegant than the romances or the schoolbooks portray. Once a prince determined or proclaimed that his cause was just, the tendency was for that fact to legitimate the most despicable and cruel behaviour, examples of which the Middle Ages no less than any other can amply offer. The war crimes of the Hundred Years War resemble those of more recent memory, including the slaying of prisoners of war and the wounded, and the mistreatment, rape and murder of the non-combatant. Medieval just war theory also allowed war against 'the other' – heretics and infidels – paralleling the rationale, or *causae*, behind modern scapegoating and ethnic hatred. The ultimate tragedy of medieval just war theory may have been its apparent impotence. Perhaps the war crime tribunals of the twenty-first century can be more effective than the papal pronouncements of earlier centuries.

Christine de Pizan on peace and on war

The single most prominent recurring theme in Christine de Pizan's political thought is the importance of peace.[21] In fact, as has been argued thus far in this work, many of Christine's political ideas, including her view of kingship, counsel, the political community and the virtue of chivalry, are the fruit of her concern over the issue of controlling the violence of the burgeoning civil war. The desperate political situation encouraged her in her essential conservatism – her nostalgia for the good rule of the 'wise' Charles V and her allegorization of the history of France. Indeed, it is all too evident that the banal appellation 'Hundred Years War' scarcely conveys the social, political and economic disintegration that characterized the reign of Charles VI in particular. The intractability of the political situation drew forth some of the most profound reflection by Christine de Pizan on the issue of peace, but it also forced her views to be multifaceted, since they were always dependent on the situation and the audience, and her patrons' willingness or inability to listen.

Looking at her political works sequentially, we see *Epistre d'Othéa, Longue estude*, *Charles V*, *Prod'homie*, *Trésor*, *Corps de policie*, *Lamentation sur la guerre civile* and finally, *Le Livre de la paix*. Each of them, in its own way and for its own audience, develops an idea of the centrality of peace. By contrast, two other works, *L'Avision Christine* and *Faits d'armes et chevalrie*, explicitly describe the characteristics of a just war. Each will be discussed in turn.

---

21 This is the subject of an important article by Berenice Carroll, 'On the Causes of War and the Quest for Peace', in Hicks, *Au champ des escriptures*, 337–58.

Epistre d'Othéa is an argument for peace within the constaints of its complex allegorical mirror form. The use of Prince Hector as the disciple of the goddess Prudence is extremely pointed. The story of the Trojan war, when read as history rather than myth, was ignited by the most idiotic and imprudent personal behaviour and had disproportionate consequences for the entire kingdom, destroying not only Hector's brother Paris, the prince of Troy whose ill-fated decision brought the wrath of Agememnon down on all of his house, but the royal house of Priam and all the people of Troy as well. This mythic tale ought to have been a powerful lesson to the reckless and foolhardy princes of France, who believed themselves to be descended from Hector of Troy. 'Never take up arms capriciously', Prudence counsels Prince Hector.[22]

Longue estude represents another step in Christine's evolution as a philosophical writer. Modelled in some ways on Dante's dream-world journey, this long and complex work brings Christine face to face with Reason. She wonders why there is so much conflict in the world, that even the birds and animals fight amongst themselves and prey on each other, so that it seems that the whole world is torn apart by war:

> So I thought of the ambitions,
> The wars, the afflictions,
> The betrayals and the treacheries
> Which exist everywhere, and of all the great evils
> That are done . . .
> I wondered what could be the reason
> That we could not have peace.[23]

Reason's response is enigmatic, only fully revealed at her court, where the character Christine is entertained by a discussion of the virtues of princes. The author's elaboration of those virtues is firmly inserted within the metaphor of the body politic and buttressed by references to her favourite authorities,[24] presenting views that will be developed more completely in her later prose works.

---

22 *Othéa*, ed. Parussa, 332. 'N'entreprens mie folles armes . . .'

23 Christine de Pizan, *Le Chemin de longue étude*, ed. A. Tarnowski (Paris: Livre de Poche, 2000), 106.

> Si pensoie aux ambicions,
> Aux guerres, aux afflictions,
> Aux traisons, aux agais faulx,
> Qui y sont et aux grans deffaulx,
> Que l'en fait, . . .
> Moy merveillant dont peut venir,
> C'on ne se peut en paix tenir.

24 Ibid., 412–49.

While Christine's pleas for peace and exhortations for royal virtues in *Othéa* and *Longue estude* are of historical interest, taken alone, they do not demonstrate a very theoretical understanding of the politics of peace. However, in *Charles V* we see the development of a revitalized notion of chivalry that reconstructs the fundamental duty of kings, and focuses on peace. Christine inverts or subverts the traditional image of the king as warrior by uncoupling chivalry (etymologically related to cavalry and *cheval*, or horse) from warfare entirely.

Using Charles V as her model, she demonstrates how the wise king epitomized both a king's obligations and his virtues. A king's powers include the regulation and enforcement of social class, through which the king ensures that the knightly class fulfils its responsibility, which is 'to watch over the defence of the humble people, of the clergy, of women, of the peasants and of the land.[25] For knights, chivalry resides in acting with justice towards those who serve the king and the common good, defending and protecting all the king's subjects. 'Chivalry consists in the faculty of overcoming enemies and those opposed to the common good', which is a paraphrase of Giles of Rome's *De regimine principum*, to which Christine adds: 'acting with justice towards those who serve him', and '[defending] his people without bloodshed'.[26] The king's leadership is accomplished through superior military strategy, which means making shrewd alliances and otherwise using pacts and treaties to get his way. The chivalrous king also appoints learned philosophers and scientists to act as his advisers and consults them frequently, as well as making his own study of political wisdom. Through his knowledge and political sense, Christine argues, Charles, the model king, was able to develop the support of his men and his people generally, which allowed him to defend his people at a much lower cost in lives. It is important to emphasize that none of these characteristics has anything to do with the traditional concept of chivalry – either as military prowess or as courtly manners. In fact, Christine has taken the term chivalry and used it to discuss normative characteristics of rule; that is, ruling for the common good, as a 'good shepherd',[27] not only because a king ought to rule this way, but also because it is prudent, preserving his kingdom, its economy and perhaps even his own life and that of his heirs.

In *Charles V*, beginning with Book II, where she discusses the historical origins of kingship and the class system, she quite naturally turns to the evolution of the warrior class and its leadership. Citing Giles of Rome, she defines chivalry as 'the capacity of vanquishing enemies and opponents to the common good'.[28]

25 *Charles V*, ed. Hicks, 112.
26 Ibid., 111–12.
27 Ibid., 194.
28 Ibid., 114.

Building on this definition, Christine structures her functional view of social class on an implicit Aristotelian naturalism. As we saw in an earlier chapter, societies are born out of human nature. But, like the Aristotelian taxonomy of good and bad regimes, not only does every society have both a ideal form and a degenerate one, so do the different estates:

> As the human soul is provided with two forces, one that pushes to follow one's own desire, the other that permits valorous resistance to a natural egoism, it follows equally that there are two kingdoms and two estates. One is made of laws that assure a just order of the public good; the other is knighthood, which protects and defends the prince, the country and the common good.[29]

Like Aristotle's schema of good and bad regimes, the difference between the ideal and the degenerate form of social class is whether or not it is directed towards the common good. As a corollary, just as each form of government has its own virtue, so too does each social class or estate. On Christine's view, chivalry, which is the virtue, or essence, of knighthood, must then be a virtue directed to the common good. Its function is the preservation of peace. It is thus extremely significant that she minimizes the notion that chivalry consists of mere physical strength and military skill or the ability to lead men into battle. Charles V, the subject of the biography, was notoriously deficient in knightly prowess and his health was far too fragile to allow him to lead his troops into war.[30] Christine argues in the biography that this does not diminish his honour, because true chivalry is not explicitly military, but in fact can prevent or avoid military engagement, thus serving the common good by protecting the weak and by recognizing the value of all the prince's subjects. Political leaders do need to be powerful, but power is not necessarily a matter of physical or military strength; on the contrary, it means having the four characteristics of chivalry: good fortune, judgement, perseverance and strength.[31] These characteristics allow the king to avoid war if possible, and to think strategically and to choose a good commander-in-chief if it is not. It is a false idea of kingly virtue, she believes, which links it to warfare, since a particularly talented soldier, like Bernard du Guesclin, could serve as commander-in-chief, who would then also serve as one of the king's counsellors.[32] Unlike rulers, chivalrous knights do have to have the appropriate expertise in arms, but that is not enough; they must have discipline as well.[33]

Found primarily in *Charles V*, the revitalization of the concept of chivalry is

29 Ibid., 115.

30 Willard, *Life*, 121–3. See also Françoise Autrand, *Charles V*.

31 *Charles V*, ed. Hicks, 115.

32 Ibid., 154–8.

33 Ibid., 116–17.

echoed in the discussions of knighthood and knightly codes of conduct in both *Corps de policie* and *Le Livre de la paix*. A vigorous yet demilitarized view of chivalry is one weapon that Christine hopes to use to ensure peace in 1402. By 1405, in the midst of her most prolific period as a political writer, she also began to articulate her views on the importance of peace in other works.

Le Livre de la prod'homie de l'homme/Prudence[34] is most often cited to prove that Christine was skilled enough in Latin to translate *Formula vitae honestae*, but at this writing it has not been examined for its political content. While *Prod'homie/Prudence* was probably valued by Christine in part because it was thought to have been written by Seneca, one of the heroes of the mirror tradition, the term 'translation' to describe this work is very misleading, because, like many medieval translations, it takes the form of text and gloss, where the gloss is the translator's interpretation and explanation of the *auctor*'s text. Like Oresme's translation of the *Politics*, Christine's translation of pseudo-Seneca ought to be considered an independent treatise in its own right. Its subject is the four cardinal virtues. The terms used in the text are prudence, magnanimity, continence and justice, all of which are extremely important but highly traditional virtues to be cultivated by anyone. In *Prod'homie*, Christine adapted the text and in her glosses explicitly underlined its applicability to kings.[35] In it, peace is an important consequence of the exercise of the virtues. A just king provides peace. In a kingdom where injustice is the norm, confusion reigns; therefore, a prudent king desires peace:

34 The manuscripts usually cited are: BNF fr. 605, the earliest of the *Prudence* MSS and one indisputably linked with the Christine workshop. Another important early MS is Brussels, Bibliothèque Royale, MS 11065–11073, which is not as readily identifiable as a Christine workshop MS, but which Eric Hicks and Christine Reno suspect might well be. For *Prod'homie*, Vatican City, Biblioteca Apostolica Vaticana, MS Reg. lat. 1238 is a product of the Christine workshop. On the advice of Eric Hicks, I have cited this version of the text. Professor Christine Reno of Vassar College kindly steered me towards the least problematic of the extant manuscripts; her article '*Le Livre du Prudence/Prod'homie de l'Homme: nouvelles perspectives*' is extremely useful. It can be found in Bernard Ribémont and Liliane Dulac (eds), *Une femme de lettres au Moyen Age: études autour de Christine de Pizan* (Orléans: Paradigme, 1995), 25–37.

35 An interesting feature of *Prod'homie* are the two appendices that Christine added to the book. The first, following on the text's discussion of wrongful use of magnanimity or courage, is a gloss entitled 'The Characteristics that the Most Worthy Knight Ought to Have', which describes the ideal. While not identical, it is very similar to the discussion of six conditions of the good knight in *Corps de policie* and Valerius Maximus. The second insertion of note is the glossary of definitions, modelled perhaps on that of Oresme's translation of the *Politics*, where Christine defines the many facets of the virtues according to 'l'opinion des hommes ecclesiastiques'.

> *Text*: [Justice] is a virtue. What is justice but a tacit composition of nature, founded for the benefit of the many. And what is this Justice but our constitution or divine law, the binding together of human company?
> *Gloss*: Justice, as Aristotle says, is a measure that renders to each his due; it is that which keeps the world in peace where it reigns; but where it is not kept everything is confusion. Oh, how justice is loved by God! And how important it is to the world! It is the bond of equity that keeps the whole polity in peace.[36]

A vision of peace is also important in Christine's works offered to women. As we have seen, in *Trésor* one of the most important roles Christine sees for a noble woman is as intecessor between her lord and his enemies. She implemented this vision in her letter of advice to the queen, dated 5 October 1405, in which she begs the queen to intervene as a mediator. Beginning in 1402, Isabeau of Bavaria was in principle to act in the king's place whenever he was incapacitated by his illness. By 1405, the growing friction between Louis of Orleans and Jean of Burgundy had resulted in thousands of troops threatening not only Paris, but also the safety of the king's young heir, Louis of Guyenne, and the fragile stability of the kingdom. Apparently, Louis of Orleans had little commitment to peace and hoped that the dissention caused by the papal schism would strengthen his hand in carving out a kingdom in Italy. In this situation verging on open civil war, Willard believes that Christine's letter was written at the request of one of the more level-headed participants, perhaps the King of Navarre, since several royal princes were working to reconcile the two dukes. The letter is written in the form of a plaint, with much gushing of tears and eyes turned upward:[37]

> Worthy lady, let it not displease you to hear recalled the piteous complaints of your grieving French supplicants at present oppressed by affliction and sorrow who with humble voice drenched in tears cry out to you . . . that you may seek and obtain a ready peace between these two worthy princes, cousins by blood and natural friends, but at present moved by a strange fortune to contention with each other.

Particularly interesting is that the reward promised the queen includes the princely and Ciceronian 'glory' or renown, and 'honour' or a place in history,

36 'Texte: [Justice] est une vertu. Qu'est Justice fors une composicion taisible de nature, trovee en l'aide de pluseurs. Et que est justice ne mais nostre constitucion ou loy divine et lian de humaine compaignie. Glose: justice, comme dit Aristote, est une mesure, qui rent a chascun son droit; c'est çe qui tient le monde en paix ou elle regne; mais ou elle est mal gardee, tout va a confusion. O comme est justice amee de Dieu! et comme elle est au monde neccessaire! C'est un lian d'equité et qui tient toute policie en ordre de paix.'

37 Willard, *Writings*, 252–3. On war and the use of the lament form by Christine, see M. Zimmerman, 'Vox Femina, Vox Politica', in Brabant (ed.), *Politics, Gender, and Genre*, 113–28.

in addition to the more predictable salvation of the queen's soul. These qualities are often characterized as chivalric and are generally depicted as the reward for princely virtue. In her search for defenders of the peace, it is significant that the idealized characteristics of knighthood have been extended by Christine to both a physically weak and non-militaristic king in *Charles V*, and to a queen, Isabeau of Bavaria.

Trésor's companion peace, *Le Livre du Corps de Policie* is also a product of this extraordinarily fruitful period for Christine, and it, too, emphasizes peace. Her hopes and aspirations for peace were directed increasingly towards the next generation; *Trésor* had been written for the young dauphine, and *Corps de Policie*, for the fourteen-year-old dauphin, Louis of Guyenne, to whom her later *Livre de la Paix* would also be dedicated.

In *Corps de policie*, all of Part Two is addressed to knights. While *ius ad bellum*, the legitimate justification for war, is not explicit in the discussion, *ius in bello* plays a significant role in this work, but not in terms of rules for combat. Rather, the real focus of her advice is on military discipline. Part Two begins with the six conditions that a good knight ought to have, borrowed from Valerius Maximus:

> The first is that they ought to love arms and the art of them perfectly, and they ought to practice that work. The second condition is that they ought to be very bold, and have such firmness and constancy in their courage that they never flee nor run from battles out of fear of death, nor spare their blood nor life, for the good of their prince and the safe keeping of their country and the republic . . . Third they ought to give heart and steadiness to each other, counseling their companions to do well, and to be firm and steadfast. The fourth is to be truthful and to uphold their fealty and oath. Fifth, they ought to love and desire honor above all worldly things. Sixth they ought to be wise and crafty against their enemies and in all deeds of arms. To those who observe them and keep these conditions well there will be honor.[38]

These six conditions combine elements of character – self-discipline, honour, shrewdness and fortitude – with purpose; the safety of ruler and ruled are not particularly original. Her choice of *exempla*, however, in this most subversive of Christine's mirrors, underlines the problem of discipline, which is by contrast a significant issue in a kingdom on the verge of civil war. Over and over, we are told stories of soldiers who are rewarded for their discipline or from whose lack of discipline terrible consequences arise:

> And although they loved arms well, they also observed knightly discipline, that is they kept right in suitable things by rules, so that they failed in nothing. Those who broke the established rules were punished. Valerius said that the discipline of chivalry, that is, keeping the rules and order appropriate to it, was the highest honor and firm

[38] *Book of the Body Politic*, trans. Forhan, 63–4.

> foundation of the empire of Rome. Moreover, he said that they won their great victories, they secured the state, and the certain position of happy peace and tranquility because they kept this discipline well.[39]

Corps de policie also discusses at length the importance of leadership, an urgent issue for two generations since Charles V had not been able physically to be a war leader, and Charles VI was not capable mentally:

> On the subject of good army leaders, Vegetius says that above all else, it is their duty to be wise and well advised in their duties, because it is a heavy responsibility to provide for so many people, that is, to think about what they might need. This means governing a large number of people for the will and good order of all, one's own honor, and the benefit of his sovereign.[40]

By 1410, with the political situation continuing to deteriorate, Christine wrote the powerful *Lamentation sur les maux de France* to the Duke of Berry. The assassination of the Duke of Orleans, the king's brother and thus Berry's nephew, had further escalated familial conflicts over the issue of controlling the two essential pawns of French political life, the incapacitated king and his young heir. Christine's attempt to persuade the elderly prince to intervene with the warring and intransigent dukes leads her to her most pointed criticisms of the damage the royal family had been inflicting on France:

> For Heaven's sake! For Heaven's sake! Mighty princes open your eyes . . . Thus you will see cities in ruins, towns and castles destroyed, fortresses thrown to the ground! And where? In the very midst of France. The noble chivalry and youth of France which as one body and soul used to stand ready to defend the crown and public good, [are] now assembled in shameful ranks against each other, father against son, brother against brother, one relative against the next, their deadly swords drenching the battlefields with blood . . .[41]

Nor was it only the loss of men at arms that she feared, but a devastated economy and popular uprisings:

> And then what next in God's name? Famine because of the pillaging and destruction of property that will follow, and failure to cultivate the fields, from which will result rebellion of the people because they are harassed by the soldiers, deprived, and too hard pressed and robbed of this and that; subversion in the cities where, for need of money it will be necessary to impose outrageous taxes on citizens.[42]

The terrible consequences of civil war led to Christine's increasingly passionate cries for peace in each of these five works. All of them are devoted to a vision

---

39 Ibid., 64.

40 Ibid., 71.

41 'Lamentation on the Woes of France', in *Writings*, trans. Willard, 304.

42 Ibid., 305.

of good rule that is contrasted with the escalating and disastrous results of prolonged warfare. Yet neither fear and hatred of the devastation of war, nor love of peace, no matter how eloquent, constitutes a theory of just war. *L'Avision Christine* and *Le Livre des fais d'armes et de chevalerie* construct a philosophy of just war.

In *L'Avision*, Christine presents the author's earliest attempt to lay out criteria for a just war in a systematic way. Although the tendency is to interpret her *Vision* as an autobiography, in fact the work is much more. Like many of her works, it has a tripartite structure and a very comprehensive and complex agenda. Rosalind Brown-Grant has pointed out that in many ways *L'Avision Christine* functions as a mirror for princes, by allowing Christine to model the appropriate soul-searching for her princely patron, and, Brown-Grant observes, the work ought to be read on the three levels that Christine herself recommends, including a political interpretation. Brown-Grant believes that like *Charles V*, this work is more than an intellectual biography or a humanistic quest for literary immortality, but is to be read as instructing the reader how to read metaphorically, and that the metaphor connects 'the political salvation of France, the moral salvation of the individual, and the salvation of humanity in general'.[43] Book I of the work is a *speculum historiale*, a kind of sacred history of France that outlines a comprehensive vision of the nation and its destiny and which reflects both an awareness of political turmoil and its consequences. In Book II, Christine explicitly articulates a theory of *ius ad bellum*. Dame Opinion states that the 'nobles following the profession of arms'

> misunderstand chivalric deeds because they do not know or want to know the proper limits which are such that it is not permissible for anyone to fight or arm himself for war except for certain reasons. That is, in defense of God's law against miscreants or heretics who oppose the faith; and for defense of the Church, his prince, his country, his land, the public good, the rights of the innocent, and his own possessions. There is no other law that permits it, nor is the fight just and approved otherwise.[44]

In this statement of *ius ad bellum*, it is significant that Christine states that anyone is authorized to fight given the correct reason, even lesser nobles. The right to declare war is not limited to kings or to the emperor but includes other rulers of subordinate ranks, a view that may have developed as much from observation of the unruly behaviour of knights as from principle. Because combat had already been engaged, perhaps the important question is not who has the right to declare war, but for what purpose they are fighting and whether their *causa* is appropriate. Jonathan Barnes characterizes Christine's view as

---

43 R. Brown-Grant, 'L'Avision Christine', in Brabant (ed.), *Politics*, 95–112.

44 *Vision*, trans. McLeod, 84.

'liberal'; and it is very likely a reflection of her usual practicality. She may not believe in the efficacy of restricting the persons who may legitimately engage in war, either because it is unrealistic or unenforceble, or because of her gender theory of complementarity. Just as women may be natural peacemakers, so men may be naturally bellicose, thus it is futile to try to restrain nobles from conflict.

This early articulation of principles of just war gives way to a more fully developed theory in *Le Livre des fais d'armes et de chevalerie*, which Christine wrote in 1410. This very influential work is a manual of warfare and chivalry and evidently was written in the hope that the dauphin, Louis of Guyenne, who was not particularly inclined to military leadership, would profit from reading it. Charity Cannon Willard speculates that Jean sans Peur, himself a gifted military commander, compensated Christine for the work willingly, since the young Louis of Guyenne needed military training and he was living under the Duke's protection at the time.[45]

Consistent with Christine's by now identifiable style, *Le livre des fais d'armes et de chevalerie* is a tapestry of the known experts in the field, interspersed with her own threads of understanding and insight. Her major authorities were several popular and widely disseminated works. The most commonplace was Vegetius, whose *De re militari* had been translated into French about 1380, and was a work she much admired. In part, this was because it was the only Roman work on the technicalities of warfare available to medieval writers, but like Valerius Maximus, whose work was also a favoured source and cited frequently, it was a rich store of information and *exempla* about the Roman army's traditions, discipline, tactics and values, which, despite their idealized form, provided a welcome model for the professionalization needed by the French army, indeed, by all medieval armies. By contrast, she relied also on the useful and interesting fourteenth-century work, the influential *Arbre des batailles*, by Honoré Bouvet (sometimes rendered Bonet).[46] In Part III of Christine's work, Bouvet appears as a dream figure to answer her questions about the rules of war, but not without first giving her permission to use his work! The character Bouvet declares: 'it is common usage among my disciples to exchange and share the flowers they take from my garden individually . . . but it is wrong to take material without acknowledgment; therein is the fault.'[47]

---

45 *Writings*, trans. Willard, 255; cf. Willard, *Life*, 183–7.

46 Honoré Bonet [Bouvet], *The Tree of Battles*, trans. G. W. Coopland (Liverpool: University Press, 1949).

47 *The Book of Deeds of Arms and of Chivalry*, trans. Sumner Willard (University Park, Pa.: Pennsylvania State University Press, 1999), 144.

Fais d'armes was one of Christine's most widely read works, so much so, that when her name was all but forgotten, the book was still valued, although its authorship was unknown.[48] *Le Livre des fais d'armes et de chevalerie* marks Christine's most significant contribution to traditional political theory. In the first four chapters, she states not only her preference for peace, and her view of war as a means to peace, but she also lays out her own contribution to just war theory, in a important advance in the emerging field of international relations. She begins with the central problem of *auctoritas*. Given the destruction and death, and all the acts of war that are both 'detestable and improper', can there ever be a just war? Citing biblical authority she argues that 'wars and battles waged for a just cause are but the proper execution of justice, to bestow right where it belongs'.[49] Both conventional and divine law are intended to control the wicked. 'Divine law grants this, as do laws drawn up by people to repress the arrogant and evildoers.'[50] The collateral effects of war – rape, pillage and the destruction of the innocent and non-combatants – are the consequence of the misuse of war, thus canon and civil law are intended to control and limit this wrongful abuse of the exercise of arms.

The classic problem of *auctoritas* is resolved by defining who has the authority to wage war. Only slightly more limited than in *L'Avision*, this authority is restricted to 'sovereign princes, which is to say, emperors, kings, dukes, and other landed lords who are duly and rightfully heads of temporal jurisdictions. No baron, or any other person, may undertake war without the express permission and will of his sovereign lord.'[51]

It is striking and significant that Christine restricts *auctoritas* so little, a point that has not gone unobserved by historians such as M. H. Keen and Jonathan Barnes.[52] The difference between *L'Avision* and *Fais d'armes* is in the audience for whom the works were prepared. Since *Fais d'armes* was explicitly designed as a technical manual on warfare, it would be irresponsible to address this central question of war without more precision than in the earlier work.

Having established the question of authority, Christine addresses just cause:

> There are five causes of war, only three of which are justifiable. The first lawful ground upon which wars may be undertaken or pursued is to sustain law and justice; the second is to counteract evildoers who befoul, injure and oppress the land [and the

48 See the discussion in the introduction by Charity Willard to the new translation of this work, ibid., and Barnes, 'Just War'.

49 *Deeds of Arms*, trans. Willard, 14.

50 Ibid.

51 Ibid., 15.

52 Keen, *Laws of War*, 77; Barnes, 'Just War', 776.

> country] and the people; the third is to recover land or lordships or other things stolen or usurped for unjust cause by others who are under the jurisdiction of the prince, the country or its subjects.[53]

For the prince to undertake war in these circumstances is not only justifiable, it is obligatory on him 'as incurred by his title to lordship'.[54] His function as ruler is to defend his people and lands, including the Church and its patrimony, but also widows, orphans and other victims of injustice. Moreover, the lesser princes under him rely on the ruler for redress of their own grievances, so only he is in a position to judge conflicts amongst his nobles.

By contrast, two causes are not justifiable but stem from the prince's own wilfulness and desires: 'one is for revenge for any loss or damage occurred; the other is to conquer and take over foreign lands or lordships'.[55] Despite the fact that such undertakings are common and even widely respected, they are not justifiable because they are both infractions of divine law. In the case of the first, God alone can take vengeance for wrongdoing, and in the case of the second, covetousness is a sin.

Yet, if a prince has incurred damage, he can desire redress as long as it is without a passion for vengeance. This is because just as it is licit for a prince to wage war to defend the rights of his subjects, 'it is lawful for the prince to keep for himself the same right that is granted to others'.[56] If he considers himself to be wronged, he should not: 'simply depart, in order to obey divine law, without taking further action . . . for divine law does not deny justice, but rather commands that it should be carried out and requires punishment for misdeeds'.[57] This is quite far removed from the idea found in many earlier theorists that the king ought to apply to the emperor for redress of his own grievances and underlines Christine's passionate conviction that justice demands the punishment of evildoers.

In a stunning departure from other theorists, what makes a war just is the process of deliberation that the prince must follow in order to wage war. This is perhaps an extension or an extrapolation of the French legal tradition that a king may not be a judge in his own case, but if so, it is implicit here only, since there is no other indication that Christine was overtly concerned about this judicial principle. The prince must gather a 'council of wise men in his parliament or in that of his sovereign if he is a subject' but he will also call on impartial third-party foreign observers, seasoned statesmen and legal advisers.

53 *Deeds of Arms*, trans. Willard, 15.

54 Ibid., 17.

55 Ibid., 16.

56 Ibid., 17.

57 Ibid.

If, after frank discussion, the prince determines that his cause is just, he must also 'summon his adversary' and lay out the case before him, and ask for restitution for the wrongs that he has experienced. If his adversary tries to make the contrary case, he should be listened to be 'heard fully . . . without willfulness or spite'.[58] If this procedure is followed, and the adversary refuses to appear 'as the law requires', then the ensuing conflict is not vengeance but the execution of due justice.

Strikingly, it is not abstract obligations or religious appeals that the work emphasizes, but rather due process, and a kind of arbitration procedure that includes both neutral foreign observers and professional jurists. It recognizes that the combatants or antagonists belong to the same international entity called 'Christendom', and that rules governing all rulers ought to apply within that entity. Of all Christine de Pizan's political works, this was perhaps the most influential, existing even today in dozens of manuscripts and early printed editions. While it might be argued that this popularity was simply because of the juxtaposition of thoughts on warfare from Honoré Bouvet and Vegetius, both of their works were widely available elsewhere. In reality, Christine's procedural and secular process of deliberation and arbitration was one of its attractions, and it was to be an important component in the rise of international law.[59]

Yet there is a marked pragmatism, even pessimism, in her words. *Fais d'armes* acknowledges that there are many reasons why rulers go to war, some better than others. It recognizes that non-combatants live precariously, dependent on protection by their lords. The degree to which they can be assumed by the antagonists to give aid and comfort to the enemy is the measure of their vulnerability to both their own and to the opposing army: 'And occasionally the poor and simple folk, who do not bear arms, are injured – and it cannot be otherwise – for weeds cannot be separated from good plants, because they are so close together that the good ones suffer.'[60] The strictures against harming them are only admonitions from an abstract ideal of justice. There is a law of war, but it has no executive power. She concludes with an admonition to take 'every precaution not to destroy' them and to shield the humble and peaceful, 'for they are Christians and not Saracens'. Yet these words are not directed against Saracens as some kind of externalized and alien other, but rather because they do not belong to the larger political community of Christian Europe, a supranational entity. Warfare is not simply the amusement or punishment of the ruling class, but its effects transcend borders and social classes. There is an

58 Ibid., 18.

59 Ibid.

60 Ibid., 171–2.

implicit recognition of an identity within a larger organism than rank or even nationality. This, tied with a deliberative process that includes foreign observers, reveals Christine de Pizan's preference for rules of war that are international in scope.

Ultimately it must be recognized, according to Christine, that sometimes justice demands war, but the evils of war stem from 'the evil will of people who misuse war'. Others, she concedes, may believe that an effort to tame war is fruitless, and thus that her work is 'the product of idleness and a waste of time'.[61] If anything is clear, however, it is her own tireless optimism that peace will be the result if each member of society behaves for the common good.

Christine's emphasis on consultation and process, on rules within a larger community than the nation, on recognition that, in addition to king or emperor, other rulers may have authority to wage wars for just cause, are steps leading to later advancements in ideas about international law, primarily in Alberico Gentili, *De jure belli* and in Hugo Grotius, *De jure belli ac pacis*. It is also significantly different from most of its predecessors and successors in one very important aspect. Christine's *Fais d'armes* is written in the vernacular, and is intended not only for knights and princes, but for ordinary men of arms who might hear it read aloud. This is a work deliberately composed 'in the plainest possible language', rather than the Latin of the jurists.[62] It was to have considerable impact on the reform of the French military system in the mid-fifteenth century.

---

61 Ibid., 14.

62 Ibid., 5–8. See also P. Haggenmacher, 'Grotius and Gentili', in H. Bull *et al.* (eds), *Hugo Grotius and International Relations* (Oxford: Clarendon Press, 1992), 133–76.

Conclusion: The Paradox of Christine de Pizan

[Fortune, t]hat false one with the double face
That one of fickle influence . . . the damage that she would bring the world . . .

As political writer and as a person Christine de Pizan presents certain paradoxes. She was one of the most prolific political writers of the Middle Ages and yet she is virtually unknown to scholars of the history of political thought. In those disciplines where her work has been recognized, especially French literature and women's studies, her political theory has largely been ignored. She provokes extreme positions: she is either France's first feminist, first female professional writer and a proto-democrat, or she is anti-feminist, a conservative, a bluestocking and a prude. Her life presents contradictions as well: she was an Italian at a French court, an educated woman at a time when the status of women had started to decline, a widow with no male 'protector' in a society where male values and privilege dominated. In a world that conferred status hierarchically, she was what we would call middle-class, since she was both the daughter and the widow of civil servants. Her style reveals other paradoxes: despite her high reputation amongst her contemporaries, the structure of many of her works is convoluted, and not infrequently her style is opaque and pedantic. She has been accused of producing a mangled hotch-potch from misunderstood and expropriated sources. Yet she speaks at times with refreshing simplicity and directness, on personal themes, as in the clearly lonely verses of her widowhood, but also when she speaks politically, as when she castigates the English and exults over their reverses. The life and ideas of this fascinating woman have stimulated what Margarete Zimmerman has wittily called 'une Querelle des Christinophiles et des Christinoclastes'.[1] How should her books, her ideas and her contribution to the history of political thought be evaluated?

Recognition that Christine de Pizan is a political theorist will resolve some of these paradoxes. To evaluate her position in the history of political thought

[1] Margarete Zimmermann, 'Christine de Pizan et les féministes autour de 1900', in Ribémont (ed.), *Sur le chemin de longue étude*, 183–204.

requires discussion of the reception of her works and of the influence of her political ideas as a whole. Machiavelli was not the first to argue that a prince can overcome fortune.

The reception of Christine de Pizan

After her death, Christine's works continued to exhibit considerable popularity, particularly her works for women. There is much evidence that these works were widely disseminated in French and in translation. While *Cité des dames* was popular at a number of European courts, *Trésor* has proven to have been broadly distributed amongst members of the middle classes throughout the fifteenth century and early into the sixteenth. With the exception of *Othéa*, however, her volumes on more conventional and explicitly political themes apparently had less widespread appeal. At present, they exist in fewer manuscript copies and early editions than do the much copied, printed and translated *Cité des dames* and *Trésor*. An inventory is rather enlightening. *Charles V* and *Fais d'armes* could once be found in seven[2] and twenty-four manuscripts respectively, *Corps de policie* exists in nine manuscripts, of which at least eight date from the fifteenth century, and in a Middle English translation that dates from the 1470s. There are only two extant manuscripts of *Le Livre de la paix*, and this important work has never been translated. *Prod'homie/Prudence* has never been published and is found today in only two manuscripts. By contrast, *Othéa* exists in some fifty manuscripts – three of which were discovered after Gianni Mombello's study of the known texts in 1967 – and in three different early English translations, as well as in a number of early printed editions.

Of course the number of extant manuscripts is not a definitive marker of the popularity of a book, and, as was the case with *Othéa*, other early copies may yet appear. Translations, early printed editions, citations and references to her works also provide a trail of information about the reception of Christine's political ideas,[3] and their relative popularity. The most significant attestation to one of Christine's books is provided by the fortunes of *Fais d'armes*, Christine's manual on warfare. Today, a fairly large number of fifteenth-century manuscript copies is complemented by an equally large number of early printed volumes and translations. Printed editions in French appeared as early as 1488

2 Three are now lost. See the introduction to Solente's edition of *Charles V.*

3 The critical editions of Christine's works enumerate the extant manuscripts, for the most part. Solente's 'Christine de Pisan', *Histoire littéraire de la France* (Paris: Imprimerie Nationale, 1974) is very helpful, as is the last chapter of Willard's *Life*. Glenda McLeod's *The Reception of Christine de Pizan from the Fifteenth to the Nineteenth Centuries* (Lewiston, NY: E. Mellen Press, 1991) complements the many twentieth-century studies of Christine.

and 1527. Caxton himself translated and printed *Fais d'armes* as *The Boke of Fayttes of Armes and of Chyualrye* in 1489, of which twenty fifteenth-century copies still exist. Yet in many cases, with the notable exception of Caxton, who was closely connected to the Burgundian court in the late fifteenth century, Christine's personal identity was lost. Fifteen of the surviving manuscripts of *Fais d'armes* present the author as a man, changing authorial references and pronouns to masculine forms.[4] As Frances Teague argues, perhaps early copyists reasoned as follows: it 'is a fine piece of work that must have been written by a man; if a woman claims authorship, something is amiss and revision is in order to show that the manuscript is a masculine work'.[5] Later sources go even further in correcting this 'mistake', as Earl Jeffrey Richards has pointed out. By the sixteenth and seventeenth centuries, Christine has become 'Christinus de Pisis, Italus natione, inter alia composuit de re militari lib.1'.[6] Yet of all Christine's political works, *Fais d'armes* is undoubtedly the most directly and obviously influential in the development of international law and in just war theory. It is difficult to avoid the conclusion that for many of its early readers, as their opinion of its value and originality increased, the possibility that it could have been written by a woman decreased, in a kind of reflexive gender bias.

Over the centuries, although it has had a significant role in providing a portrait of a model king, most of the attention that the biography of Charles V has elicited has been as a nearly contemporaneous account of an important and influential monarch. Several early historians of France admired the work, and even today many contemporary scholars cite *Charles V* as a primary source, especially Christine's descriptions of the king's personal characteristics, his coronation, his library project, and the visit of the Holy Roman Emperor, usually taken at face value, despite both propagandistic elements and errors of fact in the work. By contrast, few discuss or seem particularly interested in the work as politics or political theory.[7] Yet, the biography ought also be read as a study on rulership meant to analyse the qualities of an ideal ruler, to provide an exemplar for the new Valois dynasty, and to inspire the king's heirs to build a model kingdom. It also served as a critique of the current monarchy, yet was

---

4 Frances Teague, 'Christine de Pizan's Book of War', in McLeod (ed.), *Reception of Christine de Pizan*, 25–42.

5 Ibid., 32.

6 As quoted in Earl Jeffrey Richards, 'The Medieval "Femme auteur" as Provocation to Literary History', in McLeod (ed.), *Reception of Christine de Pizan*, 103.

7 Eric Hicks and Rosalind Brown-Grant are two exceptions that prove the rule. See Hicks's introduction to the modern French *Charles V* and Brown-Grant's excellent *Christine de Pizan and the Moral Defense of Women*.

made more palatable through its disguising conventions of hagiography and the innovations of early humanistic biography. Jacques Krynen, in his admirable work on the development of French political theory, argues that

> [t]his panegyric on Charles V was written to serve as an example to princes, but also for the political and moral formation of the dauphin. This *apologia* is a highly didactic treatise . . . This identification of a Valois with the prince developed in the mirrors is as remarkable as it is exhaustive . . . This history of Charles V in the form of the *vita* constitutes no less than the response of Christine de Pisan to political disarray.[8]

In fact, the last phrase of this citation from Krynen can serve to describe Christine's other mirrors for princes as well. All were written as a response to political turmoil. While the evidence for the direct influence of *Corps de policie* and *Le Livre de la paix* more generally is less than compelling, Christine undoubtedly did much to continue the development of the mirror genre in general and to extend its conventions to other audiences, most notably women. *Corps de policie* enriched and perpetuated the use of the corporate metaphor, signalled classical principles of good rule, and underlined the significance of all members of society for audiences both in England and in France. *Le Livre de la paix* did the same, but from a much more direct and explicit perspective, shaped by the disasters befalling France in the interval between the assassination of Louis of Orleans and the defeat at Agincourt. As her last mirror for princes, it reflected her profound disappointment in many members of the political community, and the urgent need for peace. *Paix* provided clear and compelling examples of the dangers of mob rule, drawing on a vivid image of the body politic that clearly signals interdependence gone awry:

> Let us consider the absolute folly of seeing a man driven so greatly by anger that he wants to destroy himself, his teeth tearing at his own feet, his hands striking great blows at each other, and his feet tripping each other up and kicking out his eyes, so that the whole body seemed to be in an insane spasm against itself. Indeed, one would have reason to say that such a person was completely mad. Alas, is that not the case of civil war in a country?[9]

Le Livre de la paix is in essence a valedictory piece for Christine, marking her last formal attempt to instruct the ruling classes on the nature of good government. In the critical edition of *Le Livre de la paix*, Charity Cannon Willard concluded her introduction by seeing in the work 'an effort on Christine's part to sum up her political and ethical ideas and to incorporate [them] into the new work', and in so doing she is part of a long French tradition to integrate 'the results of personal reading and experience into some set of

8 Krynen, *L'Empire du roi*, 200–201.

9 'The Book of Peace', in *Writings*, trans. Willard, 314.

beliefs'[10] that will culminate in later writers, such as Montaigne. After this work, she turned away from the mirror genre to works that were less bound by conventional topoi. While Willard's encomium situates Christine's work within the humanistic tradition, it is worth while to remember that *Le Livre de la paix* was also written by someone walking a precarious tightrope between opposing factions during a time of civil war. Since all her political theory was written in exigent circumstances, Christine worked very hard at not being perceived as a partisan of any faction despite close ties to various political actors, as Claude Gauvard has observed.[11]

While the evidence of the direct influence of specific political works is muted, Christine de Pizan's visibility during the Renaissance was high, and Earl Jeffrey Richards has found over fifty references to her or her books between 1545 and 1795, primarily in historical works. An eclipse of two or three generations ended with her rediscovery by Raimond Thomassy in 1838. Despite their later obscurity, both her mirrors for princes and her treatise on warfare earned her, in Thomassy's view, 'a legitimate and durable glory'.[12]

The legacy of Christine de Pizan

The question of Christine's legacy to women's studies is a controversial one, explored most dispassionately and thoroughly in Rosalind Brown-Grant's recent work, *Christine de Pizan and the Moral Defense of Women: Reading Beyond Gender*, and in Maureen Quilligan's magisterial *Allegory of Female Authority*. Quilligan ends her investigation into Christine's thought with an observation that, however apt, is not likely to please either Christine's proponents or her critics. Concluding that Christine is neither as retrogressive and hostile to progress as her detractors claim nor as progressive and 'modern' as her admirers allege, Quilligan avers that '[Christine] stands as a figure worthy of study (if not emulation), a pivotal early character crucial to any full accounting of women's achievements, as well as one of the first women writers of their neglected history'.[13]

In her conclusion, Brown-Grant provides a sophisticated and elegant articulation of Christine's paradoxical position in contemporary women's

---

10 *Livre de la paix*, ed. Willard, 52.

11 Claude Gauvard, 'Christine de Pizan et ses contemporains: l'engagement politique des écrivains dans le royaume de France aux XIVe et XVe siècles', in Dulac and Ribémont, *Une Femme de lettres*.

12 Raimond Thomassy, *Essai sur les écrits politiques de Christine de Pisan* (Paris: Débécourt, 1838), 87.

13 Maureen Quilligan, *The Allegory of Female Authority: Christine de Pizan's Cité des dames* (Ithaca, NY: Cornell University Press, 1991), 283.

studies. Arguing the importance of Christine's emphasis on the moral equality of women in a society unprepared to see women as the social equals of men, she contextualizes Christine's view of sexual difference within late medieval literary and moral norms. Brown-Grant concludes:

> We need to pay Christine's critique of misogyny the respect it deserves and see it as a dialogue with the society and culture of the late Middle Ages, rather than simply praising it – or denouncing it – for the extent to which it does or does not look forward to the feminist ideals and beliefs of the twentieth century. Christine's voice in defense of women is utterly different from our own, but it was in its time a dissenting voice, one which spoke out to its audience with as much urgency and vigour as that of any modern feminist today.[14]

The ambiguity of Christine's position in women's studies reveals the complexity of evaluating the ideas of someone whose world is so alien to our own.[15] By contrast, Christine's legacy as a political theorist could be judged on the basis of three criteria: first, her place in the development of Western political ideas; secondly, her contribution to the gradual development of modern democratic institutions and values; thirdly, her legitimacy as a political theorist as well as a prolific political writer.

Western political ideas

Direct citation of the political ideas and concepts in Christine's political works cannot yet be proven except in the case of *Fais d'armes*. There is no evidence to date that any later political thinker quoted directly from her works, explicitly refuted them, or named them in any way in the construction or elaboration of political views. In terms of some great chain of being of political ideas, or some orderly evolutionary flow, Christine de Pizan, cannot, with that one exception, be shown to have had any direct role in the development of Western political thought.

That said, however, she does have indirect significance in the evolution of European political ideas. First, it must be recognized that Christine's contribution to political thought in fifteenth-century France is collective as well as individual. She was one of a great wave of intellectuals who, confronted with national tragedy and incompetent rule, were concerned with the fate of France and shared observations, criticisms and ideas. Some were poets, courtiers and literati, such as Philippe de Mézières and Alain Chartier. Some were

14 Brown-Grant, *Christine de Pisan and the Moran Defense of Women*, 219.

15 On finding 'foundations' or 'otherness' in the Middle Ages, see Paul Spiegel and Gabrielle M. Freedman, 'Medievalisms Old and New: The Rediscovery of Alterity in North American Medieval Studies', *American Historical Review*, **103** (1998), 677–704.

associated with the world of church and university, such as Jean Gerson. All were moved and even distressed by the internecine relations, the stupid and covetous behaviour, and the petty jealousies and antagonisms that were tearing the country apart. There was clear evidence of both the inadequacies of the royal family and of political institutions. This chorus of voices was significant to the ultimate establishment of the nation-state and a kind of golden age of French political power and authority. The extraordinary phenomenon of poets and courtiers writing to save the nation when it was on the brink of ruin betokens a sense of engagement and respnsibility to country, which is the positive side of the development of nationalism.

Secondly, Christine's achievement as the first French woman self-consciously to write political treatises is of significance. Other women had contributed political works, including most notably the Carolingian noblewoman Duodha; Marie de France, whose fables certainly have political content; and the tremendously talented Heloise, whose stormy relationship with Peter Abelard resulted in profound reflections on the human condition.[16] However, the political content of these works was incidental to their purpose. By contrast, Christine's hallmark was her clear and singular creation of a voice with both the authority and necessity to speak out on political matters. This voice has three different characteristics: traditional humility, authorial confidence and political passion.

Her humility was both socially obligated as a result of social class and gender and a deliberate construction within the conventions of political writing. In some of her earlier works, such as *Othéa*, *Prod'homie* and *Corps de policie*, Christine's constructed identity as an unthreatening female with no important social role allowed her a kind of transparency through which the reader theoretically experienced only the wisdom of the masters. Her own message could then be clothed in the words of those authorities, and insinuated into their very texts. Thus her criticism of society, magistrates and even the king himself carried the weight of Aristotle or Bernard of Clairvaux rather than that of her 'insignificant' self. This methodology was not her own invention, rather it was a convention of medieval writing, but it was used by her with great resourcefulness. We also see the creation of an authorial persona that is in reality not humble at all. This Christine is often a character in her own works, such as *Cité des dames*, *L'Avision*, *Mutacion* and in her poetry. The reader is seduced into taking this character at face value rather than seeing her as a creation of a very skilled writer. The phenomenon of using the terms and ideas of misogyny as a weapon against it has been addressed by a number of scholars,

16 A new work on Heloise may contribute significantly to her already high reputation. See Constant J. Mews, *The Lost Love Letters of Heloise and Abelard* (New York: St Martins Press, 1999).

most notably by Nadia Margolis and Kevin Brownlee. However, Christine also speaks directly, as in her *Prison humaine* and the *Lamentation* and especially in *Le Livre de la paix* and *Jeanne d'Arc*. In these works, all of which date from later in her career and all which speak to the political situation, she is neither a character in her own work nor unduly humble. She speaks with confidence and authority as a person who has a responsibility to the kingdom to advise her rulers and the right to insist, however politely, that rulers take action. The creation of this self was more than her hope for future glory and renown, or even her awareness that writing was both her vocation and her destiny. Christine's extraordinary innovation was the appropriation of the authority to guide rulers, not on the basis of her social status or expertise, but as a 'citizen' of France. 'Je, Christine', indeed.

Thirdly, in that rising tide of intellectual ferment in which she participated, which was itself both a reflection of and catalyst for the increasing laicization and secularization of power, hers was not an insignificant voice. Her unusual character and her fearlessness in the face of power gave an exceptional quality to her participation in this stream of protest. Her voice could be tolerated by the arrogant when they were deaf to others because she was after all only 'a humble creature' and 'insignificant' to those of higher ranks.[17]

A Christinian moment?

The core of Christine's political teaching consisted of three components that indirectly shaped or contributed to the future of political ideas: her awareness of human fragility, her view of prudence as self-interest, and her functional view of the state. Christine's uniqueness as a political analyst is a consequence of her awareness of political, social and economic vulnerability. That perception translated directly into pragmatic political concepts. In a time of political chaos, justice is not an abstraction or a theoretical construct but means seeing to it that the powerful obey the law, that evildoers are punished and that the lawless are compelled to respect the lives of others. In short, justice is enforcement of the law and fair procedures applied to everyone, regardless of rank. The good community is not to be found in creating typologies of government, *pace* Aristotle, or even in constructing different institutions. Rather it means that everyone in the community has obligations to the whole. Even the lowliest person is important to the peace and stability of the totality. Those who have higher rank and privileges also have increased responsibility. The clergy and the nobility must realize that their superior status incurs burdens, but even the middle classes have civic responsibilities. For the ruler, if he cannot have peace,

17 *Book of the Body Politic*, trans. Forhan, 4.

ought to be exceedingly careful about how he chooses to fight wars. Good rule means to enforce the law and to listen to skilled advisers. It is a very practical and realistic vision.

Christine's vulnerability in life explains her conventional acceptance of social hierarchy, of monarchy, and of 'knowing her place'. Given her sex and her class, she was powerless to change institutions, nor did she have authority over those who could change them. The world was a given, and yet she had the perception to see that it might be constructed differently, including a functional view of society, a reduced political role for the clergy, and clear standards on the concepts of justice and just war. In a sense, she was utterly conventional, yet she was astoundingly insightful and optimistic within those limits. She had a clear normative vision and was able with great clarity to convey the enormous gap between what is and what ought to be. That measure is not a moral one in the abstract sense. It was fuelled by her awareness of vulnerability to the vicissitudes of fortune. In a fragile world, the only safety can be found in prudence, the prudence of self-interest. Learning from the past, being able to discern the true character of events as they occur, foresight about the future – ultimately these are the only effective weapons against the turn of Fortune's wheel. Today she is the happy young wife; tomorrow the beloved husband is dead and she is a penniless single mother, with no resources but her wits. Today the wheat shines like gold; tomorrow locusts have eaten it to the ground. Today Charles is dauphin of France; tomorrow he is on the run, hunted through the forest, a price on his head. A turn of the wheel and all is upside down. Except then, as Christine says, when the victor has become the vanquished, how he has treated his friends and his enemies in the past will come home to haunt him. This awareness of vulnerability underlies Christine's most significant innovations as a political thinker.

Awareness and sensitivity to the complete vulnerability of every individual in society, from peasant to king, underscored for Christine the importance of a functional view of the state. Since we are all vulnerable, the very survival of society is dependent on our willingness to fulfil our functions within it. If institutions are not operating adequately, each individual must play his or her role well to keep the system working. And so social hierarchy with a concomitant emphasis on the purpose or virtue of each class, its 'liberties' and obligations, is essential for the society to survive. This functional view can be seen as a precursor to the important modern norm of civic responsibility. It is not only that it takes a village to raise a child, it takes the whole village to be a village, truly and fully.

Christine's keen awareness of vulnerability has the consequence of encouraging her not only to privilege prudence as the most princely of virtues, but also as the essential virtue for everyone. Prudence is not wisdom in some abstract and theoretical sense nor is it merely discretion. Rather, prudence is foresight, expertise, shrewdness and can even include deceit. Her rich understanding of prudence looks to the modern reader very much like self-interest; to the political theorist, it resembles Machiavelli's *virtù*. Virtue and the appearance of virtue are important; the former for salvation, the latter for political survival. Self-interest, the ancient definition of tyranny, has become synonymous with good politics, a Christian development that classical and medieval theorists would condemn. Today, however, voters call it 'realistic', and woe betide the legislator who neglects local interests in favour of some abstract notion of the common good.

Over her professional career Christine emerges as a political writer who was exceptionally enmeshed in her political environment and sometimes endangered by it. Not a scholastic, nor a canon lawyer, and certainly not a political actor, Christine's significance comes from the reality that hers is a voice seldom heard in any political era; she is a subject, or in more contemporary terms, she is an ordinary citizen. She is not without self-interest herself; her writing is what allows her to make a living, but she has no safety net, no protection afforded by a countervailing power like the Church or university or a religious order or even an independent income – 500 pounds a year and a room of her own. What makes her views and insights seem so fresh is that she is the voice of the people. She is not the voice of the masses, to be sure, but of the upper middle class, the voice of everywoman in so far as it could be articulated in the period. While no one could claim that she was ordinary or typical, nor can one deny her privileged status with respect to the peasantry or artisanate, she was nevertheless the object and the victim of political decision-making. While she was extraordinary in her choices, her prodigious productivity, and her perceptiveness, to society she was 'only a woman', and the recognition she received was attenuated and contextualized with respect to her status. Christine provides the modern reader with trenchant observations of her 'betters', and gives a glimpse from the perspective of those who lack value to society. To be powerless, to be undistinguished, or to be female was a consequence of the accident of birth in a culture that inflicted preordained and predetermined social value on all, and within which there was no veil of ignorance.

Machiavelli, modernity and the mirror

Most political theorists assume that with the emergence of the ideas of Machiavelli there is a complete rupture with the ideals and values of the medieval world. Even the more muted and discriminating views of specialists of the Early Modern period mark something peculiar about Machiavelli and his confrères, writing of a 'Machiavellian moment' in the history of political thought. On the conventional account, Machiavelli's contribution to the development of political literature comes from his subversion of the traditional mirror for princes and his introduction of a *Realpolitik*, a practical and pragmatic approach to the problem of rule, rather than the high medieval emphasis on irrelevant and ineffective exhortations of virtue. Although several scholars have elaborated a more nuanced view,[18] many academics continue to affirm the commonly held opinion that his work represents a distinctive shift in political thinking, in part because of Machiavelli's confidence in his own originality and because of his view that Fortune can be controlled, even if not ultimately mastered, by the exercise of *virtù*.

There are striking similarities between the lives and ideas of Niccolò Machiavelli and Christine de Pizan. Not only did they share their Italian heritage and mother tongue, but both had knowledge and experience of court life as lay persons dependent on patronage to earn their livings. Both grew up in periods of relative peace and stability; yet both had lives disrupted by personal and political misfortune. Both began writing for political patrons after these traumatic experiences and both used writing as a means of recovery from them. Both had the desire to address diverse audiences and they both did so in the vernacular. Both used traditional genres of political writing. For Machiavelli, not only did this take the form of his highly esteemed mirror, *Il principe*, written about 1513, but also included letters, discourses and histories, much as those that Christine used to convey her views.

There are significant differences between the two writers of course, not least being gender, era, and nationality, but also very real divergences in temperment and perspective as well. But despite these differences, they were both consumed by the themes of fortune, power and political survival. The combination of intelligence, craft, foresight and skill that Christine calls prudence is analogous to Machiavelli's *virtù*, and plays the same pivotal role in the defeat of Fortune. Indeed, the evidence suggests that the two concepts prudence and *virtù* are essentially identical. His emphasis on a self-interested human nature seems to parallel her appeals to self-interest, especially in rulers, as a foundation for good government. Where they differ is in gender. Christine's prudence is female and triumphs through foresight, not domination; Machiavelli's *virtù* is male, and must 'master' Fortune by boldness. They also

18 Most notably, Quentin Skinner and J. G. A. Pocock. See for example, Skinner, *The Foundations of Modern Political Thought* (Cambridge: Cambridge University Press, 1980), i, 128–9, and Pocock, *The Machiavellian Moment: Florentine Political Thought and the Atlantic Republican Tradition* (Princeton: Princeton University Press, 1975), p. viii.

differ in their claims: Machiavelli avows originality, yet Christine often denies responsibility and relies on the prescribed authorities to insinuate her message. Our naivety as readers, in addition to our cultural preference for originality, leads us to take both rhetorical strategies at face value.

No scholar has as yet presented any evidence that Machiavelli knew or read Christine's works, at least to this writer's knowledge, although it is not impossible that he encountered them, given her Italian connections and the peripatetic circumstances of her books. Until documented, one cannot speak of a direct influence of Christine's ideas on the development of modern political ideas, with the exception of her just war theory. The evidence of any lineal connection between these two political writers is purely circumstantial.[19] It is far more likely that Christine herself represents a stage in the evolution of the mirror for princes, and that Machiavelli's contribution to political thought, while both brilliant and original, is less distinctively different from that of his predecessors than has been believed. In this sense, Christine is no anomaly, and no 'mere woman' either, but part of the general transformation of European political ideas.

Christine's greatest offering to modern readers is her ability to convey the anxieties of her era, the insecurities of someone who is almost entirely vulnerable to the vicissitudes of life, and whose ability to influence or change government was limited exclusively to her ability to criticize and to persuade. By contrast, her gift to her contemporaries was her presentation of the fact that ultimately all are vulnerable, not just the poor or the weak. It would be the duty of later writers to suggest institutional means for preserving civic life in the face of universal vulnerability – or equality – as citizens.

The final paradox of Christine is that she was both politically conservative, in the Burkean sense, and politically progressive in the modern one. She saw the purpose of government as the conservation of peace and stability. Social class and religious belief were structures that worked to preserve the community. Change was dangerous and the past was revered as more orderly, just and pleasant. By contrast, she believed in education, in social mobility based on merit, in civic and civil responsibility, in consultative politics, and in the dignity

---

19 One attempt to wrestle with this is found in an essay by Brian Pavlac, 'Machiavelli's Prince and Christine's Princess: Political Theories of the Renaissance', paper presented at CEMERS, SUNY Binghamton, October 1995. My own essay 'A Feminine Machiavelli?: Prudence meets Virtù in Christine de Pizan' will appear shortly in Maria Falco (ed.), *Feminist Views of Machiavelli* (Oxford: Oxford University Press). A recent article by Nadia Margolis alludes briefly to Machiavelli's Fortune, although in a different context. See Margolis, 'The Rhetoric of Detachment in Christine de Pizan's *Mutacion de Fortune*', *Nottingham French Studies*, **38**/2 (2000), 170–81.

of all members of society. Above all, she believed that, as a citizen of France, she had the right and the authority to speak to its rulers for the good of the nation.

Some paradoxes will never be resolved. Christine was a complex person in a difficult time. She wrote in haste too often, and sometimes with a clumsy style that testifies to a terrible sense of urgency. Like Burke, she never wrote in the abstract and she made no claim to be a philosopher. However, she was a persuasive political theorist. She reflected deeply on political life, including questions of legitimacy, authority, liberty, justice and rights. More than just punditry, her views satisfy logical criteria and are integrated into other components of her philosophical being, including ethical, metaphysical, theological and epistemological ideas. Margaret Canovan remarks that to be a political theorist means to have sustained and consistently articulated political principles,[20] and these Christine certainly had, attempting throughout her career to ensure that her concepts of justice and prudence, and her ideals of peace and order were understood in principle and applied in practice, despite her personal powerlessness. Finally, two eminent political theorists from very different traditions, John Dunn and Terence Ball,[21] have recently argued that political theory itself is a form of political action. To be a political theorist, they both maintain, although in very different ways, is to take sides, to reappraise and to analyse the communities in which we live.

More than a poet, or a historian, or a defender of women alone, Christine de Pizan is a political theorist, as she shines a mirror on those aspects of community life that demand examination and change. An attractive and courageous personality gleams through the conventional literary forms, as well as through the carefully constructed public persona. A renaissance woman in every sense, Christine de Pizan desired to speak her mind, and has thus ensured her own immortality.

20 Canovan, *Nationhood and Political Theory*, 114–34.

21 John Dunn, *The History of Political Theory and Other Essays* (Cambridge: Cambridge University Press, 1996); Terence Ball, *Reappraising Political Theory: Revisionist Studies in the History of Political Thought* (Oxford: Clarendon Press, 1995).

Selected Bibliography

Christine de Pizan: modern editions and translations

Ballades, Rondeaux, and Virelais, an Anthology, ed. Kenneth Varty ([Leicester]: Leicester University Press, 1965).

The Book of Deeds of Arms and of Chivalry, trans. Sumner Willard (University Park, Pa.: Pennsylvania State University Press, 1999).

The Book of Fayttes of Armes and of Chyualrye, trans. William Caxton (London: Published for the Early English Text Society by H. Milford, Oxford University Press, 1932; Millwood, NY: Kraus Reprint, 1988).

The Book of the Body Politic, trans. Kate Langdon Forhan (Cambridge Texts in the History of Political Thought; Cambridge and New York: Cambridge University Press, 1994).

The Book of the City of Ladies, trans. Earl Jeffrey Richards (New York: Persea Books, 1982).

The Book of the Duke of True Lovers, trans. Nadia Margolis (New York: Persea Books, 1991).

Cent ballades d'amant et de dame, ed. Jacqueline Cerquiglini-Toulet (Série 'Bibliothèque médiévale'; Paris: Union générale d'éditions, 1982).

Le Chemin de longue étude, ed. Andrea Tarnowski (Paris: Livre de Poche, 2000).

Christine de Pizan's Letter of Othéa to Hector, trans. Jane Chance (The Focus Library of Medieval Women; Newburyport, Mass.: Focus Information Group, 1990).

Christine's Vision, trans. Glenda McLeod (New York: Garland Publishing, 1993).

Le Débat sur le Roman de la Rose, ed. Eric Hicks (Paris: H. Champion, 1977).

Dit de la Rose, in *Poems of Cupid, God of Love: Christine de Pizan's Epistre au dieu d'Amours and Dit de la Rose, Thomas Hoccleve's The Letter of Cupid; editions and translations with George Sewell's The Proclamation of Cupid*, ed. and trans. Thelma S. Fenster and Mary Erler (Leiden and New York: Brill, 1990).

Ditié de Jehanne d'Arc, ed. and trans. Angus J. Kennedy and Kenneth Varty (Oxford: Society for the Study of Mediaeval Languages and Literature, 1977).

The Epistle of Othéa, trans. Stephen Scrope and Curt F. Bühler (Early English Text Society OS 264; London and New York: Oxford University Press, 1970).

The Epistle of Othéa to Hector; or, The boke of knyghthode, ed. George F. Warner and Thomas Henry Thynne, Marquess of Bath (Roxburghe Club; London: J. B. Nichols, 1904).

The Epistle of the Prison of Human Life; with, An Epistle to the Queen of France; and Lament on the Evils of the Civil War, trans. Josette A. Wisman (New York: Garland, 1984).

The Epistles on the Romance of the Rose and other Documents in the Debate, ed. Charles Frederick Ward (n.p., 1911).

Epistre au dieu d'amours, in *Poems of Cupid, God of Love: Christine de Pizan's Epistre au dieu d'Amours and Dit de la Rose, Thomas Hoccleve's The Letter of Cupid; editions and translations with George Sewell's The Proclamation of Cupid*, ed. and trans. Thelma S. Fenster and Mary Erler (Leiden and New York: Brill, 1990).

Epistre Othéa, ed. Gabriella Parussa (Textes littéraires français, 517; Geneva: Droz, 1999).

Épître d'Othéa, déese de la prudence, à Hector, chef des Troyens; reproduction des 100 miniatures du manuscrit 9392 de Jean Miélot, ed. Joseph van den Gheyn (Brussels: Vromant & Co., 1913).

Lavision-Christine: Introduction and Text, ed. Mary Louis Towner (Washington, DC: Catholic University of America Press, 1932).

Le Livre de la cité des dames, ed. Eric Hicks and Thérèse Moreau ([Paris]: Stock, 1986).

Le Livre de la mutacion de fortune, ed. Suzanne Solente (Paris: A. & J. Picard, 1959).

The 'Livre de la paix' of Christine de Pisan: A Critical Edition, ed. Charity Cannon Willard ('s-Gravenhage: Mouton, 1958).

Le Livre des faits et bonnes moeurs du roi Charles V le Sage, ed. Eric Hicks and Thérèse Moreau (Paris: Stock, 1997).

Le Livre des fais et bonnes meurs du sage roy Charles V, ed. Suzanne Solente, 2 vols. (Paris: H. Champion, 1936–40).

Le Livre des trois vertus: édition critique, ed. Charity Cannon Willard and Eric Hicks (Bibliothèque du xve siècle, 50; Paris: H. Champion, 1989).

Le Livre du corps de policie, ed. Angus J. Kennedy (Etudes christiniennes, 1; Paris: H. Champion, 1998).

Le Livre du corps de policie, édition critique, ed. Robert H. Lucas (Geneva: Droz, 1967).

Le Livre du duc des vrais amans, ed. Thelma Fenster (Medieval & Renaissance Texts & Studies, 124; Binghamton, NY: Medieval and Renaissance Texts and Studies, 1995).

The Love Debate Poems of Christine de Pizan, trans. Barbara K. Altmann (Gainesville, Fla.: University Press of Florida, 1998).

A Medieval Woman's Mirror of Honor: The Treasury of the City of Ladies, trans. Charity Cannon Willard (New York: Bard Hall Press/Persea Books, 1989).

The Middle English Translation of Christine de Pisan's Livre du corps de policie: ed. from MS C.U.L.K.1.5, ed. Diane Bornstein (Middle English Texts, 7; Heidelberg: Winter, 1977).

Œuvres poétiques de Christine de Pisan, ed. Maurice Roy, 3 vols. (Société des anciens textes français, 24; Paris: Firmin-Didot, 1886–96; repr. New York: Johnson Reprint Corp., 1965).

The Selected Writings of Christine de Pizan: New Translations, Criticism, trans. Renate Blumenfeld-Kosinski and Kevin Brownlee (New York: W. W. Norton, 1997).

Les Sept psaumes allégorisés, ed. Ruth Rea Ringland Rains (Washington, DC: Catholic University of America Press, 1965).

The Treasure of the City of Ladies, or, The Book of the Three Virtues, trans. Sarah Lawson (Harmondsworth and New York: Penguin, 1985).

The Writings of Christine de Pizan, trans. Charity Cannon Willard (New York: Persea Books, 1994).

Christine de Pizan: selected scholarly studies and monographs

Altmann, Barbara K., 'Christine de Pizan's Livre du Dit de Poissy' (PhD diss., University of Toronto, 1989).

Baird, Joseph, *The Quarrel of the Rose: Letters and Documents* (Chapel Hill: University of North Carolina Press, 1978).

Bornstein, Diane, *Ideals for Women in the Works of Christine de Pizan* (Detroit: Michigan Consortium for Medieval and Early Modern Studies, 1981).

Brabant, Margaret (ed.), *Politics, Gender, and Genre: The Political Thought of Christine de Pizan* (Boulder, Colo.: Westview Press, 1992).

Brown-Grant, Rosalind, *Christine de Pizan and the Moral Defence of Women: Reading beyond Gender* (Cambridge Studies in Medieval Literature, 40; Cambridge and New York: Cambridge University Press, 1999).

—— 'L'Avision Christine', in Brabant (ed.), *Politics, Gender, and Genre*, 95–112.

Brownlee, Kevin, *Rethinking the Romance of the Rose* (Philadelphia: University of Pennsylvania Press, 1992).

Buchanan, Carole Ann, 'The Theme of Fortune in the Works of Christine de Pizan' (Ph.D. diss., University of Glasgow, 1994).

Carroll, Berenice, 'On the Causes of War and the Quest for Peace', in Hicks (ed.), *Au champ des escriptures*, 337–58.

Delany, Sheila, 'History, Politics, and Christine Studies' in Brabant (ed.), *Politics, Gender, and Genre*, 193–206.

—— 'Mothers to Think Back Through: The Ambiguous Example of Christine de Pizan', in Laurie A. Finke and Martin B. Schichtman (eds), *Medieval Texts and Contemporary Readers* (Ithaca, NY: Cornell University Press, 1987), 177–97.

Dembinska, Maria, 'La Souffrance dans les œuvres de Christine de Pizan', *Les Cahiers de Varsovie*, **14** (1988), 137–46.

Desmond, Marilynn, *Christine de Pizan and the Categories of Difference* (Medieval Cultures, 14; Minneapolis: University of Minnesota Press, 1998).

Dulac, Liliane, and Bernard Ribémont, *Une Femme de lettres au Moyen Age: études autour de Christine de Pizan* (Orléans: Paradigme, 1995), 177–97.

Finke, Laurie A., and Martin B. Schichtman, Medieval Texts and Contemporary Readers (Ithaca, NY: Cornell University Press, 1987).

Forhan, Kate Langdon, 'Christine de Pizan and the Mirror Tradition', in M. Zimmerman (ed.), *The City of Scholars* (Berlin: DeGruyter, 1994), 189–96.

—— 'A Feminine Machiavelli?: Prudence meets Virtù in Christine de Pizan', in Maria Falco (ed.), *Feminist Views of Machiavelli* (Oxford: Oxford University Press, forthcoming).

—— 'Poets and Politics: Just War in Geoffrey Chaucer and Christine de Pizan', presented at the annual meeting of the American Political Science Association, 2000 in *Ethics of War and Peace*, ed. H. Syse (South Bend, IN: St Augustine's Press), forthcoming.

—— 'Respect, Independence, Virtue: A Medieval Theory of Toleration in the Works of Christine de Pizan', in C. J. Nederman and John C. Laursen (eds), *Difference and Dissent* (Lanham: Roman & Littlefield, 1996), 67–82.

—— 'Reading Backward: Aristotelianism in the Political Thought of Christine de Pizan', in Hicks (ed.), *Au champ des escriptures*, 359–81.

—— 'Subversion of the Princely Ideal: Prudence, Pragmatism and the Political Works of Christine de Pizan', presented at Royaume de Femynie: Femmes et Pouvoirs en France à la Renaissance, in Blois, France, 13–15 October 1995.

Gautier, A. F., *Notice sur Christine de Pisan* (Bordeaux: Henry Faye, 1844).

Gauvard, Claude, 'Christine de Pizan et ses contemporains: l'engagement politique des écrivains dans le royaume de France aux XIVe et XVe siècles', in Dulac and Ribémont, *Une Femme au Lettres*, 105–28.

Hicks, Eric (ed.), *Au champ des escriptures* (Geneva: Slatkine, 2000).

Hill, Jillian M. L., *The Medieval Debate on Jean de Meung's Roman de la Rose: Morality versus Art* (Studies in Mediaeval Literature, 4; Lewiston, NY: Edwin Mellen Press, 1991).

Hindman, Sandra, *Christine de Pizan's 'Epistre Othéa': Painting and Politics at the Court of Charles VI* (Studies and texts, 77; Toronto: Pontifical Institute of Mediaeval Studies, 1986).

Jeanneret, Sylvie, 'Texte et Enluminures dans l'Epistre d'Othea', in Hicks (ed.), *Au champ des escriptures*, 723–849.

Kennedy, Angus J., *Christine de Pizan: A Bibliographical Guide* (London: Grant & Cutler, 1984).

—— *Christine de Pizan: A Bibliographical Guide* (Research Bibliographies & Checklists, 42.1; London: Grant & Cutler, 1994).

Kosta-Thefaine, Jean-François, 'Christine de Pizan et la question des juifs', *Speculum Medii Aevii*, **3**/1–2 (1997), 39–52.

Krueger, Roberta, 'Chascune selon son estat: Women's Education and Social Class in the Conduct Books of Christine de Pizan and Anne de France', in *Papers on Seventeenth Century Literature*, **24**, alt. no. **46** (1997), 19–35.

Laidlaw, J. C., 'Christine de Pizan, the Earl of Salisbury and Henry IV', *French Studies*, **36** (1982), 129–43.

Laigle, Mathilde, *Le Livre des trois vertus de Christine de Pisan et son milieu historique et littéraire* (Paris: H. Champion, 1912).

Lunsford, Andrea A., *Reclaiming Rhetorica: Women in the Rhetorical Tradition* (Pittsburgh: University of Pittsburgh Press, 1995).

McKinley, Mary, 'The Subversive "Seulette"', in Brabant (ed.), *Politics, Gender, and Genre*, 157–70.

McLeod, Glenda (ed.), *The Reception of Christine de Pizan from the Fifteenth through the Nineteenth Centuries: Visitors to the City* (Lewiston, NY: E. Mellen Press, 1991).

—— *Virtue and Venom* (Ann Arbor: University of Michigan Press, 1991).

Margolis, Nadia, 'The Rhetoric of Detachment in Christine de Pizan's Mutacion de Fortune', *Nottingham French Studies*, **38**/2 (2000), 170–81.

Moyer, Johanna B., 'French Sumptuary Law and the Body in Medieval Thought, 1224–1571', paper presented at the fifth annual ACMRS conference, 18–20 February 1999, Tempe, Ariz.

Nys, Ernest, *Christine de Pisan et ses principales œuvres* (Brussels: Société anonyme M. Weissenbruch imprimeur du roi, 1914).

Pavlac, Brian, 'Machiavelli's Prince and Christine's Princess: Political Theories of the Renaissance', paper presented at CEMERS, SUNY Binghamton, October 1995.

Pinet, Marie Josèphe, *Christine de Pisan, 1364–1430, étude biographique et littéraire* (Bibliothèque du quinzième siècle, 35; Geneva: Slatkine Reprints, 1974).

Poirion, Daniel, and Nancy Freeman Regalado, *Contexts: Style and Values in Medieval Art and Literature* (New Haven: Yale University Press, 1991).

Quilligan, Maureen, *The Allegory of Female Authority: Christine de Pizan's Cité des dames* (Ithaca, NY: Cornell University Press, 1991).

Reno, Christine, 'Christine de Pizan: At Best a Contradictory Figure?', in Brabant (ed.), *Politics, Gender, and Genre*, 171–92.

—— '*Le Livre du Prudence/Prod'homie de l'Homme*', in Bernard Ribémont and Liliane Dulac (eds), *Une Femme de lettres au Moyen Age: études autour de Christine de Pizan* (Orléans: Paradigme, 1995), 25–37.

Ribémont, Bernard, 'Christine de Pizan et l'encyclopédisme scientifique', in Zimmermann and De Rentiis (eds), *City of Scholars*, 174–18.

—— *De natura rerum: études sur les encyclopédies médiévales* (Orléans: Paradigme, 1995).

—— (ed.), *Sur le chemin de longue étude—: actes du colloque d'Orléans, juillet 1995* (Paris: H. Champion, and Geneva: Slatkine, 1998).

Richards, Earl Jeffrey, *Christine de Pizan and Medieval French Lyric* (Gainesville, Fla.: University Press of Florida, 1998).

—— 'Christine de Pizan and Medieval Jurisprudence', paper presented at the International Christine de Pizan Society meeting, Glasgow, 2000.

—— 'The Medieval "Femme auteur" as Provocation to Literary History', in McLeod (ed.), *Reception of Christine de Pizan*, 101–26.

—— *Reinterpreting Christine de Pizan* (Athens, Ga.: University of Georgia Press, 1992).

—— 'Why is Christine not Politically Correct? Reflections on Hermeneutics, Literary Politics and Difference', paper presented at CEMERS, SUNY Binghamton, 1995.

Rigaud, Rose, *Les Idées féministes de Christine de Pisan* (Geneva: Slatkine Reprints, 1973).

Schein, Marie, 'La Pensée Politique de Christine de Pizan dans le Chemin de Long Estude' (MA thesis, University of Colorado, 1985).

Schwemm, Laura Anne, 'Christine de Pizan: Virtues and the Role of Women' (Honors thesis, Medieval Studies, Mt. Holyoke College, 1987).

Solente, Suzanne, 'Christine de Pisan', *Histoire littéraire de la France* (Paris: Imprimerie Nationale, 1974).

Teague, Frances, 'Christine de Pizan's Book of War', in McLeod (ed.), *Reception of Christine de Pizan*, 25–42.

Thomassy, Raymond, *Essai sur les écrits politiques de Christine de Pisan suivi d'une notice littéraire et de pièces inédites* (Paris: Debécourt, 1838).

Walters, Lori, 'Fortune's Double Face', *Fifteenth Century Studies*, **25** (1999), 97–114.

Wandruszka, Nikolai, 'Christine's Family Origins', in Eric Hicks, *Au champ des escritures* (Paris: Champion, 2000), 111–33.

Willard, Charity Cannon, *Christine de Pizan: Her Life and Works* (New York: Persea Books, 1984).

Yenal, Edith, *Christine de Pisan: A Bibliography of Writings by Her and about Her* (Metuchen, NJ: Scarecrow Press, 1982).

—— *Christine de Pizan: A Bibliography* (2nd edn; Metuchen, NJ: Scarecrow Press, 1989).

Zhang, Xiangyun, 'Du Miroir des Princes au Miroir des Princesses', *Fifteenth Century Studies*, **22** (1996), 55–67.

Zimmermann, Margarete, 'Christine de Pizan et les féministes autour de 1900', in B. Ribémont (ed.), *Sur le chemin de longue étude*, 183–204.

—— and Dina De Rentiis (eds), *The City of Scholars: New Approaches to Christine de Pizan* (European Cultures, 2; Berlin and New York: W. de Gruyter, 1994).

Other works

Abelard, Peter, *Peter Abelard's Ethics*, ed. and trans. D. E. Luscombe (Oxford Medieval Texts; Oxford: Clarendon Press, 1971).

Allard, Jean-Paul, 'L'Ideal communautaire selon le "Quadrilogue invectif" d'Alain Chartier', *Études indo-européennes*, **16** (1986), 1–39.

Allmand, C. T., *The Hundred Years War: England and France at War, c. 1300–c. 1450* (Cambridge Medieval Textbooks; Cambridge and New York: Cambridge University Press, 1988).

—— and George William Coopland, *War, Literature, and Politics in the Late Middle Ages* (Liverpool: Liverpool University Press, 1976).

Ambrisco, Alan S., 'Cannibalism and Cultural Encounters in Richard Coeur de Lion', *Journal of Medieval and Early Modern Studies*, **29** (1999), 499–528.

Aquinas, Thomas, *Summa theologica* (New York: Benziger Bros., 1947).

Aristotle, *The Nicomachean Ethics*, trans. H. Rackham (new and rev. edn; Cambridge, Mass. and London: Harvard University Press, 1982).

—— *The Politics*, trans. H. Rackham (The Loeb Classical Library; London: W. Heinemann, 1932).

—— *The Politics*, ed. and trans. E. Barker (Oxford: Oxford University Press, 1946).

Augustine, *Political Writings*, trans. Michael W. Tkacz, Douglas Kries, Ernest L. Fortin and Roland Gunn (Indianapolis, Ind.: Hackett, 1994).

Autrand, Françoise, *Charles V: le sage* (Paris: Fayard, 1994).

—— *Charles VI: la folie du roi* (Paris: Fayard, 1986).

—— *Naissance d'un grand corps de l'État: les gens du Parlement de Paris, 1345–1454* (Paris: Université de Paris I, Panthéon Sorbonne, 1981).

—— *Pouvoir et société en France, XIVe–XVe siècles* (Paris: Presses universitaires de France, 1974).

Babbitt, Susan M., *Oresme's Livre de politiques and the France of Charles V* (Transactions of the American Philosophical Society, 75, pt. 1; Philadelphia: American Philosophical Society, 1985).

Bagge, Sverre, *The Political Thought of The King's Mirror* (Mediaeval Scandinavia Supplements, 3; Odense: Odense University Press, 1987).

Baldwin, John W., *Aristocratic Life in Medieval France: The Romances of Jean Renart and Gerbert de Montreuil, 1190–1230* (Baltimore: Johns Hopkins University Press, 2000).

—— *The Government of Philip Augustus: Foundations of French Royal Power in the Middle Ages* (Berkeley: University of California Press, 1986).

Ball, Terence, *Reappraising Political Theory: Revisionist Studies in the History of Political Thought* (Oxford: Clarendon Press, 1995).

Barlow, Claude W., *Iberian Fathers* (Washington, DC: Catholic University of America Press, 1969).

Barnes, Jonathan, 'The Just War', in *Cambridge History of Later Medieval Philosophy* (Cambridge: Cambridge University Press, 1982), 771–84.

Bartholomew of Lucca, *On the Government of Rulers: De regimine principum*, trans. James M. Blythe (The Middle Ages Series; Philadelphia: University of Pennsylvania Press, 1997).

Beaumanoir, Philippe de, *The 'Coutumes de Beauvaisis' of Philippe de Beaumanoir*, trans. F. R. P. Akehurst (Philadelphia: University of Pennsylvania Press, 1992).

Beaune, Colette, *Journal d'un bourgeois de Paris: de 1405 à 1449* (Lettres gothiques; Paris: Livre de Poche, 1990).

—— Fredric L. Cheyette and Susan Ross Huston, *The Birth of an Ideology: Myths and Symbols of Nation in Late-Medieval France* (Berkeley: University of California Press, 1991).

Bell, David A., 'Recent Works on Early Modern French National Identity', *Journal of Modern History*, **68** (1996), 84–113.

Bell, Dora M., *Étude sur le Songe du vieil pèlerin de Philippe de Mézières (1327–1405) d'apres le manuscrit français B.N. 22542; document historique et moral du règne de Charles VI* (Geneva: E. Droz, 1955).

—— *L'Idéal éthique de la royauté en France au Moyen Age* (Geneva: E. Droz, 1962).

Benson, R. L., and Giles Constable (eds), *Renaissance and Renewal in the Twelfth Century* (Cambridge, Mass.: Harvard University Press, 1982).

Berges, Wilhelm, *Die Fürstenspiegel des hohen und späten Mittelalters* (Stuttgart: Hiersemann, 1952).

Bisson, Lillian M., *Chaucer and the Late Medieval World* (New York: St. Martin's Press, 1998).

Black, Antony, *Council and Commune: The Conciliar Movement and the Fifteenth-Century Heritage* (London: Burns & Oates, and Shepherdstown: Patmos Press, 1979).

—— *Political Thought in Europe 1250–1450* (Cambridge and New York: Cambridge University Press, 1992).

Bloch, Marc Léopold Benjamin, *Les Rois thaumaturges: étude sur le caractère surnaturel attribué à la puissance royale, particulièrement en France et en Angleterre* (Publications de la Faculté des lettres de l'Université de Strasbourg, 19; Strasbourg: Librairie Istra; London: H. Milford, Oxford University Press, 1924).

Blythe, James M., *Ideal Government and the Mixed Constitution in the Middle Ages* (Princeton: Princeton University Press, 1992).

Bonet, Honoré, *The Tree of Battles*, ed. George William Coopland (Liverpool: Liverpool University Press, 1949).

Born, Leslie K., 'The Perfect Prince', *Speculum*, **3** (1928), 470–504.

Bouchard, Constance Britain, *'Strong of Body, Brave and Noble': Chivalry and Society in Medieval France* (Ithaca, NY and London: Cornell University Press, 1998).

Bradley, Ritamary, 'Backgrounds of the Title *Speculum* in Medieval Literature', *Speculum*, **29** (1954), 100–15.

Briggs, Charles F., *Giles of Rome's De regimine principum: Reading and Writing Politics at Court and University, c. 1275–c.1525* (Cambridge Studies in Palaeography and Codicology, 5; Cambridge and New York: Cambridge University Press, 1999).

Brown, Alfred L., *The Governance of Late Medieval England, 1272–1461* (The Governance of England, 3; Stanford, Calif.: Stanford University Press, 1989).

Brown, Cynthia J., 'Allegorical Design and Image Making in Fifteenth-Century France: Alain Chartier's Joan of Arc', *French Studies*, **53** (1999), 385–404.

Buescu, Ana Isabel, 'The Utopia of a Perfect Prince: Recurrences in Modern Europe's "Mirrors for the Prince"', *History of European Ideas*, **16**/4–6 (1993), 599–606.

Bull, Hedley, Benedict Kingsbury and Adam Roberts, *Hugo Grotius and International Relations* (Oxford: Clarendon Press, 1992).

Burns, J. H. (ed.), *The Cambridge History of Medieval Political Thought c. 350–c. 1450* (Cambridge and New York: Cambridge University Press, 1988).

Cachey, T. J., *Dante now: Current Trends in Dante Studies* (The William and Katherine Devers series in Dante studies, 1; Notre Dame: University of Notre Dame Press, 1995).

Camille, Michael, 'The Luttrell Psalter and the Making of "Merrie England"', *History Today*, **48**/9 (1998), 13–19.

Canning, Joseph, *A History of Medieval Political Thought, 300–1450* (London and New York: Routledge, 1996).

Canovan, Margaret, *Nationhood and Political Theory* (Cheltenham and Brookfield, Vt.: Edward Elgar, 1996).

Carlyle, Robert Warrand, and A. J. Carlyle, *A History of Mediæval Political Theory in the West* (Edinburgh and London: W. Blackwood and Sons, 1903).

Carpentier, Elisabeth, and J-P. Arrignan, *La France et les Français, XIVe et XVe siècles* (Paris: Orphrys, 1993).

—— and Michel Le Mené, *La France du XIe au XVe siècle: population, société, économie* (ed. Thémis, Histoire. Paris: Presses universitaires de France, 1996).

Carroll, Berenice A., Dorothy Gies McGuigan and Peggy Ann Kusnerz, *The Role of Women in Conflict and Peace: Papers* (Ann Arbor: University of Michigan Center for Continuing Education of Women, 1977).

Cerquiglini-Toulet, Jacqueline, 'L'Imaginaire du livre à la fin du Moyen Age: pratiques de lecture, théorie de l'écriture', *MLN* **108** (1993), 680–95.

Cherewatuk, Karen, and Ulrike Wiethaus, *Dear Sister: Medieval Women and the Epistolary Genre* (Philadelphia: University of Pennsylvania Press, 1993).

Cicero, Marcus Tullius, *De officiis*, trans. Walter Miller (The Loeb Classical Library; London: W. Heinemann, 1913).

—— *De re publica; De legibus*, trans. Clinton Walker Keyes (The Loeb Classical Library; London: Heineman, 1928).

—— *De senectute, De amicitia, De divinatione*, trans. William Armistead Falconer (Cambridge, Mass.: Harvard University Press, 1964).

—— *Selected Works*, trans. Michael Grant (repr. with revisions, Harmondsworth and New York: Penguin Books, 1971).

Clogan, Paul Maurice, *Civil Strife and National Identity in the Middle Ages* (Medievalia et humanistica, NS 26; Lanham, Md.: Rowman & Littlefield Publishers, 1999).

Coleman, Janet, *Ancient and Medieval Memories: Studies in the Reconstruction of the Past* (Cambridge and New York: Cambridge University Press, 1992).

—— *A History of Political Thought: From the Middle Ages to the Renaissance* (Malden, Mass. and Oxford: Blackwell Publishers, 2000).

—— *Medieval Readers and Writers, 1350–1400* (New York: Columbia University Press, 1981).

Colish, Marcia L., *Medieval Foundations of the Western Intellectual Tradition, 400–1400* (Yale Intellectual History of the West; New Haven: Yale University Press, 1997).

Contamine, Philippe, *La Guerre de cent ans* (Paris: Presses universitaires de France, 1968).

—— *Guerre et société en France, en Angleterre et en Bourgogne, XIVe–XVe siècle*, ed. Maurice Hugh Keen and Charles Giry-Deloison (Collection 'Histoire et littérature régionales', 8; Villeneuve d'Ascq (Nord): Centre d'histoire de la région du Nord et de l'Europe du Nord-Ouest: Université Charles de Gaulle Lille III, 1991).

—— *La Noblesse au royaume de France de Philippe le Bel à Louis XII: essai de synthèse* (Paris: Presses universitaires de France, 1997).

—— *War in the Middle Ages* (New York: Blackwell, 1984).

Copeland, Rita, *Criticism and Dissent in the Middle Ages* (Cambridge and New York: Cambridge University Press, 1996).

Coville, Alfred, *Jean Petit: la question du tyrannicide au commencement du XVe siècle* (Paris: A. Picard, 1932).

Dante, Alighieri, *Monarchia*, trans. and ed. Prue Shaw (Cambridge Medieval Classics, 4; Cambridge and New York: Cambridge University Press, 1995).

Delisle, Léopold Victor, *Recherches sur la librairie de Charles V, roi de France, 1337–1380* (Amsterdam: G. Th. van Heusden, 1967).

Denifle, Heinrich, *La Désolation des églises, monastères et hôpitaux en France pendant la guerre de cent ans* (Brussels: Culture et civilisation, 1965).

Denton, Jeffrey Howard, *Orders and Hierarchies in Late Medieval and Renaissance Europe* (Toronto: University of Toronto Press, 1999).

Derville, Alain, *L'Économie française au moyen âge* (Paris: Ophrys, 1995).

Deschamps, Eustache, *L'Art de dictier*, ed. and trans. Deborah M. Sinnreich-Levi (Medieval Texts and Studies, 13; East Lansing, Mich.: Colleagues Press, 1994).

—— *Œuvres complètes de Eustache Deschamps*, ed. Auguste Queux de Saint-Hilaire and Gaston Raynaud, 11 vols (Société des anciens textes français; Paris: Firmin-Didot, 1878–1903).

Duby, Georges, *Le Chevalier, la femme et le prêtre: le mariage dans la France féodale* (Paris: Hachette littérature générale, 1981).

—— *The Chivalrous Society* (Berkeley: University of California Press, 1977).

—— *France in the Middle Ages 987–1460: From Hugh Capet to Joan of Arc* (A History of France; Oxford and Cambridge, Mass.: B. Blackwell, 1991).

—— *Histoire de la France urbaine* (L'Univers historique [Paris]: Seuil, 1980).

Dunn, John, *The History of Political Theory and Other Essays* (Cambridge and New York: Cambridge University Press, 1996).

Elshtain, Jean Bethke, *Just War Theory* (Readings in Social and Political Theory; New York: New York University Press, 1992).

Ertman, Thomas, *Birth of the Leviathan: Building States and Regimes in Medieval and Early Modern Europe* (Cambridge and New York: Cambridge University Press, 1997).

Evergates, Theodore, *Aristocratic Women in Medieval France* (Middle Ages Series; Philadelphia: University of Pennsylvania Press, 1999).

Famiglietti, R. C., 'The French Monarchy in Crisis 1392–1415' (Ph.D. diss., City University of New York, 1982).

Favier, Jean, and Françoise Autrand, *La France médiévale* ([Paris]: Fayard, 1983).

Ferster, Judith, *Fictions of Advice: The Literature and Politics of Counsel in Late Medieval England* (Middle Ages Series; Philadelphia: University of Pennsylvania Press, 1996).

Finnis, John, *Aquinas: Moral, Political, and Legal Theory* (Founders of Modern Political and Social Thought; Oxford and New York: Oxford University Press, 1998).

Forde, Simon, Lesley Johnson and Alan V. Murray, *Concepts of National Identity in the Middle Ages* (Leeds Texts and Monographs, NS 14; Leeds: School of English, University of Leeds, 1995).

Forhan, Kate Langdon, 'The Ciceronian Prince: Text and Image in the Mirror of Princes', paper presented at the annual meeting of the American Political Science Association, Washington, DC, 1991.

—— 'The Not-So-Divided Self: Reading Augustine in the Twelfth Century', *Augustiniana*, **42** (1992), 95–110.

—— 'Salisburian Stakes', *History of Political Thought*, **11** (1990), 397–407.

—— 'The Twelfth-Century "Bureaucrat" and the Life of the Mind: John of Salisbury's Policraticus' (Ph.D. diss., Johns Hopkins University, 1987).

Fowler, Kenneth Alan, Wim Swaan and Edwin Smith, *The Age of Plantagenet and Valois: The Struggle for Supremacy, 1328–1498* (New York: Putnam, 1967).

Fraioli, Deborah, 'The Literary Image of Joan of Arc: Prior Influences', *Speculum*, **56** (1981), 811–30.

Freedman, Paul, and Gabrielle Peters, 'Medievalisms Old and New', *American Historical Review*, **103** (1998), 677–704.

Froissart, Jean, *Chroniques*, ed. George T. Diller (Geneva: Droz, 1991).

Gentili, Alberico, *De iure belli libri tres*, ed. John CarewRolfe and Coleman Phillipson (Oxford and London: Clarendon Press; H. Milford, 1933).

Gerson, Jean, *Early Works*, trans. Brian Patrick McGuire (New York: Paulist Press, 1998).

—— *Jean Gerson: Selections from A Deo exivit, Contra curiositatem studentium and De mystica theologia speculativa*, ed. Steven E. Ozment (Textus minores, 38; Leiden: E. J. Brill, 1969).

—— *Œuvres complètes*, ed. Palémon Glorieux (Paris and New York: Desclée, 1960).

Gierke, Otto Friedrich von, *Political Theories of the Middle Ages* (1900; repr. Cambridge: Cambridge University Press, 1987).

Giles of Rome, *De regimine principum libri III*, ed. Samaritanius Hieronymus (Aalen: Scientia Verlag, 1967).

—— *Li Livres du gouvernement des rois: A XIIIth Century French Version of Egidio Colonna's Treatise De regimine principum, now first published from the Kerr MS*, ed. Samuel Paul Molenaer (New York: AMS Press, 1966).

—— *The Governance of Kings and Princes: John Trevisa's Middle English Translation of the De regimine principum of Aegidius Romanus*, ed. David C. Fowler, Charles F. Briggs and Paul G. Remley (New York: Garland Publishing, 1997).

Goldberg, Benjamin, *The Mirror and Man* (Charlottesville: University of Virginia Press, 1985).

Goodman, Anthony, and James L. Gillespie, *Richard II: The Art of Kingship* (Oxford: Clarendon Press, 1999).

Grotius, Hugo, *Hugonis Grotii in tres libros De iure belli ac pacis. Prolegomena* ('s-Gravenhage: M. Nijhoff, 1952).

Grudin, Michaela Paasche, *Chaucer and the Politics of Discourse* (Columbia, SC: University of South Carolina Press, 1996).

Haggenmacher, P., 'Grotius and Gentili', in H. Bull *et al.* (eds), *Hugo Grotius and International Relations* (Oxford: Clarendon Press, 1992), 133–76.

Hanley, Sarah, 'Identity Politics and Rulership in France: Female Political Place and the Fraudulent Salic Law in Christine de Pizan and Jean de Montreuil', in M. Wolfe (ed.), *Changing Identities in Early Modern France* (Durham, NC: Duke University Press, 1997), 78–94.

—— *The Lit de Justice of the Kings of France: Constitutional Ideology in Legend, Ritual, and Discourse* (Princeton: Princeton University Press, 1983).

Hill, Jillian M. L., *The Medieval Debate on Jean de Meung's Roman de la Rose: Morality versus Art* (Studies in Mediaeval Literature, 4; Lewiston: Edwin Mellen Press, 1991).

Hollister, C. Warren, and John W. Baldwin, 'The Rise of Administrative Kingship', *American Historical Review*, **83** (1978), 867–905.

Huizinga, Johan, *The Autumn of the Middle Ages* (Chicago: University of Chicago Press, 1996).

—— *The Waning of the Middle Ages: A Study of the Forms of Life, Thought, and Art in France and the Netherlands in the XIVth and XVth centuries* (Garden City, NY, 1954).

Huppert, George, *After the Black Death: A Social History of Early Modern Europe* (Interdisciplinary Studies in History; Bloomington: Indiana University Press, 1986).

The Institutes of Justinian, trans. B. Moyle (Oxford: Oxford University Press, 1896).

Jaeger, C. Stephen, *The Origins of Courtliness: Civilizing Trends and the Formation of Courtly Ideals, 939–1210* (The Middle Ages; Philadelphia: University of Pennsylvania Press, 1985).

Jászi, Oszkár, and John D. Lewis, *Against the Tyrant: The Tradition and Theory of Tyrannicide* (Glencoe, Ill.: Free Press, 1957).

John of Salisbury, *Policraticus*, ed. C. C. I. Webb (Oxford: Oxford University Press, 1909).

—— *Policraticus I–IV*, ed. K. S. B. Keats-Rohan (Corpus Christianorum Continuatio Mediaevalis, 118; Turnholt: Brépols, 1993).

—— *Le Policraticus de Jean de Salisbury (1372) (manuscrit no 24287 de la B.N.), livre IV*, trans. Denis Foulechat and Charles Brucker (Travaux du C.R.A.L., no 3; Nancy: Presses universitaires de Nancy, 1985).

—— *Policraticus: Of the Frivolities of Courtiers and the Footprints of Philosophers*, trans. Cary J. Nederman (Cambridge Texts in the History of Political Thought; Cambridge and New York: Cambridge University Press, 1990).

—— *Le Policratique de Jean de Salisbury (1372) Livres I–III*, trans. Denis Foulechat and Charles Brucker (Publications romanes et françaises, 209; Geneva: Librairie Droz, 1994).

—— *The Statesman's Book of John of Salisbury, being the Fourth, Fifth, and Sixth Books, and Selections from the Seventh and Eighth Books, of the Policraticus*, trans. John Dickenson (New York: Russell & Russell, 1963).

—— *Tyrans, princes et prêtres: Jean de Salisbury, Policratique IV et VIII*, trans. Denis Foulechat and Charles Brucker (Montréal: Ceres, 1987).

Johnson, James Turner, *Just War Tradition and the Restraint of War: A Moral and Historical Inquiry* (Princeton: Princeton University Press, 1981).

—— *The Quest for Peace: Three Moral Traditions in Western Cultural History* (Princeton: Princeton University Press, 1987).

Jones, Terry, *Chaucer's Knight: The Portrait of a Medieval Mercenary* (New York: Methuen, 1985).

Jordan, William C., *The Great Famine: Northern Europe in the Early Fourteenth Century* (Princeton: Princeton University Press, 1996).

Kaeuper, Richard W., *War, Justice, and Public Order: England and France in the Later Middle Ages* (Oxford: Clarendon Press, 1988).

Kantorowicz, Ernst Hartwig, *The King's Two Bodies: A Study in Mediaeval Political Theology* (Princeton: Princeton University Press, 1957).

Kay, Sarah, *The Chansons de Geste in the Age of Romance: Political Fictions* (Oxford: Clarendon Press, 1995).

Kaye, Joel, *Economy and Nature in the Fourteenth Century: Money, Market Exchange, and the Emergence of Scientific Thought* (Cambridge: Cambridge University Press, 1998).

Keen, Maurice Hugh, *Chivalry* (New Haven: Yale University Press, 1984).

—— *England in the Later Middle Ages: A Political History* (London: Methuen, 1973).

—— *English Society in the Later Middle Ages, 1348–1500* (London: Allen Lane, 1990).

—— *The Laws of War in the Late Middle Ages* (London: Routledge & Kegan Paul, 1965).

—— *Nobles, Knights, and Men-at-arms in the Middle Ages* (London and Rio Grande, Ohio: Hambledon Press, 1996).

—— 'The Political Thought of the Fourteenth-Century Civilians', in Beryl Smalley and P. R. L. Brown (eds), *Trends in Medieval Political Thought* (Oxford: Blackwell, 1965), 105–26.

Kempshall, M. S., *The Common Good in Late Medieval Political Thought* (Oxford: Clarendon Press, 1999).

Kent, Bonnie, *The Virtues of the Will* (Washington, DC: Catholic University Press, 1998).

Kerhervé, Jean, *Histoire de la France: la naissance de l'Etat moderne 1180–1492* (Carré Histoire, 44; Paris: Hachette, 1998).

Kretzmann, Norman, Anthony John Patrick Kenny and Jan Pinborg (eds), *The Cambridge History of Later Medieval Philosophy: From the Rediscovery of Aristotle to the Disintegration of Scholasticism, 1100–1600* (Cambridge and New York: Cambridge University Press, 1982).

Krynen, Jacques, *L'Empire du roi: idées et croyances politiques en France, XIII*[e]*–XV*[e] *siècle* ([Paris]: Gallimard, 1993).

—— *Idéal du prince et pouvoir royal en France à la fin du Moyen Age, 1380–1440: étude de la littérature politique du temps* (Paris: Editions A. et J. Picard, 1981).

Latini, Brunetto, *The Book of the Treasure*, trans. Paul Barrette and Spurgeon Baldwin (New York: Garland Publishing, 1993).

—— *Li Livres dou tresor*, ed. Francis J. Carmody (Berkeley: University of California Press, 1947).

Laursen, John Christian, and Cary J. Nederman, *Beyond the Persecuting Society: Religious Toleration before the Enlightenment* (Philadelphia: University of Pennsylvania Press, 1998).

Lewis, John D., 'Medieval Theories of Resistance', in Oszkár Jászi and John D. Lewis, *Against the Tyrant: The Tradition and Theory of Tyrannicide* (Glencoe: Free Press, 1957), 17–34.

Lewis, P. S., *Essays in Later Medieval French History* (London: Hambledon Press, 1985).

—— *Later Medieval France: The Polity* (London: Macmillan, 1968).

—— *The Recovery of France in the Fifteenth Century* (London: Macmillan, 1971).

Liebeschütz, Hans, *Mediaeval Humanism in the Life and Writings of John of Salisbury* (Studies of the Warburg Institute, 17; London: Warburg Institute, University of London, 1950).

Linder, Amnon, 'The Knowledge of John of Salisbury in the Late Middle Ages', *Studi medievali*, ser. 3, **18** (1977), 319–22.

Lunsford, Andrea A., *Reclaiming Rhetorica: Women in the Rhetorical Tradition* (Pittsburgh: University of Pittsburgh Press, 1995).

Luscombe, D. E., *Peter Abelard* (London: Historical Association, 1979).

Machiavelli, Niccolò, *The Prince*, trans. Russell Price, ed. Quentin Skinner, (Cambridge: Cambridge University Press, 1988).

Macrobius, Ambrosius Aurelius Theodosius, *Commentary on the Dream of Scipio*, trans. William Harris Stahl (Records of Civilization: Sources and Studies, 48; New York: Columbia University Press, 1952).

Major, J. Russell, *From Renaissance Monarchy to Absolute Monarchy: French Kings, Nobles, and Estates* (Baltimore: Johns Hopkins University Press, 1994).

—— *Representative Institutions in Renaissance France, 1421–1559* (Madison: University of Wisconsin Press, 1960).

—— and Mack P. Holt, *Society and Institutions in Early Modern France* (Athens, Ga.: University of Georgia Press, 1991).

Marsilius of Padua, *Writings on the Empire: Defensor minor and De translatione Imperii*, ed. and trans. Cary J. Nederman (Cambridge Texts in the History of Political Thought; Cambridge and New York: Cambridge University Press, 1993).

Mate, Mavis E., *Daughters, Wives, and Widows after the Black Death: Women in Sussex, 1350–1535* (Woodbridge and Rochester, NY: Boydell Press, 1998).

Mews, Constant J., *The Lost Love Letters of Heloise and Abelard* (New York: St. Martin's Press, 1999).

Mézières, Philippe de, *Le Songe du Vieil Pelerin*, ed. George William Coopland (London: Cambridge University Press, 1969).

Miller, David, *On Nationality* (Oxford Political Theory; Oxford: Clarendon Press, 1995).

Mollat, Michel, *Genèse médiévale de la France moderne: XIVe–XVe siècle* (Paris: Arthaud, 1977).

—— *The Poor in the Middle Ages: An Essay in Social History* (New Haven: Yale University Press, 1986).

Moyer, Joanna B., 'French Sumptuary Law and the Body in Medieval Thought, 1224–1571', paper presented at the fifth annual ACMRS conference, February 18–20, 1999, Tempe, Arizona.

Muir, Lynette R., *Literature and Society in Medieval France: The Mirror and the Image, 1100–1500* (New York: St. Martin's Press, 1985).

Nederman, Cary J., *Community and Consent: The Secular Political Theory of Marsiglio of Padua's Defensor pacis* (Lanham, Md.: Rowman & Littlefield, 1995).

—— 'A Duty to Kill', *Review of Politics*, **50** (1988), 365–89.

—— *Medieval Aristotelianism and its Limits: Classical Traditions in Moral and Political Philosophy, 12th–15th Centuries* (Variorum; Aldershot: Ashgate, 1997).

—— 'The Mirror Crack'd: The Speculum Principum as Political and Social Criticism in the Late Middle Ages', *The European Legacy*, **3**/3 (1998), 18–38.

—— 'State and Political Theory in France and England, 1250–1350' (Ph.D. diss., York University, 1984).

—— and Kate Langdon Forhan (eds), *Medieval Political Theory: A Reader. The Quest for the Body Politic, 1100–1400* (London and New York: Routledge, 1993; repr. as *Readings in Medieval Political Theory: 1100–1400* Indianapolis: Hackett, 2000).

—— and John Christian Laursen, *Difference and Dissent: Theories of Toleration in Medieval and Early Modern Europe* (Lanham, Md.: Rowman & Littlefield, 1996).

Nys, Ernest, *Les Origines du droit international* (Brussels: A. Castaigne, 1894).

—— *Les Théories politiques et le droit international en France jusqu'au 18e siècle* (Geneva: Slatkine Reprints, 1970).

Oresme, Nicole, *Le Livre de éthiques d'Aristote*, ed. Albert Douglas Menut (New York: G. E. Stechert, 1940).

—— *Le Livre de politiques d'Aristote*, ed. Albert Douglas Menut (Transactions of the American Philosophical Society, NS 60, pt. 6; Philadelphia: American Philosophical Society, 1970).

—— *Maistre Nicole Oresme: Le livre de yconomique d'Aristote; critical edition of the French text from the Avranches manuscript with the original Latin version, introduction and English translation*, ed. and trans. Albert Douglas Menut (Transactions of the American Philosophical Society; NS 47, pt. 5; Philadelphia: American Philosophical Society, 1957).

—— *Le Livre du ciel du monde*, ed. Albert Douglas Menut (Madison: University of Wisconsin Press, 1968).

Orme, Nicholas, *From Childhood to Chivalry: The Education of the English Kings and Aristocracy, 1066–1530* (London and New York: Methuen, 1984).

Ozment, Steven E., *The Age of Reform (1250–1550): An Intellectual and Religious History of Late Medieval and Reformation Europe* (New Haven: Yale University Press, 1980).

Pascoe, Louis B., *Jean Gerson: Principles of Church Reform* (Studies in Medieval and Reformation Thought, 7; Leiden: Brill, 1973).

Pennington, Kenneth, *The Prince and the Law, 1200–1600: Sovereignty and Rights in the Western Legal Tradition* (Berkeley: University of California Press, 1993).

Peters, Edward, and Walter P. Simons, 'The New Huizinga and the Old Middle Ages', *Speculum*, **74** (1999), 587–620.

Pirenne, Henri, *Histoire économique de l'Occident médiéval* ([Bruges]: Desclée De Brouwer, 1951).

—— *Medieval Cities: Their Origins and the Revival of Trade* (Princeton: Princeton University Press, 1969).

—— *Economic and Social History of Medieval Europe*, trans. Ivy E. Clegg (New York: Harcourt Brace, 1937).

Pocock, J. G. A., *The Machiavellian Moment: Florentine Political Thought and the Atlantic Republican Tradition* (Princeton: Princeton University Press, 1975).

Poirion, Daniel, *Le Poète et le prince: l'évolution du lyrisme courtois de Guillaume de Machaut à Charles d'Orléans* (Paris: Presses universitaires de France, 1965).

—— Nancy Freeman Regalado, *Contexts: Style and Values in Medieval Art and Literature* (New Haven: Yale University Press, 1991).

Roberts, Anna, *Violence against Women in Medieval Texts* (Gainesville, Fla.: University Press of Florida, 1998).

Rosenwein, Barbara H., *Anger's Past: The Social Uses of an Emotion in the Middle Ages* (Ithaca, NY: Cornell University Press, 1998).

Roux, Pierre-Jean, 'Alain Chartier devant la crise du pouvoir royal au debut du xve siècle', in Louis Terreaux (ed.), *Culture et pouvoir au temps de l'Humanisme et de la Renaissance* (Geneva: Slatkine, 1978), 7–16.

Rubin, Miri, *Charity and Community in Medieval Cambridge* (Cambridge Studies in Medieval Life and Thought, 4th ser., 4; Cambridge and New York: Cambridge University Press, 1987).

—— *The Work of Jacques Le Goff and the Challenges of Medieval History* (Woodbridge and Rochester, NY: Boydell Press, 1997).

Russell, Frederick H., *The Just War in the Middle Ages* (Cambridge Studies in Medieval Life and Thought, 3d ser., 8; Cambridge and New York: Cambridge University Press, 1975).

Scaglione, Aldo D., *Knights at Court: Courtliness, Chivalry and Courtesy from Ottonian Germany to the Italian Renaissance* (Berkeley: University of California Press, 1991).

Scales, Len, 'Medieval Barbarism?', *History Today*, **49**/10 (1999), 42–4.

Schulze, Hagen, *States, Nations, and Nationalism* (London: Blackwell, 1996).

Seward, Desmond, *The Hundred Years War: The English in France, 1337–1453* (New York: Athenaeum, 1982).

Shepard, Laurie, *Courting Power: Persuasion and Politics in the Early Thirteenth Century* (Garland Studies in Medieval Literature,17; New York: Garland Publishing, 1999).

Sherman, Claire Richter, *Imaging Aristotle: Verbal and Visual Representation in Fourteenth-Century France* (Berkeley: University of California Press, 1995).

—— *The Portraits of Charles V of France (1338–1380)* (Monographs on Archaeology and Fine Arts, 20; New York: Published by New York University Press for the College Art Association of America, 1969).

Sigmund, Paul E., *Nicholas of Cusa and Medieval Political Thought* (Harvard Political Studies; Cambridge, Mass.: Harvard University Press, 1963).

Skinner, Quentin, *The Foundations of Modern Political Thought* (Cambridge and New York: Cambridge University Press, 1978).

Smalley, Beryl, and P. R. L. Brown, *Trends in Medieval Political Thought* (Oxford: Blackwell, 1965).

Solterer, Helen, *The Master and Minerva* (Berkeley: University of California Press, 1995).

Spiegel, Paul, and Gabrielle M. Freedman, 'Medievalisms Old and New: The Rediscovery of Alterity in North American Medieval Studies', *American Historical Review*, **103** (1998), 677–704.

Stein, P. G., 'Roman Law', in J. H. Burns (ed.), *Medieval Political Thought* (Cambridge: Cambridge University Press, 1988), 37–50.

Strayer, Joseph, *Medieval Statecraft and the Perspectives of History* (Princeton: Princeton University Press, 1971).

Suomela-Harma, Elina, 'Les Temps de la fin dans quelques textes de la première moitié du XVe siècle (Alain Chartier, Juvenal des Ursins, Le Bourgeois de Paris)', in *Fin des temps et temps de la fin dans l'univers medieval* (Aix-en-Provence: Université de Provence, 1993), 475–92.

Swanson, R. N., *Religion and Devotion in Europe, c.1215–c.1515* (Cambridge Medieval Textbooks; Cambridge and New York: Cambridge University Press, 1995).

—— *Universities, Academics and the Great Schism* (Cambridge Studies in Medieval Life and Thought, 3d ser., 12 (Cambridge and New York: Cambridge University Press, 1979).

Taber, Douglass, *The Theologian and the Schism: A Study of the Political Thought of Jean Gerson (1363–1429)*, 2 vols (Ann Arbor, Mich.: University Microfilms International, 1986).

Thomas, Antoine, *Jean de Gerson et l'éducation des dauphins de France: étude critique, suivie du texte de deux de ses opuscules et de documents inédits sur Jean Majoris, précepteur de Louis XI* (Paris: E. Droz, 1930).

Tierney, Brian, *The Crisis of Church and State, 1050–1300. With Selected Documents* (Englewood Cliffs, NJ: Prentice-Hall, 1964).

—— *Foundations of the Conciliar Theory: The Contribution of the Medieval Canonists from Gratian to the Great Schism* (enl. new edn; Studies in the History of Christian Thought, 81; Leiden and New York: Brill, 1998).

—— *Religion, Law, and the Growth of Constitutional Thought, 1150–1650* (Wiles lectures, 1979; Cambridge and New York: Cambridge University Press, 1982).

Tuchman, Barbara Wertheim, *A Distant Mirror: The Calamitous Fourteenth Century* (New York: Knopf, 1978).

Ullmann, Walter, *The Growth of Papal Government in the Middle Ages* ([2nd] edn, London: Methuen, 1962).

—— *The Individual and Society in the Middle Ages* (Baltimore: Johns Hopkins Press, 1966).

—— *The Origins of the Great Schism: A Study in Fourteenth-Century Ecclesiastical History* ([Hamden, Conn.]: Archon Books, 1967).

—— *The Papacy and Political Ideas in the Middle Ages* (London: Variorum Reprints, 1976).

Vale, M. G. A., *The Angevin Legacy and the Hundred Years War, 1250–1340* (Oxford and Cambridge, Mass.: Blackwell, 1990).

—— *English Gascony, 1399–1453: A Study of War, Government and Politics during the Later Stages of the Hundred Years' War* (London: Oxford University Press, 1970).

Venette, Jean de, *The Chronicle of Jean de Venette*, trans. Richard Newhall (Records of Civilization, Sources and Studies, 50; New York: Columbia University Press, 1953).

Verdon, Jean, *Les Françaises pendant la guerre de Cent Ans: début du XIVe siècle–milieu du XVe siècle* (Paris: Perrin, 1991).

Verger, Jacques, *Les universités françaises au Moyen Age* (Education and Society in the Middle Ages and Renaissance, 7; Leiden and New York: E. J. Brill, 1995).

Vincent of Beauvais, *Vincenti Belvacensis De morali principis institutione*, ed. Robert J. Schneider (Turnhout: Brepols, 1995).

Walzer, Michael, *Just and Unjust Wars: A Moral Argument with Historical Illustrations* (New York: Basic Books, 1992).

Webb, Clement Charles Julian, *John of Salisbury* (London: Methuen, 1932).

Wilkinson, Bertie, *The Creation of Medieval Parliaments* (New York: Wiley, 1972).

Wilks, Michael, *The World of John of Salisbury* (Studies in Church History, Subsidia, 3; Oxford: Basil Blackwell for the Ecclesiastical History Society, 1984).

Witt, Ronald G., *'In the footsteps of the ancients': The Origins of Humanism from Lovato to Bruni* (Studies in Medieval and Reformation Thought, 74; Leiden and Boston: Brill, 2000).

Wolfe, Michael, *Changing Identities in Early Modern France* (Durham, NC: Duke University Press, 1997).

Wood, Neal, *Cicero's Social and Political Thought* (Berkeley: University of California Press, 1988).

Wright, Nicholas, *Knights and Peasants: The Hundred Years War in the French Countryside* (Woodbridge and Rochester, NY: Boydell and Brewer, 1998).

Young, Iris Marion, *Justice and the Politics of Difference* (Princeton: Princeton University Press, 1990).

Zetterbaum, Marvin, 'Self and Subjectivity in Political Theory', *Review of Politics*, **44**/1 (Jan. 1982), 59–82.

Ziegler, Philip, *The Black Death* (New York: Harper & Row, 1971).

Index